C-4992   CAREER EXAMINATION SERIES

This is your
PASSBOOK for...

Real Estate Specialist II

Test Preparation Study Guide
Questions & Answers

COPYRIGHT NOTICE

This book is SOLELY intended for, is sold ONLY to, and its use is RESTRICTED to individual, bona fide applicants or candidates who qualify by virtue of having seriously filed applications for appropriate license, certificate, professional and/or promotional advancement, higher school matriculation, scholarship, or other legitimate requirements of education and/or governmental authorities.

This book is NOT intended for use, class instruction, tutoring, training, duplication, copying, reprinting, excerption, or adaptation, etc., by:

1) Other publishers
2) Proprietors and/or Instructors of "Coaching" and/or Preparatory Courses
3) Personnel and/or Training Divisions of commercial, industrial, and governmental organizations
4) Schools, colleges, or universities and/or their departments and staffs, including teachers and other personnel
5) Testing Agencies or Bureaus
6) Study groups which seek by the purchase of a single volume to copy and/or duplicate and/or adapt this material for use by the group as a whole without having purchased individual volumes for each of the members of the group
7) Et al.

Such persons would be in violation of appropriate Federal and State statutes.

PROVISION OF LICENSING AGREEMENTS – Recognized educational, commercial, industrial, and governmental institutions and organizations, and others legitimately engaged in educational pursuits, including training, testing, and measurement activities, may address request for a licensing agreement to the copyright owners, who will determine whether, and under what conditions, including fees and charges, the materials in this book may be used them. In other words, a licensing facility exists for the legitimate use of the material in this book on other than an individual basis. However, it is asseverated and affirmed here that the material in this book CANNOT be used without the receipt of the express permission of such a licensing agreement from the Publishers. Inquiries re licensing should be addressed to the company, attention rights and permissions department.

All rights reserved, including the right of reproduction in whole or in part, in any form or by any means, electronic or mechanical, including photocopying, recording, or by any information storage and retrieval system, without permission in writing from the Publisher.

Copyright © 2025 by
National Learning Corporation

212 Michael Drive, Syosset, NY 11791
(516) 921-8888 • www.passbooks.com
E-mail: info@passbooks.com

PASSBOOK® SERIES

THE *PASSBOOK® SERIES* has been created to prepare applicants and candidates for the ultimate academic battlefield – the examination room.

At some time in our lives, each and every one of us may be required to take an examination – for validation, matriculation, admission, qualification, registration, certification, or licensure.

Based on the assumption that every applicant or candidate has met the basic formal educational standards, has taken the required number of courses, and read the necessary texts, the *PASSBOOK® SERIES* furnishes the one special preparation which may assure passing with confidence, instead of failing with insecurity. Examination questions – together with answers – are furnished as the basic vehicle for study so that the mysteries of the examination and its compounding difficulties may be eliminated or diminished by a sure method.

This book is meant to help you pass your examination provided that you qualify and are serious in your objective.

The entire field is reviewed through the huge store of content information which is succinctly presented through a provocative and challenging approach – the question-and-answer method.

A climate of success is established by furnishing the correct answers at the end of each test.

You soon learn to recognize types of questions, forms of questions, and patterns of questioning. You may even begin to anticipate expected outcomes.

You perceive that many questions are repeated or adapted so that you can gain acute insights, which may enable you to score many sure points.

You learn how to confront new questions, or types of questions, and to attack them confidently and work out the correct answers.

You note objectives and emphases, and recognize pitfalls and dangers, so that you may make positive educational adjustments.

Moreover, you are kept fully informed in relation to new concepts, methods, practices, and directions in the field.

You discover that you are actually taking the examination all the time: you are preparing for the examination by "taking" an examination, not by reading extraneous and/or supererogatory textbooks.

In short, this PASSBOOK®, used directedly, should be an important factor in helping you to pass your test.

REAL ESTATE SPECIALIST II

DUTIES
As a Real Estate Specialist II, you would supervise staff, including coordinating the work flow of a unit and/or provide oversight and direction to outside consultants. You may be responsible for an agency's statewide or regional program, serving as the agency's expert for acquisition, disposition, negotiations, relocation assistance, valuations, or property management. You would also be responsible for performing the more complicated real estate transactions.

SCOPE OF THE EXAMINATION
The written test will cover knowledge, skills and/or abilities in such areas as:

1. **Preparing written material** - These questions test for the ability to present information clearly and accurately, and to organize paragraphs logically and comprehensibly. For some questions, you will be given information in two or three sentences followed by four restatements of the information. You must then choose the best version. For other questions, you will be given paragraphs with their sentences out of order. You must then choose, from four suggestions, the best order for the sentences.
2. **Principles and techniques of real property appraisal** - These questions test for a knowledge of principles and practices used in the appraisal of agricultural, commercial, and residential real property including knowledge of the three approaches to value; sales comparison, income, and cost estimation.
3. **Supervision** - These questions test for knowledge of the principles and practices employed in planning, organizing, and controlling the activities of a work unit toward predetermined objectives. The concepts covered, usually in a situational question format, include such topics as assigning and reviewing work; evaluating performance; maintaining work standards; motivating and developing subordinates; implementing procedural change; increasing efficiency; and dealing with problems of absenteeism, morale, and discipline.
4. **Understanding and interpreting tax maps and site plans** - These questions test for the ability to read, analyze and perform computations based on various types of maps and plans, and may include tax maps, deed descriptions, site plans, survey maps and building layouts. All the information needed to answer the questions will be provided in the maps, plans, layouts or related written material. A calculator and magnifying glass may be helpful for answering some of these questions. Candidates may bring their own calculator and magnifying glass if they so choose.
5. **Real property acquisition, appraisal, negotiations, relocation, property management and applicable state and federal laws, rules and regulations** - These questions test for knowledge of terms, principles and processes relating to the State's ability to acquire and sell real property. They cover such subjects as the role of negotiators in real property acquisition; right of landowners and tenants when the State acquires property; factors influencing property value determinations and rent determinations; types and characteristics of leasing agreements; eligibility for relocation payments and calculation of payment amounts; and management of State property as an asset, including disposition. The information needed to answer some of these questions can be found in the Eminent Domain Procedure Law and State Highway Law.

HOW TO TAKE A TEST

I. YOU MUST PASS AN EXAMINATION

A. *WHAT EVERY CANDIDATE SHOULD KNOW*

Examination applicants often ask us for help in preparing for the written test. What can I study in advance? What kinds of questions will be asked? How will the test be given? How will the papers be graded?

As an applicant for a civil service examination, you may be wondering about some of these things. Our purpose here is to suggest effective methods of advance study and to describe civil service examinations.

Your chances for success on this examination can be increased if you know how to prepare. Those "pre-examination jitters" can be reduced if you know what to expect. You can even experience an adventure in good citizenship if you know why civil service exams are given.

B. *WHY ARE CIVIL SERVICE EXAMINATIONS GIVEN?*

Civil service examinations are important to you in two ways. As a citizen, you want public jobs filled by employees who know how to do their work. As a job seeker, you want a fair chance to compete for that job on an equal footing with other candidates. The best-known means of accomplishing this two-fold goal is the competitive examination.

Exams are widely publicized throughout the nation. They may be administered for jobs in federal, state, city, municipal, town or village governments or agencies.

Any citizen may apply, with some limitations, such as the age or residence of applicants. Your experience and education may be reviewed to see whether you meet the requirements for the particular examination. When these requirements exist, they are reasonable and applied consistently to all applicants. Thus, a competitive examination may cause you some uneasiness now, but it is your privilege and safeguard.

C. *HOW ARE CIVIL SERVICE EXAMS DEVELOPED?*

Examinations are carefully written by trained technicians who are specialists in the field known as "psychological measurement," in consultation with recognized authorities in the field of work that the test will cover. These experts recommend the subject matter areas or skills to be tested; only those knowledges or skills important to your success on the job are included. The most reliable books and source materials available are used as references. Together, the experts and technicians judge the difficulty level of the questions.

Test technicians know how to phrase questions so that the problem is clearly stated. Their ethics do not permit "trick" or "catch" questions. Questions may have been tried out on sample groups, or subjected to statistical analysis, to determine their usefulness.

Written tests are often used in combination with performance tests, ratings of training and experience, and oral interviews. All of these measures combine to form the best-known means of finding the right person for the right job.

II. HOW TO PASS THE WRITTEN TEST

A. NATURE OF THE EXAMINATION

To prepare intelligently for civil service examinations, you should know how they differ from school examinations you have taken. In school you were assigned certain definite pages to read or subjects to cover. The examination questions were quite detailed and usually emphasized memory. Civil service exams, on the other hand, try to discover your present ability to perform the duties of a position, plus your potentiality to learn these duties. In other words, a civil service exam attempts to predict how successful you will be. Questions cover such a broad area that they cannot be as minute and detailed as school exam questions.

In the public service similar kinds of work, or positions, are grouped together in one "class." This process is known as *position-classification*. All the positions in a class are paid according to the salary range for that class. One class title covers all of these positions, and they are all tested by the same examination.

B. FOUR BASIC STEPS

1) Study the announcement

How, then, can you know what subjects to study? Our best answer is: "Learn as much as possible about the class of positions for which you've applied." The exam will test the knowledge, skills and abilities needed to do the work.

Your most valuable source of information about the position you want is the official exam announcement. This announcement lists the training and experience qualifications. Check these standards and apply only if you come reasonably close to meeting them.

The brief description of the position in the examination announcement offers some clues to the subjects which will be tested. Think about the job itself. Review the duties in your mind. Can you perform them, or are there some in which you are rusty? Fill in the blank spots in your preparation.

Many jurisdictions preview the written test in the exam announcement by including a section called "Knowledge and Abilities Required," "Scope of the Examination," or some similar heading. Here you will find out specifically what fields will be tested.

2) Review your own background

Once you learn in general what the position is all about, and what you need to know to do the work, ask yourself which subjects you already know fairly well and which need improvement. You may wonder whether to concentrate on improving your strong areas or on building some background in your fields of weakness. When the announcement has specified "some knowledge" or "considerable knowledge," or has used adjectives like "beginning principles of…" or "advanced … methods," you can get a clue as to the number and difficulty of questions to be asked in any given field. More questions, and hence broader coverage, would be included for those subjects which are more important in the work. Now weigh your strengths and weaknesses against the job requirements and prepare accordingly.

3) Determine the level of the position

Another way to tell how intensively you should prepare is to understand the level of the job for which you are applying. Is it the entering level? In other words, is this the position in which beginners in a field of work are hired? Or is it an intermediate or advanced level? Sometimes this is indicated by such words as "Junior" or "Senior" in the class title. Other jurisdictions use Roman numerals to designate the level – Clerk I, Clerk II, for example. The word "Supervisor" sometimes appears in the title. If the level is not indicated by the title, check the description of duties. Will you be working under very close supervision, or will you have responsibility for independent decisions in this work?

4) Choose appropriate study materials

Now that you know the subjects to be examined and the relative amount of each subject to be covered, you can choose suitable study materials. For beginning level jobs, or even advanced ones, if you have a pronounced weakness in some aspect of your training, read a modern, standard textbook in that field. Be sure it is up to date and has general coverage. Such books are normally available at your library, and the librarian will be glad to help you locate one. For entry-level positions, questions of appropriate difficulty are chosen – neither highly advanced questions, nor those too simple. Such questions require careful thought but not advanced training.

If the position for which you are applying is technical or advanced, you will read more advanced, specialized material. If you are already familiar with the basic principles of your field, elementary textbooks would waste your time. Concentrate on advanced textbooks and technical periodicals. Think through the concepts and review difficult problems in your field.

These are all general sources. You can get more ideas on your own initiative, following these leads. For example, training manuals and publications of the government agency which employs workers in your field can be useful, particularly for technical and professional positions. A letter or visit to the government department involved may result in more specific study suggestions, and certainly will provide you with a more definite idea of the exact nature of the position you are seeking.

III. KINDS OF TESTS

Tests are used for purposes other than measuring knowledge and ability to perform specified duties. For some positions, it is equally important to test ability to make adjustments to new situations or to profit from training. In others, basic mental abilities not dependent on information are essential. Questions which test these things may not appear as pertinent to the duties of the position as those which test for knowledge and information. Yet they are often highly important parts of a fair examination. For very general questions, it is almost impossible to help you direct your study efforts. What we can do is to point out some of the more common of these general abilities needed in public service positions and describe some typical questions.

1) General information

Broad, general information has been found useful for predicting job success in some kinds of work. This is tested in a variety of ways, from vocabulary lists to questions about current events. Basic background in some field of work, such as sociology or economics, may be sampled in a group of questions. Often these are principles which have become familiar to most persons through exposure rather than through formal training. It is difficult to advise you how to study for these questions; being alert to the world around you is our best suggestion.

2) Verbal ability

An example of an ability needed in many positions is verbal or language ability. Verbal ability is, in brief, the ability to use and understand words. Vocabulary and grammar tests are typical measures of this ability. Reading comprehension or paragraph interpretation questions are common in many kinds of civil service tests. You are given a paragraph of written material and asked to find its central meaning.

3) Numerical ability

Number skills can be tested by the familiar arithmetic problem, by checking paired lists of numbers to see which are alike and which are different, or by interpreting charts and graphs. In the latter test, a graph may be printed in the test booklet which you are asked to use as the basis for answering questions.

4) Observation

A popular test for law-enforcement positions is the observation test. A picture is shown to you for several minutes, then taken away. Questions about the picture test your ability to observe both details and larger elements.

5) Following directions

In many positions in the public service, the employee must be able to carry out written instructions dependably and accurately. You may be given a chart with several columns, each column listing a variety of information. The questions require you to carry out directions involving the information given in the chart.

6) Skills and aptitudes

Performance tests effectively measure some manual skills and aptitudes. When the skill is one in which you are trained, such as typing or shorthand, you can practice. These tests are often very much like those given in business school or high school courses. For many of the other skills and aptitudes, however, no short-time preparation can be made. Skills and abilities natural to you or that you have developed throughout your lifetime are being tested.

Many of the general questions just described provide all the data needed to answer the questions and ask you to use your reasoning ability to find the answers. Your best preparation for these tests, as well as for tests of facts and ideas, is to be at your physical and mental best. You, no doubt, have your own methods of getting into an exam-taking mood and keeping "in shape." The next section lists some ideas on this subject.

IV. KINDS OF QUESTIONS

Only rarely is the "essay" question, which you answer in narrative form, used in civil service tests. Civil service tests are usually of the short-answer type. Full instructions for answering these questions will be given to you at the examination. But in case this is your first experience with short-answer questions and separate answer sheets, here is what you need to know:

1) Multiple-choice Questions

Most popular of the short-answer questions is the "multiple choice" or "best answer" question. It can be used, for example, to test for factual knowledge, ability to solve problems or judgment in meeting situations found at work.

A multiple-choice question is normally one of three types—
- It can begin with an incomplete statement followed by several possible endings. You are to find the one ending which *best* completes the statement, although some of the others may not be entirely wrong.
- It can also be a complete statement in the form of a question which is answered by choosing one of the statements listed.

- It can be in the form of a problem – again you select the best answer.

Here is an example of a multiple-choice question with a discussion which should give you some clues as to the method for choosing the right answer:

When an employee has a complaint about his assignment, the action which will *best* help him overcome his difficulty is to
    A. discuss his difficulty with his coworkers
    B. take the problem to the head of the organization
    C. take the problem to the person who gave him the assignment
    D. say nothing to anyone about his complaint

In answering this question, you should study each of the choices to find which is best. Consider choice "A" – Certainly an employee may discuss his complaint with fellow employees, but no change or improvement can result, and the complaint remains unresolved. Choice "B" is a poor choice since the head of the organization probably does not know what assignment you have been given, and taking your problem to him is known as "going over the head" of the supervisor. The supervisor, or person who made the assignment, is the person who can clarify it or correct any injustice. Choice "C" is, therefore, correct. To say nothing, as in choice "D," is unwise. Supervisors have and interest in knowing the problems employees are facing, and the employee is seeking a solution to his problem.

2) True/False Questions

The "true/false" or "right/wrong" form of question is sometimes used. Here a complete statement is given. Your job is to decide whether the statement is right or wrong.

SAMPLE: A roaming cell-phone call to a nearby city costs less than a non-roaming call to a distant city.

This statement is wrong, or false, since roaming calls are more expensive.

This is not a complete list of all possible question forms, although most of the others are variations of these common types. You will always get complete directions for answering questions. Be sure you understand *how* to mark your answers – ask questions until you do.

V. RECORDING YOUR ANSWERS

Computer terminals are used more and more today for many different kinds of exams.
For an examination with very few applicants, you may be told to record your answers in the test booklet itself. Separate answer sheets are much more common. If this separate answer sheet is to be scored by machine – and this is often the case – it is highly important that you mark your answers correctly in order to get credit.
An electronic scoring machine is often used in civil service offices because of the speed with which papers can be scored. Machine-scored answer sheets must be marked with a pencil, which will be given to you. This pencil has a high graphite content which responds to the electronic scoring machine. As a matter of fact, stray dots may register as answers, so do not let your pencil rest on the answer sheet while you are pondering the correct answer. Also, if your pencil lead breaks or is otherwise defective, ask for another.

Since the answer sheet will be dropped in a slot in the scoring machine, be careful not to bend the corners or get the paper crumpled.

The answer sheet normally has five vertical columns of numbers, with 30 numbers to a column. These numbers correspond to the question numbers in your test booklet. After each number, going across the page are four or five pairs of dotted lines. These short dotted lines have small letters or numbers above them. The first two pairs may also have a "T" or "F" above the letters. This indicates that the first two pairs only are to be used if the questions are of the true-false type. If the questions are multiple choice, disregard the "T" and "F" and pay attention only to the small letters or numbers.

Answer your questions in the manner of the sample that follows:

32. The largest city in the United States is
    A. Washington, D.C.
    B. New York City
    C. Chicago
    D. Detroit
    E. San Francisco

1) Choose the answer you think is best. (New York City is the largest, so "B" is correct.)
2) Find the row of dotted lines numbered the same as the question you are answering. (Find row number 32)
3) Find the pair of dotted lines corresponding to the answer. (Find the pair of lines under the mark "B.")
4) Make a solid black mark between the dotted lines.

VI. BEFORE THE TEST

Common sense will help you find procedures to follow to get ready for an examination. Too many of us, however, overlook these sensible measures. Indeed, nervousness and fatigue have been found to be the most serious reasons why applicants fail to do their best on civil service tests. Here is a list of reminders:

- Begin your preparation early – Don't wait until the last minute to go scurrying around for books and materials or to find out what the position is all about.
- Prepare continuously – An hour a night for a week is better than an all-night cram session. This has been definitely established. What is more, a night a week for a month will return better dividends than crowding your study into a shorter period of time.
- Locate the place of the exam – You have been sent a notice telling you when and where to report for the examination. If the location is in a different town or otherwise unfamiliar to you, it would be well to inquire the best route and learn something about the building.
- Relax the night before the test – Allow your mind to rest. Do not study at all that night. Plan some mild recreation or diversion; then go to bed early and get a good night's sleep.
- Get up early enough to make a leisurely trip to the place for the test – This way unforeseen events, traffic snarls, unfamiliar buildings, etc. will not upset you.
- Dress comfortably – A written test is not a fashion show. You will be known by number and not by name, so wear something comfortable.

- Leave excess paraphernalia at home – Shopping bags and odd bundles will get in your way. You need bring only the items mentioned in the official notice you received; usually everything you need is provided. Do not bring reference books to the exam. They will only confuse those last minutes and be taken away from you when in the test room.
- Arrive somewhat ahead of time – If because of transportation schedules you must get there very early, bring a newspaper or magazine to take your mind off yourself while waiting.
- Locate the examination room – When you have found the proper room, you will be directed to the seat or part of the room where you will sit. Sometimes you are given a sheet of instructions to read while you are waiting. Do not fill out any forms until you are told to do so; just read them and be prepared.
- Relax and prepare to listen to the instructions
- If you have any physical problem that may keep you from doing your best, be sure to tell the test administrator. If you are sick or in poor health, you really cannot do your best on the exam. You can come back and take the test some other time.

VII. AT THE TEST

The day of the test is here and you have the test booklet in your hand. The temptation to get going is very strong. Caution! There is more to success than knowing the right answers. You must know how to identify your papers and understand variations in the type of short-answer question used in this particular examination. Follow these suggestions for maximum results from your efforts:

1) Cooperate with the monitor

The test administrator has a duty to create a situation in which you can be as much at ease as possible. He will give instructions, tell you when to begin, check to see that you are marking your answer sheet correctly, and so on. He is not there to guard you, although he will see that your competitors do not take unfair advantage. He wants to help you do your best.

2) Listen to all instructions

Don't jump the gun! Wait until you understand all directions. In most civil service tests you get more time than you need to answer the questions. So don't be in a hurry. Read each word of instructions until you clearly understand the meaning. Study the examples, listen to all announcements and follow directions. Ask questions if you do not understand what to do.

3) Identify your papers

Civil service exams are usually identified by number only. You will be assigned a number; you must not put your name on your test papers. Be sure to copy your number correctly. Since more than one exam may be given, copy your exact examination title.

4) Plan your time

Unless you are told that a test is a "speed" or "rate of work" test, speed itself is usually not important. Time enough to answer all the questions will be provided, but this does not mean that you have all day. An overall time limit has been set. Divide the total time (in minutes) by the number of questions to determine the approximate time you have for each question.

5) Do not linger over difficult questions

If you come across a difficult question, mark it with a paper clip (useful to have along) and come back to it when you have been through the booklet. One caution if you do this – be sure to skip a number on your answer sheet as well. Check often to be sure that you have not lost your place and that you are marking in the row numbered the same as the question you are answering.

6) Read the questions

Be sure you know what the question asks! Many capable people are unsuccessful because they failed to *read* the questions correctly.

7) Answer all questions

Unless you have been instructed that a penalty will be deducted for incorrect answers, it is better to guess than to omit a question.

8) Speed tests

It is often better NOT to guess on speed tests. It has been found that on timed tests people are tempted to spend the last few seconds before time is called in marking answers at random – without even reading them – in the hope of picking up a few extra points. To discourage this practice, the instructions may warn you that your score will be "corrected" for guessing. That is, a penalty will be applied. The incorrect answers will be deducted from the correct ones, or some other penalty formula will be used.

9) Review your answers

If you finish before time is called, go back to the questions you guessed or omitted to give them further thought. Review other answers if you have time.

10) Return your test materials

If you are ready to leave before others have finished or time is called, take ALL your materials to the monitor and leave quietly. Never take any test material with you. The monitor can discover whose papers are not complete, and taking a test booklet may be grounds for disqualification.

VIII. EXAMINATION TECHNIQUES

1) Read the general instructions carefully. These are usually printed on the first page of the exam booklet. As a rule, these instructions refer to the timing of the examination; the fact that you should not start work until the signal and must stop work at a signal, etc. If there are any *special* instructions, such as a choice of questions to be answered, make sure that you note this instruction carefully.

2) When you are ready to start work on the examination, that is as soon as the signal has been given, read the instructions to each question booklet, underline any key words or phrases, such as *least, best, outline, describe* and the like. In this way you will tend to answer as requested rather than discover on reviewing your paper that you *listed without describing*, that you selected the *worst* choice rather than the *best* choice, etc.

3) If the examination is of the objective or multiple-choice type – that is, each question will also give a series of possible answers: A, B, C or D, and you are called upon to select the best answer and write the letter next to that answer on your answer paper – it is advisable to start answering each question in turn. There may be anywhere from 50 to 100 such questions in the three or four hours allotted and you can see how much time would be taken if you read through all the questions before beginning to answer any. Furthermore, if you come across a question or group of questions which you know would be difficult to answer, it would undoubtedly affect your handling of all the other questions.

4) If the examination is of the essay type and contains but a few questions, it is a moot point as to whether you should read all the questions before starting to answer any one. Of course, if you are given a choice – say five out of seven and the like – then it is essential to read all the questions so you can eliminate the two that are most difficult. If, however, you are asked to answer all the questions, there may be danger in trying to answer the easiest one first because you may find that you will spend too much time on it. The best technique is to answer the first question, then proceed to the second, etc.

5) Time your answers. Before the exam begins, write down the time it started, then add the time allowed for the examination and write down the time it must be completed, then divide the time available somewhat as follows:
   - If 3-1/2 hours are allowed, that would be 210 minutes. If you have 80 objective-type questions, that would be an average of 2-1/2 minutes per question. Allow yourself no more than 2 minutes per question, or a total of 160 minutes, which will permit about 50 minutes to review.
   - If for the time allotment of 210 minutes there are 7 essay questions to answer, that would average about 30 minutes a question. Give yourself only 25 minutes per question so that you have about 35 minutes to review.

6) The most important instruction is to *read each question* and make sure you know what is wanted. The second most important instruction is to *time yourself properly* so that you answer every question. The third most important instruction is to *answer every question*. Guess if you have to but include something for each question. Remember that you will receive no credit for a blank and will probably receive some credit if you write something in answer to an essay question. If you guess a letter – say "B" for a multiple-choice question – you may have guessed right. If you leave a blank as an answer to a multiple-choice question, the examiners may respect your feelings but it will not add a point to your score. Some exams may penalize you for wrong answers, so in such cases *only*, you may not want to guess unless you have some basis for your answer.

7) Suggestions
   a. Objective-type questions
      1. Examine the question booklet for proper sequence of pages and questions
      2. Read all instructions carefully
      3. Skip any question which seems too difficult; return to it after all other questions have been answered
      4. Apportion your time properly; do not spend too much time on any single question or group of questions

5. Note and underline key words – *all, most, fewest, least, best, worst, same, opposite,* etc.
6. Pay particular attention to negatives
7. Note unusual option, e.g., unduly long, short, complex, different or similar in content to the body of the question
8. Observe the use of "hedging" words – *probably, may, most likely,* etc.
9. Make sure that your answer is put next to the same number as the question
10. Do not second-guess unless you have good reason to believe the second answer is definitely more correct
11. Cross out original answer if you decide another answer is more accurate; do not erase until you are ready to hand your paper in
12. Answer all questions; guess unless instructed otherwise
13. Leave time for review

  b. Essay questions
1. Read each question carefully
2. Determine exactly what is wanted. Underline key words or phrases.
3. Decide on outline or paragraph answer
4. Include many different points and elements unless asked to develop any one or two points or elements
5. Show impartiality by giving pros and cons unless directed to select one side only
6. Make and write down any assumptions you find necessary to answer the questions
7. Watch your English, grammar, punctuation and choice of words
8. Time your answers; don't crowd material

8) Answering the essay question

Most essay questions can be answered by framing the specific response around several key words or ideas. Here are a few such key words or ideas:

M's: manpower, materials, methods, money, management
P's: purpose, program, policy, plan, procedure, practice, problems, pitfalls, personnel, public relations

  a. Six basic steps in handling problems:
1. Preliminary plan and background development
2. Collect information, data and facts
3. Analyze and interpret information, data and facts
4. Analyze and develop solutions as well as make recommendations
5. Prepare report and sell recommendations
6. Install recommendations and follow up effectiveness

  b. Pitfalls to avoid
1. *Taking things for granted* – A statement of the situation does not necessarily imply that each of the elements is necessarily true; for example, a complaint may be invalid and biased so that all that can be taken for granted is that a complaint has been registered

2. *Considering only one side of a situation* – Wherever possible, indicate several alternatives and then point out the reasons you selected the best one
3. *Failing to indicate follow up* – Whenever your answer indicates action on your part, make certain that you will take proper follow-up action to see how successful your recommendations, procedures or actions turn out to be
4. *Taking too long in answering any single question* – Remember to time your answers properly

IX. AFTER THE TEST

Scoring procedures differ in detail among civil service jurisdictions although the general principles are the same. Whether the papers are hand-scored or graded by machine we have described, they are nearly always graded by number. That is, the person who marks the paper knows only the number – never the name – of the applicant. Not until all the papers have been graded will they be matched with names. If other tests, such as training and experience or oral interview ratings have been given, scores will be combined. Different parts of the examination usually have different weights. For example, the written test might count 60 percent of the final grade, and a rating of training and experience 40 percent. In many jurisdictions, veterans will have a certain number of points added to their grades.

After the final grade has been determined, the names are placed in grade order and an eligible list is established. There are various methods for resolving ties between those who get the same final grade – probably the most common is to place first the name of the person whose application was received first. Job offers are made from the eligible list in the order the names appear on it. You will be notified of your grade and your rank as soon as all these computations have been made. This will be done as rapidly as possible.

People who are found to meet the requirements in the announcement are called "eligibles." Their names are put on a list of eligible candidates. An eligible's chances of getting a job depend on how high he stands on this list and how fast agencies are filling jobs from the list.

When a job is to be filled from a list of eligibles, the agency asks for the names of people on the list of eligibles for that job. When the civil service commission receives this request, it sends to the agency the names of the three people highest on this list. Or, if the job to be filled has specialized requirements, the office sends the agency the names of the top three persons who meet these requirements from the general list.

The appointing officer makes a choice from among the three people whose names were sent to him. If the selected person accepts the appointment, the names of the others are put back on the list to be considered for future openings.

That is the rule in hiring from all kinds of eligible lists, whether they are for typist, carpenter, chemist, or something else. For every vacancy, the appointing officer has his choice of any one of the top three eligibles on the list. This explains why the person whose name is on top of the list sometimes does not get an appointment when some of the persons lower on the list do. If the appointing officer chooses the second or third eligible, the No. 1 eligible does not get a job at once, but stays on the list until he is appointed or the list is terminated.

X. HOW TO PASS THE INTERVIEW TEST

The examination for which you applied requires an oral interview test. You have already taken the written test and you are now being called for the interview test – the final part of the formal examination.

You may think that it is not possible to prepare for an interview test and that there are no procedures to follow during an interview. Our purpose is to point out some things you can do in advance that will help you and some good rules to follow and pitfalls to avoid while you are being interviewed.

What is an interview supposed to test?

The written examination is designed to test the technical knowledge and competence of the candidate; the oral is designed to evaluate intangible qualities, not readily measured otherwise, and to establish a list showing the relative fitness of each candidate – as measured against his competitors – for the position sought. Scoring is not on the basis of "right" and "wrong," but on a sliding scale of values ranging from "not passable" to "outstanding." As a matter of fact, it is possible to achieve a relatively low score without a single "incorrect" answer because of evident weakness in the qualities being measured.

Occasionally, an examination may consist entirely of an oral test – either an individual or a group oral. In such cases, information is sought concerning the technical knowledges and abilities of the candidate, since there has been no written examination for this purpose. More commonly, however, an oral test is used to supplement a written examination.

Who conducts interviews?

The composition of oral boards varies among different jurisdictions. In nearly all, a representative of the personnel department serves as chairman. One of the members of the board may be a representative of the department in which the candidate would work. In some cases, "outside experts" are used, and, frequently, a businessman or some other representative of the general public is asked to serve. Labor and management or other special groups may be represented. The aim is to secure the services of experts in the appropriate field.

However the board is composed, it is a good idea (and not at all improper or unethical) to ascertain in advance of the interview who the members are and what groups they represent. When you are introduced to them, you will have some idea of their backgrounds and interests, and at least you will not stutter and stammer over their names.

What should be done before the interview?

While knowledge about the board members is useful and takes some of the surprise element out of the interview, there is other preparation which is more substantive. It *is* possible to prepare for an oral interview – in several ways:

1) Keep a copy of your application and review it carefully before the interview

This may be the only document before the oral board, and the starting point of the interview. Know what education and experience you have listed there, and the sequence and dates of all of it. Sometimes the board will ask you to review the highlights of your experience for them; you should not have to hem and haw doing it.

2) Study the class specification and the examination announcement

Usually, the oral board has one or both of these to guide them. The qualities, characteristics or knowledges required by the position sought are stated in these documents. They offer valuable clues as to the nature of the oral interview. For example, if the job involves supervisory responsibilities, the announcement will usually indicate that knowledge of modern supervisory methods and the qualifications of the candidate as a supervisor will be tested. If so, you can expect such questions, frequently in the form of a hypothetical situation which you are expected to solve. NEVER go into an oral without knowledge of the duties and responsibilities of the job you seek.

3) Think through each qualification required

Try to visualize the kind of questions you would ask if you were a board member. How well could you answer them? Try especially to appraise your own knowledge and background in each area, *measured against the job sought*, and identify any areas in which you are weak. Be critical and realistic – do not flatter yourself.

4) Do some general reading in areas in which you feel you may be weak

For example, if the job involves supervision and your past experience has NOT, some general reading in supervisory methods and practices, particularly in the field of human relations, might be useful. Do NOT study agency procedures or detailed manuals. The oral board will be testing your understanding and capacity, not your memory.

5) Get a good night's sleep and watch your general health and mental attitude

You will want a clear head at the interview. Take care of a cold or any other minor ailment, and of course, no hangovers.

What should be done on the day of the interview?

Now comes the day of the interview itself. Give yourself plenty of time to get there. Plan to arrive somewhat ahead of the scheduled time, particularly if your appointment is in the fore part of the day. If a previous candidate fails to appear, the board might be ready for you a bit early. By early afternoon an oral board is almost invariably behind schedule if there are many candidates, and you may have to wait. Take along a book or magazine to read, or your application to review, but leave any extraneous material in the waiting room when you go in for your interview. In any event, relax and compose yourself.

The matter of dress is important. The board is forming impressions about you – from your experience, your manners, your attitude, and your appearance. Give your personal appearance careful attention. Dress your best, but not your flashiest. Choose conservative, appropriate clothing, and be sure it is immaculate. This is a business interview, and your appearance should indicate that you regard it as such. Besides, being well groomed and properly dressed will help boost your confidence.

Sooner or later, someone will call your name and escort you into the interview room. *This is it.* From here on you are on your own. It is too late for any more preparation. But remember, you asked for this opportunity to prove your fitness, and you are here because your request was granted.

What happens when you go in?

The usual sequence of events will be as follows: The clerk (who is often the board stenographer) will introduce you to the chairman of the oral board, who will introduce you to the other members of the board. Acknowledge the introductions before you sit down. Do not be surprised if you find a microphone facing you or a stenotypist sitting by. Oral interviews are usually recorded in the event of an appeal or other review.

Usually the chairman of the board will open the interview by reviewing the highlights of your education and work experience from your application – primarily for the benefit of the other members of the board, as well as to get the material into the record. Do not interrupt or comment unless there is an error or significant misinterpretation; if that is the case, do not hesitate. But do not quibble about insignificant matters. Also, he will usually ask you some question about your education, experience or your present job – partly to get you to start talking and to establish the interviewing "rapport." He may start the actual questioning, or turn it over to one of the other members. Frequently, each member undertakes the questioning on a particular area, one in which he is perhaps most competent, so you can expect each member to participate in the examination. Because time is limited, you may also expect some rather abrupt switches in the direction the questioning takes, so do not be upset by it. Normally, a board member will not pursue a single line of questioning unless he discovers a particular strength or weakness.

After each member has participated, the chairman will usually ask whether any member has any further questions, then will ask you if you have anything you wish to add. Unless you are expecting this question, it may floor you. Worse, it may start you off on an extended, extemporaneous speech. The board is not usually seeking more information. The question is principally to offer you a last opportunity to present further qualifications or to indicate that you have nothing to add. So, if you feel that a significant qualification or characteristic has been overlooked, it is proper to point it out in a sentence or so. Do not compliment the board on the thoroughness of their examination – they have been sketchy, and you know it. If you wish, merely say, "No thank you, I have nothing further to add." This is a point where you can "talk yourself out" of a good impression or fail to present an important bit of information. Remember, *you close the interview yourself.*

The chairman will then say, "That is all, Mr. _____, thank you." Do not be startled; the interview is over, and quicker than you think. Thank him, gather your belongings and take your leave. Save your sigh of relief for the other side of the door.

How to put your best foot forward

Throughout this entire process, you may feel that the board individually and collectively is trying to pierce your defenses, seek out your hidden weaknesses and embarrass and confuse you. Actually, this is not true. They are obliged to make an appraisal of your qualifications for the job you are seeking, and they want to see you in your best light. Remember, they must interview all candidates and a non-cooperative candidate may become a failure in spite of their best efforts to bring out his qualifications. Here are 15 suggestions that will help you:

1) Be natural – Keep your attitude confident, not cocky

If you are not confident that you can do the job, do not expect the board to be. Do not apologize for your weaknesses, try to bring out your strong points. The board is interested in a positive, not negative, presentation. Cockiness will antagonize any board member and make him wonder if you are covering up a weakness by a false show of strength.

2) Get comfortable, but don't lounge or sprawl

Sit erectly but not stiffly. A careless posture may lead the board to conclude that you are careless in other things, or at least that you are not impressed by the importance of the occasion. Either conclusion is natural, even if incorrect. Do not fuss with your clothing, a pencil or an ashtray. Your hands may occasionally be useful to emphasize a point; do not let them become a point of distraction.

3) Do not wisecrack or make small talk

This is a serious situation, and your attitude should show that you consider it as such. Further, the time of the board is limited – they do not want to waste it, and neither should you.

4) Do not exaggerate your experience or abilities

In the first place, from information in the application or other interviews and sources, the board may know more about you than you think. Secondly, you probably will not get away with it. An experienced board is rather adept at spotting such a situation, so do not take the chance.

5) If you know a board member, do not make a point of it, yet do not hide it

Certainly you are not fooling him, and probably not the other members of the board. Do not try to take advantage of your acquaintanceship – it will probably do you little good.

6) Do not dominate the interview

Let the board do that. They will give you the clues – do not assume that you have to do all the talking. Realize that the board has a number of questions to ask you, and do not try to take up all the interview time by showing off your extensive knowledge of the answer to the first one.

7) Be attentive

You only have 20 minutes or so, and you should keep your attention at its sharpest throughout. When a member is addressing a problem or question to you, give him your undivided attention. Address your reply principally to him, but do not exclude the other board members.

8) Do not interrupt

A board member may be stating a problem for you to analyze. He will ask you a question when the time comes. Let him state the problem, and wait for the question.

9) Make sure you understand the question

Do not try to answer until you are sure what the question is. If it is not clear, restate it in your own words or ask the board member to clarify it for you. However, do not haggle about minor elements.

10) Reply promptly but not hastily

A common entry on oral board rating sheets is "candidate responded readily," or "candidate hesitated in replies." Respond as promptly and quickly as you can, but do not jump to a hasty, ill-considered answer.

11) Do not be peremptory in your answers

A brief answer is proper – but do not fire your answer back. That is a losing game from your point of view. The board member can probably ask questions much faster than you can answer them.

12) Do not try to create the answer you think the board member wants

He is interested in what kind of mind you have and how it works – not in playing games. Furthermore, he can usually spot this practice and will actually grade you down on it.

13) Do not switch sides in your reply merely to agree with a board member

Frequently, a member will take a contrary position merely to draw you out and to see if you are willing and able to defend your point of view. Do not start a debate, yet do not surrender a good position. If a position is worth taking, it is worth defending.

14) Do not be afraid to admit an error in judgment if you are shown to be wrong
The board knows that you are forced to reply without any opportunity for careful consideration. Your answer may be demonstrably wrong. If so, admit it and get on with the interview.

15) Do not dwell at length on your present job
The opening question may relate to your present assignment. Answer the question but do not go into an extended discussion. You are being examined for a *new* job, not your present one. As a matter of fact, try to phrase ALL your answers in terms of the job for which you are being examined.

Basis of Rating
Probably you will forget most of these "do's" and "don'ts" when you walk into the oral interview room. Even remembering them all will not ensure you a passing grade. Perhaps you did not have the qualifications in the first place. But remembering them will help you to put your best foot forward, without treading on the toes of the board members.

Rumor and popular opinion to the contrary notwithstanding, an oral board wants you to make the best appearance possible. They know you are under pressure – but they also want to see how you respond to it as a guide to what your reaction would be under the pressures of the job you seek. They will be influenced by the degree of poise you display, the personal traits you show and the manner in which you respond.

ABOUT THIS BOOK

This book contains tests divided into Examination Sections. Go through each test, answering every question in the margin. We have also attached a sample answer sheet at the back of the book that can be removed and used. At the end of each test look at the answer key and check your answers. On the ones you got wrong, look at the right answer choice and learn. Do not fill in the answers first. Do not memorize the questions and answers, but understand the answer and principles involved. On your test, the questions will likely be different from the samples. Questions are changed and new ones added. If you understand these past questions you should have success with any changes that arise. Tests may consist of several types of questions. We have additional books on each subject should more study be advisable or necessary for you. Finally, the more you study, the better prepared you will be. This book is intended to be the last thing you study before you walk into the examination room. Prior study of relevant texts is also recommended. NLC publishes some of these in our Fundamental Series. Knowledge and good sense are important factors in passing your exam. Good luck also helps. So now study this Passbook, absorb the material contained within and take that knowledge into the examination. Then do your best to pass that exam.

EXAMINATION SECTION

EXAMINATION SECTION
TEST 1

DIRECTIONS: Each question or incomplete statement is followed by several suggested answers or completions. Select the one that *BEST* answers the question or completes the statement. *PRINT THE LETTER OF THE CORRECT ANSWER IN THE SPACE AT THE RIGHT.*

1. It has been stated that in renting there is no substitute for accompanying a prospect to the space you are trying to rent. Of the following, the MOST important reason for this is that 1.____

    A. prospects are not likely to be willing to inspect space unless they are accompanied
    B. prospects are likely to see the least attractive points of the available space unless skillfully diverted from them
    C. the real estate manager is able to exhibit the good points of the space
    D. the presence of the real estate manager alerts the staff to the necessity for making a good impression

2. As real estate manager, you have commercial space for rent which contains a certain defect which is known to you. In showing the space to a prospective tenant it would be *ADVISABLE tor* you to 2.____

    A. attempt to ignore the defect and disparage its importance if it is mentioned by the prospect
    B. explain the defect in advance of showing the space to the prospect
    C. ignore the defect and immediately change the subject if it is mentioned by the prospect
    D. show the space at a time when the defect may not be apparent

3. The owner of a building containing commercial space has informed his renting agent of the rent he expects to receive for this commercial space. When shown the space and told of the rent, a prospective tenant, of good reputation, agrees immediately and without argument to rent the space. It would be *BEST* for the renting agent to 3.____

    A. indicate that he has made an error and ask for a somewhat higher rent which the prospect may be willing to pay
    B. make immediate arrangements to close the deal on the basis of the rent already discussed
    C. set conditions of leasing, other than rent, which are disadvantageous to the prospect, indicating that these conditions may be withdrawn if a higher rent is agreed upon
    D. make no binding commitment until he has an opportunity to look for other prospective tenants who might be willing to pay a higher rental

4. Assume that approximately 7% of the commercial rental space in a neighborhood is vacant and that this and other rental conditions are the same now as they were when certain commercial space, for which you are managing agent, was last rented. The lease is about to expire on the commercial space. Faced with the problem of renting the space to a new tenant or renewing the occupancy of the present tenant, it is *USUALLY* true that 4.____

1

A. new tenants are willing to pay higher rents than old tenants
B. new tenants make fewer demands than old tenants if the real estate agent is of good reputation
C. old tenants make fewer demands than new tenants if the real estate agent has properly handled their requests while under the old lease
D. it is more desirable to get a new tenant than retain an old one

5. The one of the following factors to which you should give LEAST consideration in determining the rental value of office space in a building under your management is

A. accessibility of the building to means of transportation
B. height of the ceilings in the office space
C. prestige value of tenancy in the building
D. rental value of office space in other buildings in the neighborhood

6. The LEAST accurate of the following statements concerning the determination of the rental value of office space within an office building is:

A. Space along the side of the building is less valuable than space on a corner.
B. The better the view from windows in the space, the more valuable is the space.
C. Above the eighth floor, the higher the floor, the less valuable the space.
D. The more accessible space is to the toilet facilities (of modern design), the more valuable it is.

7. One of the factors to be considered in renting apartments is the likelihood that the prospective tenant may later wish to renew his lease. In a building in a stable neighborhood, the one of the following types of families which a real estate manager should LEAST expect to want to remain after the expiration of the lease is a

A. single person, age about 67 years
B. young couple, age about 25 years
C. couple, age about 40 years, with two children, age 7 and 9 years
D. couple, age about 45 years, with four children age 7, 8, 9 and 12 years

8. Assume that a great deal of building is going on in a neighborhood where there is much unimproved land in order to take care of an increasing population. It is to be expected that real estate values in this neighborhood are

A. decreasing
B. increasing
C. increasing for existing buildings while decreasing for unimproved land
D. remaining relatively constant

9. In a neighborhood where there is a trend toward increasing population due to conversions of private dwellings into rooming houses, the value of neighborhood real estate will generally be

A. decreasing
B. increasing
C. increasing for unimproved land but decreasing for land having residential buildings
D. unaffected

10. An apartment consists of the following: a living room 12 ft. X 14 ft.; a bedroom 8 ft. X 8 ft.; a bathroom 6 ft. X 6 ft.; a bedroom 11 ft. X 12 ft.; a kitchen 6 ft. X 10 ft., at one end of which is a dining area 6 ft. X 6 ft. separated from the kitchen by room dividers in the form of 5 ft. high cabinets; a hallway 4 ft. X 15 ft.; two closets 2 1/2 ft. X 5 ft.; and a closet 4 ft. X 7 ft. The only windows in the apartment are in the bedrooms, living room, kitchen, and bathroom. According to the system of calculation generally used, the number of rooms in this apartment is

    A. 3 1/2   B. 4 1/2   C. 4 3/4   D. 5 1/4

11. The one of the following statements which is NOT a valid reason for demanding a security deposit of a month's rent as part of the lease agreement is:

    A. Ability to pay a security deposit as well as the first month's rent before taking occupancy tends to indicate that a tenant is solvent.
    B. Current expenses of the building may in part be defrayed by security deposits.
    C. If a tenant moves before the expiration of his lease, the security deposit reduces the loss due to vacancy that is likely to occur.
    D. Loss of income will be minimized in the event that action to evict a tenant for non-payment of rent becomes necessary.

12. At the expiration of a lease on commercial space where the tenant has installed sinks and toilets, it is the USUAL practice that ownership of these fixtures

    A. passes to the landlord
    B. passes to the landlord, with the tenant retaining the right of purchase at a price equal to the original cost less depreciation
    C. remains with the tenant
    D. remains with the tenant, unless otherwise specified in the lease

13. The term "percentage lease," when used in connection with leasing of a store, refers USUALLY to an agreement

    A. to assume the remaining portion of an existing lease and at its termination to renew the lease at an agreed percentage increase
    B. to lease a percentage portion of previously undivided premises and to erect suitable partitions
    C. to pay a fixed rent plus a percentage of the tenant's gross receipts above an agreed amount
    D. among several lessees of one premises, each to assume responsibility for a percentage portion of an undivided premises and a percentage portion of the lease

14. The term "title insurance" refers to insurance that protects a

    A. prospective purchaser with a preliminary purchase agreement against refusal of the owner to convey title of the property
    B. purchaser against any outstanding taxes or liens against the property prior to the transfer of title
    C. purchaser against damage to property between the time of the agreement to purchase and the final transfer of title
    D. purchaser against the discovery of a defect in the seller's title to the property

15. Where a store or commercial establishment which uses water is situated in a residential building, the MAJORITY of commercial lease agreements provide that

    A. a fixed amount be paid with the rent to the landlord to cover water use
    B. a fixed percentage of the water charge for the building be paid by the commercial tenant
    C. water charges be paid by the landlord
    D. water charges, dependent upon water use, be paid separately by the commercial tenant

16. The LEAST amount of time that it will take to have a tenant removed from an apartment for non-payment of rent, from the date that the owner decides to evict the tenant, who is already more than one month delinquent in the payment of his rent, is GENERALLY

    A. less than 7 days
    B. between 13 and 19 days
    C. between 17 and 30 days
    D. not less than 10 months

17. The one of the following which is NOT provided for by Workmen's Compensation Insurance is payment

    A. for hospitalization of the injured employee
    B. for medicines and crutches or other implements that may be necessary to restore the employee's health
    C. when an injury is due to the employee's being under the influence of alcohol
    D. when an injury is due to the employee's own negligence

18. Public liability insurance GENERALLY protects the insured, landlord when

    A. a tenant's property is damaged by water used to put out a fire in another tenant's apartment
    B. a visitor to one of the tenants is injured by falling over a worn and broken step at the entrance to the building
    C. an employee is injured while performing his assigned duties
    D. damage to the building has been caused by an airplane crash

19. Assuming that sufficient fire insurance is carried, the MOST important factor considered by fire insurance companies in making a settlement after a fire has destroyed a building is the _____ of the building.

    A. assessed valuation
    B. most recent sale price
    C. original construction cost
    D. replacement cost

20. In purchasing fire insurance in your State, it should be realized that

    A. all members of the Board of Fire Underwriters will charge the same rates, while non-member companies may have different rates
    B. insurance companies incorporated in your State all charge the rates which are fixed by law, while out-of-state companies are free to charge any rates that they deem appropriate
    C. insurance rates are determined by bargaining between the insurance broker and the prospective customer as in any free market
    D. no rate agreements exist, each insurance company individually determining its own rates based upon such factors as past experience, profit margins, and competitive position

21. The owner of a building in a city of over one million population proposes to carry one percent co-insurance to protect himself against loss by fire. It would generally be *BEST* for a real estate agent to recommend that

    A. a greater amount of insurance be purchased if the replacement cost of the building is greater than the original construction cost
    B. a lesser amount be purchased because total loss of a building in this city by fire is unlikely
    C. a lesser amount be purchased since insurance companies will not sell insurance for the full value of a building
    D. the insurance be purchased if the owner has the funds available to pay the premiums

22. From the point of view of good real estate management, a tenant should *FIRST be* told of the necessity to pay his rent on time

    A. when he makes application for a lease
    B. whenever he is more than one week delinquent in the payment of his rent
    C. whenever he is more than three days delinquent in the payment of his rent
    D. within the first month after the lease becomes operative

23. If a tenant refuses to pay his rent until the real estate manager has had an inexpensive but necessary repair made, it would be *BEST* for the real estate manager to

    A. refuse even to consider the repair until the rent is paid
    B. explain to the tenant that he has an obligation to pay rent but agree to investigate the need for the repair, insisting that rent be paid after the investigation is completed
    C. have the repair made and then insist on the payment of rent
    D. insist that the rent be paid, refusing to couple consideration of the need for the repair with the payment of rent

24. Examination of the public hallways of a building containing tile floors reveals that a blackened and dirty area exists along the base of the walls, extending up the walls for a couple of inches. The MOST likely of the following explanations for this condition is that

    A. children have been scuffing their feet along the walls
    B. it is a normal development caused by the traffic of dirty feet in the halls, elimination of the dirty area being impractical because of the expense
    C. the floors have been cleaned with a mop which was not sufficiently clean
    D. there is a structural fault in the flooring or walls requiring immediate attention from an expert

25. The charge for water supplied by cities of over one million population to an apartment house with no commercial tenants is GENERALLY made on the basis of

    A. assessed valuation of the building
    B. frontage and number of apartments
    C. frontage, number of stories, and number and type of water outlets
    D. water meter readings

KEY (CORRECT ANSWERS)

1. C
2. B
3. B
4. C
5. B

6. C
7. B
8. B
9. A
10. B

11. B
12. A
13. C
14. D
15. D

16. B
17. C
18. B
19. D
20. A

21. B
22. A
23. D
24. C
25. C

TEST 2

DIRECTIONS: Each question or incomplete statement is followed by several suggested answers or completions. Select the one that *BEST* answers the question or completes the statement. *PRINT THE LETTER OF THE CORRECT ANSWER IN THE SPACE AT THE RIGHT.*

1. The term HATCH DOOR is generally used to describe a door   1.____

   A. between the outdoors and the basement
   B. giving access from the boiler room to the fire tubes of a boiler
   C. giving access to the roof from the top of the stairway
   D. giving entrance from the hallway to the elevator shaft

2. A *PARAPET* is   2.____

   A. a device through which a fine spray of oil enters the firebox of an oil burner
   B. a hot water drain used mornings to bleed off cold water which has accumulated overnight
   C. a protective low wall at the edge of a roof
   D. the primary support of an arch

3. *2-4-D is* used to designate   3.____

   A. an oil moisture used to start an oil burner in operation
   B. a size of threaded pipe of the type used to carry waste water
   C. a type of weed killer for use on lawns
   D. a type of pre-mixed cement for patching walks

4. A *CONDENSER* is a part of a   4.____

   A. boiler where the oil is preheated
   B. fertilizer spreader where concentrated fertilizer is mixed with water
   C. radiator where the return water forms from steam
   D. refrigerator where the refrigerant takes liquid form

5. A *LOW WATER CUT-OFF* is usually a device to   5.____

   A. close the waste line opening when the waste has flushed out of the toilet bowl
   B. shut down the automatic lawn-watering system when the moisture level in the lawn reaches a predetermined level of saturation
   C. stop a sump pump when the water level is below floor level in the sump well
   D. stop an oil burner motor when the water level in the system falls below a predetermined level

6. The purpose of a *CHECK VALVE* is to   6.____

   A. interrupt the flow of electricity in an overloaded circuit
   B. limit the amount of electrical current which can fl flow from a main line into a branch circuit
   C. prevent water from flowing in a pipe system in a direction opposite to that desired
   D. stop the flow of water when the water in a system reaches a predetermined level

7. An investigation has been made of a broken window pane in an apartment on the third floor which the tenant claims was broken by children playing outside. The investigation disclosed that there were several small holes in the window pane. Each hole is approximately cone shaped and is about 3/16 inch in diameter on the inside of the glass (room side) and about 1/2 inch in diameter on the outside. Cracks connected some of these holes. On the basis of this information, the tenant should

    A. be charged for the window pane since the damage is not normal wear and tear and it is not possible to substantiate the tenant's claim
    B. be charged for the window pane since the nature of the damage indicates that it was caused from inside
    C. not be charged for the window pane since it is not possible to determine the cause of the damage and the low floor involved does not tend to support the tenant's explanation
    D. not be charged for the window pane since the nature of the damage indicates that it was caused from outside

8. The one of the following which has come into common use for the extermination of roaches and silverfish is

    A. 2-4 D   B. chlordane   C. paris green   D. red squill

9. When the building superintendent tells you that the transformer of one of the oil burners is defective, he is referring to the device which

    A. atomizes the liquid oil prior to ignition
    B. changes low pressure steam to high pressure steam
    C. increases the voltage for oil ignition
    D. regulates oil temperature prior to atomization

10. When a building superintendent reports corroded flashings resulting in leakage, the part of the building he is referring to is the

    A. basement piping   B. boiler room
    C. pavement adjoining building D. roof

11. If an automatic elevator is not leveling properly at floor stops, the proper action to take is to

    A. allow the car to remain in service only if the distance between the car floor and floor landing is 3 inches or less
    B. post signs to that effect in the elevator car to warn passengers
    C. station a maintenance man near the ground floor stop to warn passengers
    D. take the car out of service during slow periods to make necessary adjustments

12. Although rock salt is commonly used on the walks when they are iced or heavily packed with snow, the *CHIEF* disadvantage of its use is that it

    A. creates a very slushy condition
    B. generally causes deterioration of concrete walks
    C. increases cleaning costs if used intensively
    D. is harmful to adjacent trees and shrubs

13. When instructing tenants how to clean enamel-painted woodwork, the tenant should be advised to wash the surfaces with   13._____

    A. ammonia water
    B. mild soap and water solution
    C. plain warm water
    D. strong soda solution

14. Of the following items included in the work schedule of porters, the one that should be assigned as a daily duty is   14._____

    A. cleaning incinerators
    B. cleaning stairhall windows and woodwork
    C. mopping all assigned stairhalls
    D. sweeping all stair landings

15. A building has a coal-fired steam boiler as the heating plant. While using the boiler, proper examination of the water gauge fails to reveal the presence of any water. Of the following, it would be best that   15._____

    A. a small amount of water be let into the boiler immediately, increasing the amount of water gradually until the proper level is reached
    B. the fire be put out immediately by covering with sand
    C. the fire be put out immediately by spraying with warm water
    D. the required amount of water be put into the boiler immediately

---

KEY (CORRECT ANSWERS)

1. D
2. C
3. C
4. D
5. D

6. C
7. B
8. B
9. C
10. D

11. D
12. D
13. B
14. D
15. B

EXAMINATION SECTION
TEST 1

DIRECTIONS: Each question or incomplete statement is followed by several suggested answers or completions. Select the one that BEST answers the question or completes the statement. *PRINT THE LETTER OF THE CORRECT ANSWER IN THE SPACE AT THE RIGHT.*

1. During an interview with a tenant at your office, he confides to you that he would rather find his own apartment for his family than move into public housing. He asks for your advice in this matter.
   The BEST thing you can do is

   A. advise that he look only to public housing since these are the best apartments
   B. tell him that you cannot advise him in such personal matters and then refer him to Social Services
   C. discuss with him the different ways he might find an apartment, including one in public housing
   D. suggest that he talk over his decision more carefully with his family

2. While inspecting conditions around a site, you notice that some of the garbage cans are not covered.
   Which of the following BEST explains why this condition should be corrected? To

   A. prevent the garbage cans from getting lost
   B. prevent garbage from cans spreading onto the street
   C. allow sanitation men to handle the cans without spillage
   D. keep dogs and cats from knocking garbage cans over

3. While interviewing tenants, an assistant may find that a tenant will be silent for a short time before answering questions.
   In order to get the required information from the tenant when this happens, the assistant should GENERALLY

   A. repeat the same question to make the tenant stop hesitating
   B. ask the tenant to write out his answer
   C. ask the tenant to answer quickly because other tenants are waiting to see you
   D. wait patiently and not pressure the tenant into quick, undeveloped answers

4. A tenant that you have been trying to encourage to apply for public housing comes to your desk at the site office. He is talking in a very angry and excited way about the lack of heat in his apartment. He says he will not pay his rent until there is heat.
   The BEST thing for you to do at this time is to

   A. tell him that he should have applied for public housing as you suggested
   B. immediately let your supervisor know that he is refusing to pay his rent
   C. let him talk until he finishes and then discuss his problem with him
   D. tell him that you will not talk to him until he stops yelling

5. You have been informed that no determination has yet been made on the eligibility of a certain tenant for public housing. The decision will depend upon further checking. When you see the tenant, he seems to be quite worried, and he asks you whether his application has been accepted.
   What would be BEST for you to do under these circumstances? Tell him

   A. you can't talk to him because there is no definite information and you are very busy
   B. to put his question in writing and send it to your manager so that it will be on record
   C. you don't know yet but that he should not worry since you are quite sure he will be accepted
   D. his application is being checked, and you will let him know the final result

6. An assistant is interviewing a high priority applicant who, contrary to usual experience, is extremely well-prepared and supplied with all the information the assistant is seeking. Which of the following possible actions by the assistant is MOST suitable under these circumstances?

   A. Directly showing a willingness to review the information carefully and promptly
   B. Exercising extreme caution about the credibility of the facts presented
   C. Showing his awareness that the applicant is trying to trick him with false information
   D. Accepting all of the candidate's information because of his obviously high level of intelligence

7. One of the tenants to be relocated is an extremely alert but elderly man who resists your every attempt to discuss with him the necessity for moving. He has lived in this building for almost thirty years, and he states flatly that he will NOT move.
   Of the following, the MOST acceptable action for you to take is to

   A. tell him he is being unreasonable and selfish
   B. forcibly have him removed from the premises
   C. refer his case to a social worker
   D. advise him to take his case to the Legal Aid Society

8. Suppose you telephone to set up an important appointment with a tenant for a specific day on your calendar. He refuses to meet with you on that day because he claims the day is his religious holiday.
   What is the BEST way of handling this situation?

   A. Tell him it is against his interest not to meet with you on that day
   B. Give up any idea now of meeting with him and go on to arranging your next appointment
   C. Ask when he will be able to meet with you and indicate to him what the subject is
   D. Indicate to him that you know the holiday cannot be important since city employees do not officially have that day off

9. In a building slated for demolition but still inhabited by tenants, an assistant sees some children of tenants pulling on a pipe in the hall. He tells them to stop but they say that the building is being torn down anyway. What should the assistant do FIRST?

   A. Explain to the children that although this is true, they are causing danger to tenants still in the building.

B. Go immediately to the parents and tell them to punish their children for their misbehavior.
C. Say nothing else to the children but go to the site office and report the problem to his supervisor.
D. Go outside and call a policeman but tell the policeman to treat the children gently.

10. When interviewing a tenant who is to be relocated, the FIRST of the following actions for you to take is to

    A. inform the tenant that your office will help only if he cooperates
    B. advise the tenant that you must see proof for all statements he makes
    C. assure the tenant that every effort will be made to find suitable housing
    D. tell the tenant he will have no trouble finding new housing facilities

10.____

11. During interviews, people give information about themselves in several ways. Of the following, which would usually give the LEAST amount of information about the person being questioned? His

    A. spoken words
    B. tone of voice
    C. facial expression
    D. body position

11.____

12. Suppose that while you are interviewing a tenant about the condition of his apartment, he becomes angered by your questioning and begins to use abusive language. Which of the following is the BEST way for you to react to him?

    A. Use the same kind of language as he does to show him that you are neither impressed nor upset by his speech.
    B. Interrupt him and tell him that you are not required to listen to such language.
    C. Lower your voice and speak more slowly in an attempt to set an example that will calm him.
    D. Let him continue to use abusive language but insist that he answer your questions at once.

12.____

13. Of the following characteristics, the one which would be MOST helpful for an assistant when helping an angry applicant understand why he has been turned down for public housing would be the ability to

    A. state the rules exactly as they are written
    B. show examples of other cases where the same thing happened
    C. remain patient and understanding of the person's position
    D. remain uninvolved and cold to individual personal problems

13.____

Questions 14-19.

DIRECTIONS: Answer Questions 14 through 19 on the basis of the information given in the paragraphs below.

Three year's ago, a city introduced a program of reduced transit rates for the elderly. It was hoped that this program would increase the travel of the elderly and help them maintain a greater measure of independence. About 600,000 of the 800,000 eligible residents are currently enrolled in the program. To be eligible, a person must be 65 years of age or older and not employed full-time. Riding for reduced fare is permitted between 10:00 M. and 4:00 P.M. and between 7:00 P.M. and midnight on weekdays and 24 hours a day on Saturdays, Sundays, and holidays.

In a city university study based on a sampling of 728 enrollees interviewed, it was learned that 51 percent are able to travel more, and 30.8 percent had been able to save enough money to make a noticeable difference in their budgets as a result of the reduced-fare program.

It has been recommended that reduced-fare programs be extended to encourage the use of transit Lines in off-hours by other groups such as the poor, the very young, housewives, and the physically handicapped. To implement this recommendation, it would be necessary for the Federal government to increase transit subsidies.

14. Which one of the following would be the BEST title for the passage above?

    A. A Program of Reduced Transit Rates for the Elderly
    B. Recommendations for Extending Programs for the Elderly
    C. City University Study on the Relationship of Age and Travel
    D. Eligibility Requirements for the Reduced Rate Program

15. *Approximately* what percentage of the eligible residents is currently enrolled in the reduced-fare program?

    A. 25%   B. 50%   C. 65%   D. 75%

16. Which one of the following persons is NOT eligible for the reduced-fare program? A

    A. Woman, age 67, employed part-time as a stenographer
    B. Handicapped man, age 62
    C. Blind man, age 66, employed part-time as a transcribing typist
    D. Housewife, age 70

17. At which one of the following times would the reduced-fare NOT be permitted for an eligible elderly person?

    A. Sunday, 6:00 P.M.   B. Christmas Day, 2:00 M.
    C. Tuesday, 9:00 M.   D. Thursday, 8:00 P.M.

18. Of the 728 enrollees interviewed in a city university study of the reduced-fare program, it was found that

    A. the majority traveled more and saved money at the same time
    B. more than half traveled less and therefore saved money
    C. about half traveled more and about one-third saved money
    D. the majority saved money but traveled the same rate as before

19. According to the passage above, what would be necessary to extend the reduced-fare program to other groups of people?   19.____

    A. Increasing the eligible age to 68
    B. Reducing the hours when half-fare is permitted
    C. Increasing the fare for other riders
    D. Increasing the transit subsidies by the Federal government

20. Reports are made MOST often in order to   20.____

    A. suggest new ideas
    B. give information
    C. issue orders to workers
    D. show that work is being done

21. An assistant is reporting a loose floor board in a certain apartment building on the site. The MOST important thing he should report in order to get immediate repairs is   21.____

    A. how the floor board became loose
    B. when the floor board became loose
    C. the type of material and the number of men needed to make the repair
    D. in which apartment the loose floor board is located

22. Suppose you receive a phone call from a tenant about a problem that requires you to look up the information and call her back. Although the tenant had given you her name earlier and you can say the name, you are not sure that you can spell it correctly. Which of the following would be MOST likely to insure that you spell the name correctly?   22.____

    A. Say the name slowly and ask her if you are saying it correctly.
    B. Spell her name as you have been saying it.
    C. Ask her to spell the name so that you can write it.
    D. Look through your files for a similar name and copy the spelling.

23. When tenants relocate, a report is made. This report is in the form of a standard form instead of a fully written report.   23.____
    The MOST important advantage of using a standard form for certain information is that

    A. one can be sure that the report will be sent in as soon as possible
    B. anyone can write out the report without directions from a supervisor
    C. needed information is less likely to be left out of the report
    D. information that is written up this way is less likely to be false

24. Suppose you are filling out a section of a form to describe an incident which will be read by a social worker but you run out of space before finishing. It would be BEST for you to   24.____

    A. leave out whatever information you consider unimportant
    B. write what you can on the form and attach another sheet with the rest of the information
    C. cross out what you wrote on the form and write on a separate sheet of paper which you attach to the form
    D. write what you can on the form and tell your supervisor or the social worker the rest of it

25. It is part of an assistant's job to help a manager enter various items of information on a monthly report. This information may be, for example, the number of tenants relocated to different types of housing and the number of tenants left on the site.
    The assistant must be careful NOT to make mistakes on his entries about tenants because

    A. mistakes will show his supervisor that his work is poor
    B. records must not be too difficult to read
    C. these mistakes are hard to notice and correct
    D. correct records are needed for the department to operate smoothly

26. For tenants who are not eligible for public housing and who are unable to find a new apartment, the relocation agency

    A. refers the case to the Human Rights Commission
    B. seeks to obtain private housing for the family
    C. advises the family to move in with relatives and friends
    D. arranges sleeping quarters at the site office

27. The MAXIMUM amount of money a relocated family can receive for moving expenses is

    A. under $500
    B. $500 - 750
    C. $751 - 1000
    D. $1001 - 1500

28. Of the following conditions that are often present in slum buildings, the one which is MOST likely to cause lead poisoning in children is

    A. exposed rusty nails in floors
    B. uncovered garbage cans containing old pencils
    C. paint flaking off walls and window sills
    D. the escape of fumes from faulty oil burners

29. An assistant would be correct to advise a tenant that it is ILLEGAL to throw which of the following into an incinerator?

    A. Compactly wrapped bundles
    B. Empty plastic bags
    C. Loose vacuum or carpet sweepings
    D. Soapy rags

30. A housing project is being built on Site X.
    Of the following, the people who are given priority for apartments in the project if they meet eligibility requirements are

    A. former tenants of Site X
    B. welfare recipients
    C. minority groups with the lowest income
    D. families with the most children

31. A family which occupied a 4 1/2 room apartment at an urban renewal site moved to an off-site 5-room apartment. They were eligible for a 6-room apartment, but it was unavailable.
    The family is now entitled to reimbursement for moving expenses based on

A. a 4-room apartment
B. a 5-room apartment
C. a 6-room apartment
D. actual cost of the move in an unlimited amount

32. During inspection of a tenant's apartment, you observe that the grids and burners of the stove are greasy and heavily caked with spilled food. Because of this, the burners do not produce an even flame from all the ga.s openings.
Of the following, the BEST thing to tell the tenant FIRST is that she should

   A. scrape off the caked-on drippings and then poke open all the clogged openings so the gas. will burn evenly
   B. remove the soiled parts of the burner and soak them in hot water with a mild cleaner to remove the dirt
   C. learn how to use the stove properly so that her food does not boil over or splatter onto the grids
   D. stop using the range until someone from the management office comes to adjust the flame

33. While inspecting a tenant's apartment, one of the things you should check is the drainage of the sinks. In testing the kitchen sink, you observe that there are coffee grinds and a film of grease in the drain basket.
Of the following, the BEST instructions to give the tenant are to

   A. throw coffee grinds in the garbage and wash oils down the drain
   B. collect oil in a can and put it in the garbage, but wash coffee grinds down with cold water
   C. avoid clogging, wash both coffee grinds and oil down the sink with hot, soapy water
   D. collect and dispose of coffee grinds and oils by putting them in the garbage and not in the sink

34. Mrs. Mary Jones and her family live in a 5-room apartment in a building on an urban renewal site. A public housing development is planned for this site. You are interviewing her with regard to relocation. During the interview, you learn that Mrs. Jones is divorced, unemployed, and receiving public assistance. Her four children are all under eight years of age, she is from a. small town in North Carolina, and she has lived in the city for over 2 1/2 years.
From 'your questions, what should you *immediately* know regarding relocation possibilities?
She is

   A. *eligible* for high priority in a public housing development
   B. *eligible* for public housing but not for another two months
   C. *not eligible* for public housing
   D. *not eligible* for public housing for another six months

35. You are about to visit a tenant to encourage him to move from the site when a neighbor tells you that for the last week the tenant has been quarreling loudly and constantly with his wife and children. When you knock on his door, he tells you to go away. You try several times to visit this apartment, but with no success.
What is the BEST thing to do in an effort to solve this problem?

A. Ask the neighbor to encourage him to let you in since he probably has confidence in the neighbor
B. Report the problem to your supervisor since the services of a social worker may be needed
C. Leave a note in the door telling the tenant to come to the site office
D. Call the police and tell them of the unusual difficulty you are having with this man

36. Which one of the following is the BEST kind of evidence presented by a tenant to prove that he actually lives at his current address?

    A. change-of-address form that the tenant has filled out for a creditor
    B. letter with the tenant's name and present address on it
    C. library card
    D. receipt

37. As an assistant, you could be asked to make a recommendation regarding the type of lighting fixtures a tenant should use.
If you were concerned with not overburdening the present electrical circuits, a recommendation to use fluorescent lights rather than incandescent lights would be

    A. *good,* because fluorescent lights flicker less than , incandescent bulbs
    B. *good,* because fluorescent lights draw less current than incandescent bulbs
    C. *poor,* because fluorescent lights are very hard to install in a system designed for incandescent lights
    D. *poor,* because incandescent lights use less current than fluorescent lights

38. If a tenant had to move more than one time, moving expenses would be paid for all of the following combinations of moves EXCEPT

    A. an intrasite move and a subsequent move to a tenant-found apartment
    B. a move to another site and a subsequent move to public housing
    C. two moves to another site and a subsequent move to a tenant-found apartment
    D. a move-out to a tenant-found apartment and a subsequent move to public housing

39. The step of eviction of an on-site tenant is *generally* considered

    A. when a tenant has failed to pay a month's rent
    B. only when a tenant has refused to move into public housing
    C. as a last step in solving any housing problems of a tenant
    D. as a warning to an on-site tenant who is allowing more relatives to live with him than is noted on the S.O.R. card

40. Suppose that a tenant tells you her moving expenses will come to more than the amount she is eligible to receive. You WOULD tell her to

    A. pay the extra expense herself
    B. ask the Social Service Department for help
    C. submit a moving bill from the mover
    D. leave behind all broken furniture

KEY (CORRECT ANSWERS)

1.	C	11.	D	21.	D	31.	A
2.	B	12.	C	22.	C	32.	B
3.	D	13.	C	23.	C	33.	D
4.	C	14.	A	24.	D	34.	A
5.	D	15.	D	25.	B	35.	B
6.	A	16.	B	26.	B	36.	D
7.	C	17.	C	27.	A	37.	B
8.	C	18.	C	28.	C	38.	D
9.	A	19.	D	29.	C	39.	C
10.	C	20.	B	30.	A	40.	C

TEST 2

DIRECTIONS: Each question or incomplete statement is followed by several suggested answers or completions. Select the one that BEST answers the question or completes the statement. *PRINT THE LETTER OF THE CORRECT ANSWER IN THE SPACE AT THE RIGHT.*

1. Housing officials and experts have long suggested changing slum tenements into cooperatives.
   The PROBABLE reason that the advocates of tenement cooperatives feel that tenant-owners would be more likely than absentee landlords to keep buildings in good condition is that

   A. the tenant-owners would be living there while an absentee landlord would not
   B. the tenants in cooperatives want to demonstrate the advantages of cooperative living
   C. absentee landlords do not understand inner city problems
   D. absentee landlords have no reason to provide good maintenance

   1.___

2. A three-part plan to control the loss of an estimated sixty million dollars a year in welfare monies has been proposed.
   Which one of the following proposals would LEAST likely be part of this plan?

   A. Identification cards with photographs of the welfare client
   B. Face-to-face interviews with the welfare clients
   C. Computerized processing of welfare money records
   D. Individual cash payments to each member of a family

   2.___

3. Which one of the following statements describes the purpose of the Equal Rights Amendment which was passed by Congress but was not ratified by the required number of states?
   To

   A. eliminate state-enforced racial discrimination in public schools through extensive use of busing
   B. guarantee to aliens living in the United States the right to hold Civil Service jobs
   C. prohibit sex discrimination by any law or action of the government
   D. extend the right to vote to those previously ineligible by requiring only thirty days residency in a state

   3.___

4. In dealing with members of different ethnic groups in the area he serves, the assistant should give

   A. individuals the services required by his agency
   B. less service to those he judges to be more advantaged
   C. better service to groups with which he sympathizes most
   D. better service to groups with political *muscle*

   4.___

5. The MAJOR reason for joining a professional group such as The National Association of Housing and Redevelopment Officials, The Citizens Housing and Planning Council, or The National Housing Conference is to

   5.___

A. keep yourself informed about current ideas and
B. directions in the housing field · put it on your resume
C. get promoted
D. gain respect from fellow workers

6. Suppose you are interviewing a tenant whose clothing is sloppy, strange, or out of fashion.
   Which of the following is MOST certain to be an appropriate action taken toward this tenant?

   A. Tell him he will get better service when he dresses better.
   B. Refer him to the Department of Social Services for help.
   C. Refer his children to the Bureau of Child Welfare.
   D. Treat him as respectfully as you treat other tenants.

7. An assistant may initiate an order that a tenant's welfare check be *rent-restricted* if that tenant has mismanaged his welfare check and not paid his rent.
   Taking this action assures that

   A. all of the tenant's next welfare checks will be sent to the Urban Renewal Site as payment on account
   B. the Urban Renewal Site will receive a certain portion of the tenant's next welfare check and the tenant will receive the remainder
   C. the welfare center will send the Urban Renewal Site full payment for the rent and will require that the tenant repay this amount
   D. the welfare center will hold payment of checks from the tenant until they are notified by the assistant that the rent has been paid

8. For six months, a family lived in a 4-room apartment where they paid $376 a month. They made an intrasite move to a 4-room apartment where they paid $92 per room a month for six months.
   Comparing the two six-month periods, the TOTAL amount of money the family saved by making the intrasite move was

   A. $48   B. $58   C. $86   D. $118

9. To calculate a tenant's usable income, you should make tax deductions of 4.4 percent on salary up to a maximum of $9,000 and state disability deductions of .5 percent on salary up to $3,000.
   What does a tenant's COMBINED deduction amount to if his annual salary is $6,700?

   A. $228.00   B. $284.30   C. $309.80   D. $350.00

10. If the temporary relocation expenses for housing are set at $27 per day for one adult and $15 per day for each additional person in a room, how much money is allowed for a woman and four children temporarily relocated in one room for a period of six days?

    A. $252   B. $522   C. $567   D. $777

11. According to relocation policy, a family relocating to private housing from federally-aided or certain other sites will be granted a relocation payment. This payment equals the difference between 1/5 of the family's yearly income and the scheduled yearly rent for a standard apartment for their size family.
   Suppose a two-person family whose yearly income is $6,450 has been unable to obtain public housing and so finds a one-bedroom private apartment. The scheduled rent for a one-bedroom apartment appropriate for their occupancy is $120 a month. What payment will they receive?

   A. $120   B. $144   C. $150   D. $205

12. A family on a housing relocation site is paying $240 per month for rent. This represents 25% of their gross monthly income.
   If the husband earns 4/5 of their total combined monthly income, how much does the WIFE earn per month?

   A. $192   B. $324   C. $768   D. $960

13. In a nearly vacant building, there are only a few tenants left who are waiting to move into public housing. When you visit them to check their present conditions, you notice that some of the *tinned-up* apartments have the sheet metal partly pulled off the doors. The tenants tell you that they think that the many men who come and go frequently are drug addicts.
   The BEST action for you to take is to

   A. ignore the incident since all tenants will be moving out soon
   B. visit the site when you think someone might actually be selling drugs
   C. put up a sign warning these men that the building will be knocked down shortly
   D. report all your observations and the reports of the tenants to your supervisor

Questions 14-19.

DIRECTIONS: Answer Questions 14 through 19 on the basis of the information given in the passage below.

The City of X has set up a Maximum Base Rent Program for all rent-controlled apartments. The objective is to insure that the landlord will get a fair, but not excessive, profit on his building to stem the great tide of buildings being abandoned by their owners and to encourage landlords to continue the upkeep of their property. The Maximum Base Rent Program permits the landlord to raise rents under carefully devised standards, while practically no raises in rents in this City were permitted under previous guidelines.

Under this plan, the City determines a Maximum Ease Rent amount by means of a formula which takes into account the age of the building, the number of apartments, total rents received from the building, the amount of expenses, and labor costs. The Maximum Base Rent amount is to be recomputed every two years to allow for increases or decreases in building costs.

The Maximum Base Rent, which will allow the landlord to make a "fair return" on his investment, may not be collected immediately, however, since no rent increases over 7.5 percent will be permitted in any one year. The highest actual rent for each apartment during a given year will be called the Maximum Collectible Rent. This will be computed so that the increase over the present rent is not more . than 7.5 percent ($7.50 on every $100.00). Sometimes it may be less. Therefore, collectible rents will increase each year until the Maximum Base Rent is reached.

14. According to the above passage, the Maximum Base Rent is determined by the   14.____

    A. landlord
    B. Mayor
    C. Rent Commissioner
    D. City

15. Which of the following, according to the passage, permits a *fair return* on the landlord's investment?   15.____
    The _____ Rent Program.

    A. Minimum Base
    B. Maximum Base
    C. Minimum Collectible
    D. Maximum Collectible

16. It may be concluded from the passage that the City of X hopes that insuring fair profits for landlords will be followed by   16.____

    A. good upkeep of apartment buildings
    B. decreased interest rates on home mortgages
    C. lower rents in the future
    D. a better formula for determining rents

17. According to the passage, guidelines for determining rents previous to the Maximum Base Rent Program resulted in   17.____

    A. practically no raises in rents being made
    B. rent increases of approximately 10 percent a year
    C. a *fair return* to landlords from most rents
    D. landlords making too much money on their property

18. Based on the above passage, which is the MOST correct description of the kinds of facts that are taken into consideration when determining the Maximum Base Rent? Facts about   18.____

    A. labor costs and politics
    B. the landlord and labor costs
    C. the building and labor costs
    D. the building and the landlord

19. According to the above passage, the MAXIMUM annual Increase In rent for a tenant In rent-controlled housing under the Maximum Base Rent Program is   19.____

    A. 7.5 percent each year for ten years
    B. 7.5 percent each year until the Maximum Base Rent is reached
    C. always under 7.5 percent a year
    D. $7.50 each year until it reaches $100.00

Questions 20-25.

DIRECTIONS: Answer Questions 20 through 25 on the basis of the information in the following form.

METROPOLITAN CITY

Last Name	First Name	Middle Initial
Smith	John	G.

Street		Apartment
758 Reason Street		1C

Borough or Town	State	Zip Code
Bronx	New York	10403

Monthly Rent	Number of Rooms	
$110.00	5	

E.

FAMILY COMPOSITION

	Name	Relation to Head	Birth Date Mo./Yr.	Annual Income	Employer or School
1.	Smith, John G.	Head	7/58	$10,400	Harris Chemical
2.	Smith, Ethel S.	Wife	3/61	0	
3.	Smith, Lucy M.	Daughter	4/81	0	P.S. 172
4.	Smith, John G., Jr.	Son	8/83	0	P.S. 172
5.	Smith, Susan F.	Daughter	1/88	0	
6.	Simmons, Sylvia T.	Mother-in-law	4/40	$4,680	F.W. Woolworth (part-time)
7.					

Total Annual Income	$15,080
Total Assets: Small Savings Accounts. Mr. Smith.	$5,000 life insurance on
Additional Information	

20. The occupants of the Smith apartment are Mr. Smith, Mrs. Smith, ____ mother, their ____ and ____.

    A. her; son; daughters
    B. his; son; daughters
    C. her; sons; daughter
    D. her; sons; daughters

21. The income of the Smith household comes from the earnings of the father, the

    A. mother, the mother-in-law, and the children
    B. mother, and the children, but not the mother-in-law
    C. mother-in-law, and the children, but not the mother
    D. mother-in-law, but not the mother and children

22. From the information given about the Smith family, their apartment seems to be

    A. too small
    B. the right size
    C. a little large
    D. much too large

23. If an assistant goes to the Smiths' apartment to discuss their relocation and everyone is home except Mr. Smith, with whom should the assistant talk about relocation?

    A. John Jr. and Ethel Smith
    B. Ethel Smith and Sylvia Simmons
    C. Lucy and Ethel Smith
    D. John Smith, Jr. and Sylvia Simmons

24. The reason why the last column was left blank for Susan Smith is PROBABLY that

    A. the assistant forgot to ask for this information
    B. Susan's parents would not give this information
    C. Susan is too young to go to school
    D. Susan does not live at home

25. The section for Additional Information was left blank MOST probably because

    A. the assistant did not have time to ask for more information
    B. the Smith family is sufficiently well-described by the other information on the form
    C. the Additional Information section is not an important part of the form
    D. unfavorable facts have been purposely left out

26. Whenever a tenant moves into a private apartment for which a finder's fee is to be paid, this fee is payable to the

    A. landlord or broker
    B. tenant
    C. local site office
    D. Housing and Development Administration

27. When a relocated tenant moves into public housing in the city, all rents must be paid DIRECTLY to the

    A. Relocation and Management Services Office
    B. Housing and Redevelopment Administration

C. Model Cities Administration
D. City Housing Authority

28. According to relocation rules and regulations, in order for an apartment to be considered *standard,* it is LEAST important that the apartment

A. not be overcrowded
B. have a bathroom with a shower
C. have hot and cold running water
D. be free of hazardous violations

29. The PRIMARY purpose of the Finder's Fee Program is to

A. provide a listing of private home owners willing to take in tenants during emergencies
B. establish a link between private contractors and public housing
C. arrange housing for those forced to vacate because of boiler breakdowns
D. provide a listing of housing facilities in private housing

30. Which one of the following would MOST likely cause the GREATEST amount of damage to the asphalt tiles on apartment floors?

A. Protective furniture casters
B. Wet mopping
C. Liquid wax
D. Grease

31. The rents for three families in a relocation site come to a total of $0,720 per year. If Family A pays $3,480 per year and Family B pays $2,400 per year, how much does Family C pay?

A. $2,760   B. $3,840   C. $4,200   D. $5,800

32. Of 180 families that relocated in a given month, one-fifth moved into Finder's Fee apartments, one-quarter moved into tenant-found apartments, one-third moved into public housing, and the rest moved out of the city.
How many moved out of the city?

A. 36   B. 39   C. 45   D. 60

33. If a tenant earns $5,280 a year and his rent is 25% of his annual income, the amount of rent he pays each month is

A. $110   B. $115   C. $120   D. $135

34. The word *recycling* has become a popular one as used by those who are concerned with saving the environment. This word USUALLY refers to an interest in

A. using bicycles again instead of automobiles for transportation
B. the chemical treatment of rain water for drinking purposes
C. collecting used bottles, cans, and newspaper which will be sold, treated, and re-used
D. reorganizing public transportation routes in the city so that noise and traffic will be reduced

35. Recent accusations of fraud involving FHA-insured mortgages in various American cities have brought to light the fact that 35.____

    A. blockbusting has become the favorite tactic of real estate brokers
    B. families with incomes of $16,000 - $20,000 have been prevented from obtaining mortgages
    C. homes bought through false credit ratings at inflated prices were quickly lost by low income owners
    D. the bad design of homes involved has helped pollute the urban environment

---

KEY (CORRECT ANSWERS)

1.	A	16.	A
2.	D	17.	A
3.	C	18.	C
4.	A	19.	B
5.	A	20.	A
6.	D	21.	D
7.	B	22.	A
8.	A	23.	B
9.	C	24.	C
10.	B	25.	B
11.	C	26.	A
12.	A	27.	D
13.	D	28.	B
14.	D	29.	D
15.	B	30.	D

31. B
32. B
33. A
34. C
35. C

EXAMINATION SECTION
TEST 1

DIRECTIONS: Each question consists of a statement. You are to indicate whether the statement is TRUE (T) or FALSE (F). *PRINT THE LETTER OF THE CORRECT ANSWER IN THE SPACE AT THE RIGHT.*

1. All of the property of the Thirteen Colonies was described by metes and bounds. 1.____

2. This means that the legal description was by direction and measurement from some designated starting point called a *monument*. 2.____

3. After the unit of measurement became the township, a block of land six miles square, this was further divided into sections one mile square. 3.____

4. After a township has been surveyed, the sections are numbered beginning at the southeast corner and numbering east and then back until all of the 36 sections are numbered. 4.____

5. Each township is made up of 11 full sections and 25 fractional sections. 5.____

6. Since the numbering of the sections always begins at the northeast corner, this section is always numbered 36. 6.____

7. The rectangular system provides a comprehensive and complete system for the prompt location of any land in any area. 7.____

8. In a metes and bounds description, the piece of land is described by giving its boundaries. 8.____

9. If natural objects such as trees, streams, or stone monuments are used to form the boundary, no attempt is made at an accurate measurement as to distance and angles. This is called a formal description. 9.____

10. The first requisite of a metes and bounds description is a definite and stable starting point; e.g., the intersection of the center lines of two streets. 10.____

11. A metes and bounds description which encloses a tract of land is fatally defective. 11.____

12. The bearing of a line is its angular deviation measured in degrees, minutes, and seconds from a true north and south line. 12.____

13. Land is unlike any other commodity in that it is lacking in segmentation or natural divisions. 13.____

14. The accuracy and sufficiency of the description will barely affect the success or failure of a real estate transaction. 14.____

15. If it is necessary to use a street address, the dimensions of the tract should be specified. 15.____

16. The use of the tax lot number is a sure way to identify the parcel. 16.____

17. A reference to an earnest money receipt is an infallible method of identifying land. 17.____

18. A reference to a recorded document such as a deed or mortgage which contains a correct legal description is an acceptable method of describing a particular parcel.   18.____

19. Land development quite generally means the creation of a subdivision.   19.____

20. A plat is a temporary map, diagram, drawing, replat or other writing containing all the descriptions, locations, specifications, dedications, provisions, and information concerning a subdivision.   20.____

21. The initial point of all plats must be marked with a monument.   21.____

22. No name of a plat of a town or an addition to a town may have a name the same as, similar to, or pronounced the same as any other town or addition in the same county.   22.____

23. A typical description in a plat might be, *Lot Seven (7), Block Eleven (11), Smith Addition to the city of Ann Arbor, Washtenaw County, Michigan.*   23.____

24. It is illegal to divide any lot of any recorded plat for the purpose of sale or building development if the resulting parcels do not conform to the requirements of the state, the municipality where they are located, and other governmental units.   24.____

25. When the transaction involves only a portion of the land owned by a party at a particular location, a description based on reference to outside facts is especially invulnerable to attack.   25.____

KEY (CORRECT ANSWERS)

1.	T	11.	F
2.	T	12.	T
3.	T	13.	T
4.	F	14.	F
5.	F	15.	T
6.	F	16.	F
7.	T	17.	F
8.	T	18.	T
9.	F	19.	T
10.	T	20.	F
21.	T		
22.	T		
23.	T		
24.	T		
25.	F		

TEST 2

DIRECTIONS: Each question consists of a statement. You are to indicate whether the statement is TRUE (T) or FALSE (F). *PRINT THE LETTER OF THE CORRECT ANSWER IN THE SPACE AT THE RIGHT.*

1. Unless one is able through the description to locate the property on the ground, the whole contract fails to meet the requirements of the statute of frauds. 1.____

2. Where the description describes lots and blocks of an unrecorded plot, or a street number, or *My farm on Whirlpool Ridge,* oral testimony is not admitted to clarify the intention of the parties, but oral testimony as to the terms of the contract itself is admitted. 2.____

3. Contracts should always describe the property with references, to recorded instruments or plots, or by metes and bounds, referable to some well-established point or line. 3.____

4. The writing of metes and bounds descriptions in a deed can safely and surely be done by any licensed, experienced real estate broker. 4.____

5. Describing lands according to regular government surveys is easy. 5.____

6. Fundamentally, the government survey consists, in part, of certain lines in an East and West direction, called PRINCIPAL MERIDIANS, and other lines in a North and South direction called BASE LINES, to which all descriptions within several hundred miles are referred. 6.____

7. The spherical shape of the earth causes all North and South lines to converge as they run toward the Poles, so that a township, if accurately laid down on the ground, must necessarily be narrower on the North line than on the South line; and the East and West line, when laid down on the earth's surface, must be a curved line having a radius equal to the distance from the North Pole, in this latitude. 7.____

8. The effects of the spherical shape of the earth have resulted in fractional sections along the North and West sides of a township. 8.____

9. The ranges and townships are numbered consecutively East and West, and North and South, of the base line and principle meridian, respectively. 9.____

10. In every description under the government survey system, the concluding words are *Township .... South, Range .... East,* or, as customarily abbreviated, *T .... S, R. .... E.* (Of course, if the area is North of the base line or West of the principal meridian, those words or symbols are used.) 10.____

11. The sections were numbered from 1 to 36, beginning in the North East corner of a township. 11.____

12. Section 1 was in the North East Corner, section 6 in the South East corner, section 31 in the North West corner, and section 36 in the South West Corner. 12.____

13. The numbering proceeds South from sections 1 to 6, West to section 7, South to section 12, East to section 13, South to section 18, West to section 19, South to section 24, East to section 25, South to section 30, West to section 31, and East to section 36. 13.____

31

14. The boundaries of the sections are rarely exactly North, South, East, and West in direction, rarely one mile square and rarely contain exactly 640 acres.   14.__

15. If less than a section is to be conveyed, it is divided first (using the usual abbreviations) into N.E. 1/4, a N.W. 1/4, a S.W. 1/4 and a S.E. 1/4, each containing approximately 160 acres.   15.__

16. Next, if one of these quarters is, in turn, divided into sixteenths, on *forties*, it may be correctly described as, for example, the N.E. 1/4 of the N.E. 1/4, the N.W. 1/4 of the N.E. 1/4, the S.W. 1/4 of the N.E. 1/4, and the S.E. 1/4 of the N.E. 1/4.   16.__

17. If one half of one of the subdivisions described in the preceding question is to be conveyed, that is, the 20 acre tract having its longer dimension East and West, and bounded on the North by the North line of the section, and on the East by the East line of the section, it MAY be correctly described as *the N 1/2 of the N.E. 1/4 of the N.E. 1/4* of the section, followed by *of Sec. ... T, ... N., R. ... E.*, or the like.   17.__

18. An adequate or good land description is one which describes a general class of property.   18.__

19. The metes and bounds description should be used as a first resort due to its many advantages.   19.__

20. Surveyors drafting descriptions today always give distances in chains, links, rods, or furlongs.   20.__

21. The public domain is divided into north and south lines, six miles apart, called *township* lines, and into east and west lines, also six miles apart, called *ranges*.   21.__

22. The intersection of the base line and meridian is the starting point of calculations east or west, north or south, to locate a definite township.   22.__

23. Ranges are numbered east or west from a principal meridian, while townships are numbered north or south from the principal base line.   23.__

24. Deed descriptions, in order to eliminate error, usually spell out directions and the fractional part of the section, followed by the abbreviation in parentheses, or vice versa.   24.__

25. The abbreviations for a deed description of *the southwest quarter of the northeast quarter of Section 6, Township 7 South, Range 14 East, Mt. Diablo Base and Meridian,* are to be correctly written as *the SW 1/4 of the NE 1/4 of Sec. 6, T7S, R14E, M.D.B.& M.*   25.__

KEY (CORRECT ANSWERS)

1.	T	11.	T
2.	F	12.	F
3.	T	13.	F
4.	F	14.	T
5.	T	15.	T
6.	F	16.	T
7.	T	17.	T
8.	T	18.	F
9.	T	19.	F
10.	T	20.	F

21. F
22. T
23. T
24. T
25. T

TEST 3

DIRECTIONS: Each question consists of a statement. You are to indicate whether the statement is TRUE (T) or FALSE (F). *PRINT THE LETTER OF THE CORRECT ANSWER IN THE SPACE AT THE RIGHT.*

1. An insufficient description in a listing agreement may result in a denial of an agent's commission when he sells the property. 1.___

2. An insufficient description in an offer to purchase may serve as the basis of an action by either buyer or seller to break the contract. 2.___

3. An insufficient description in an offer to purchase may serve as the basis of an action by the buyer for damages for misrepresentation. 3.___

4. The governmental survey responsible for the checkerboard pattern of real estate in the western United States uses the northern boundary of the state as its baseline. 4.___

5. Parallels to the baseline are spaced 8 miles apart. 5.___

6. Townships drawn as the result of the government survey are always 6-mile squares. 6.___

7. Townships are numbered north from the base line. 7.___

8. The measurement east or west of the principal meridian is referred to as township. 8.___

9. The distance north of the base line is referred to as range. 9.___

10. T 3 N, R 4 E means Township 3 North, Range 4 East. 10.___

11. Townships are divided into sections, each 1 mile square. 11.___

12. Sections are always numbered starting in the northeast corner of the township. 12.___

13. Sections are always rigidly uniform. 13.___

14. If a township included a lake or river, there were parcels of land along the shore which were not large enough to be considered sections; these partial sections were called government lots and were USUALLY identified by number. 14.___

15. A metes-and-bounds description is any description which describes a parcel of land by starting from a known point and following the outside boundaries of the parcel, giving the direction and length of each side. 15.___

16. The typical known points in metes-and-bounds descriptions of rural land are section corners or quarter corners. 16.___

17. The typical known points in metes-and-bounds descriptions of platted land are lot corners. 17.___

18. Street or road intersections are never used as known points in metes-and-bounds descriptions. 18.___

19. Metes-and-bounds descriptions can not be used when a parcel has irregular or curved boundaries. 19.___

20. Today, drafting descriptions will always be given in chains, links, rods, or furlongs. 20._____

21. One mile is equal in length to 8 furlongs. 21._____

22. Eighty chains is equal in length to 320 rods. 22._____

23. When a parcel of land is platted, it is surveyed and divided into lots and blocks, each of which is given a number. 23._____

24. After property is divided into lots and blocks, the lot and block numbers are a sufficient description of the land. 24._____

25. A parcel of land can never be described by its street address. 25._____

KEY (CORRECT ANSWERS)

1.	T	11.	T
2.	T	12.	T
3.	T	13.	F
4.	F	14.	T
5.	F	15.	T
6.	T	16.	T
7.	T	17.	T
8.	F	18.	F
9.	F	19.	F
10.	T	20.	F

21. T
22. T
23. T
24. T
25. F

EXAMINATION SECTION
TEST 1

DIRECTIONS: Each question or incomplete statement is followed by several suggested answers or completions. Select the one that *BEST* answers the question or completes the statement. *PRINT THE LETTER OF THE CORRECT ANSWER IN THE SPACE AT THE RIGHT.*

1. Gross income of a property less vacancy and bad debt allowance is known as   1.____

   A. net operating income
   B. contract rent
   C. gross rental profit
   D. effective gross income

2. All other factors being the same, as the neighborhood in which an income property is located deteriorates, the capitalization rate used for the property will be   2.____

   A. higher   B. lower   C. unstable   D. less reliable

3. The present cost to reproduce a shopping center, less depreciation and including the value of the land, is $2 million. An economic analysis of the income yield indicates a value of $1,500,000. The property was recently sold in a legitimate open marketplace transaction for $1,700,000, subject to a purchase money mortgage of $1,200,000. In assessing the value of the property, the assessor should give the GREATEST weight to the   3.____

   A. purchase money mortgage
   B. economic analysis
   C. recent sale price
   D. cost to reproduce less depreciation

4. There are types of expenses incurred by an owner which are usually made an expense of ownership rather than being an expense of the real estate. The one of the following which is an expense of the real estate is   4.____

   A. mortgage interest
   B. depreciation on the building
   C. reserves for replacement of short-lived building components
   D. income tax

5. In valuing an old investment type of property, the MOST appropriate method for an assessor to use is   5.____

   A. capitalization of income
   B. replacement cost less depreciation
   C. mortgages on the property
   D. gross to net income ratios

6. The sales comparison method which is used in appraising real estate has its basis in in the principle of   6.____

   A. contribution   B. change   C. substitution   D. balance

7. The cost approach is the MOST valid approach to use in deriving an assessed value when

   A. construction costs are low
   B. a building is new
   C. the cost of the property is justified by the economic value
   D. the cost of the property is lower than the economic value

8. Which one of the following items is usually *excluded* ___ when computing the net square feet of an individual apartment in a multi-family building? All

   A. columns whether enclosed or not
   B. ducts and risers
   C. balconies exterior to the apartment
   D. areas within the perimeter walls of the apartment

9. Residential neighborhoods frequently give early warning signs of decline. Which one of the following is LEAST important as an indicator of neighborhood decline?

   A. Change in the nature of the population
   B. Unusual number of "For Sale" signs where permitted
   C. Conversion of large homes into rooming houses
   D. Lack of enforcement of zoning regulations and deed restrictions

10. Marble or stone chips set in Portland cement and polished to a smooth surface is known as

    A. terra cotta
    B. crushed limestone
    C. terrazzo
    D. expanded slag

11. According to the capitalization of income approach to value, if all factors of income, interest rate, and recapture and reversion are the same, the use of a 40-year income projection will bear what relationship to the use of a 10-year income projection?

    A. The use of a 40-year income projection will produce a higher value than the use of a 10-year projection
    B. The decline in gross and net income as the properties become older results in a lower value over 40 years
    C. A 10-year income projection will produce the same value as a 40-year income projection
    D. They would bear no direct relationship to each other since the courts in certiorari cases are abandoning building residual techniques for assessing purposes

12. The one of the following factors which LEAST influences the character of the income stream in the appraisal of income-producing properties is the

    A. amount of income which is expected
    B. certainty of receiving the expected income
    C. timing of the receipt of each component in the expected income stream
    D. reinvestment rate of return on the anticipated net income

13. The capitalization technique used by assessors known as the building residual technique with straight line recapture involves several appraisal assumptions. Which one of the following assumptions is NOT inherent in the use of this technique?

    A. The land value will vary over the economic life of the property
    B. It is necessary for the assessor to predict the remaining economic life of the building
    C. The property value is at its peak at the date the appraisal is made and will continue to decline during the economic life of the property
    D. Income attributable to the building declines year by year over the economic life of the property

14. Assume that you are estimating the replacement costs of a building. Which one of the following would be of GREATEST value to you in making this estimate?

    A. Knowledge of a building's content (cubic capacity)
    B. Zoning floor area ratio (in square feet)
    C. Energy saving devices (in units of energy)
    D. Name of the builder

15. Two homes which are adjacent to each other are identical to each other in every respect, and, therefore, have the same market value of $40,000. Home "A" is assessed $12,500 for land and $40,000 total. Home "B" is assessed $10,000 for land and $40,000 total. The owner of Home "A" files for a reduction of his assessment. Of the following, the MOST appropriate response to the request for reduction is that

    A. because of the difference in land value assessments, a reduction will be made in the total assessed value
    B. no reduction is warranted as the total assessed values are the same
    C. the difference in land value assessments is due to the fact that owner "A" has a larger parcel of land
    D. no reduction is warranted because it will disturb the equality of assessment of other similar parcels in the block

16. A main structural element which sustains the joists of a floor is known as a

    A. girder   B. column   C. mullion   D. ridge piece

17. Low ceiling heights in a factory building are a form of depreciation known as

    A. economic obsolescence   B. physical deterioration
    C. accrued depreciation   D. functional obsolescence

18. Crucial to the validity of the principle that reproduction cost, less depreciation, plus land value ordinarily sets an upper limit on value, is the

    A. assumption of little delay in the construction process
    B. accuracy of the cost and depreciation estimate
    C. supply-demand relationship at the time of the appraisal
    D. inclusion of both "hard" and "soft" costs in the cost estimate

19. Suppose that a property with a net income of $100,000 can be purchased for all cash at $1,000,000.
    If it were to be purchased with $250,000 cash plus a 25-year mortgage at 8% interest in the amount of $750,000 (annual constant 9.37%), the pre-income tax equity rate of return would be, most nearly,

    A. 9.3%   B. 10.5%   C. 11.1%   D. 11.9 %

4 (#1)

20. Suppose that an apartment house has an effective gross income of $250,000 and total operating expenses of $150,000. Of the operating expenses, 66 2/3% are considered to be variable and 33 1/3% are considered to be fixed.
If both the effective gross income and the variable expenses increase by 10%, the net operating income will

20.____

A. increase by 10%
B. increase by 15%
C. increase by 16 2/3%
D. not increase

21. Suppose that income producing property sells at an indicated overall capitalization rate of 9%.
If the net income ratio for this property is 50%, the gross income multiplier is, most nearly,

21.____

A. 4.5   B. 5.5   C. 6.0   D. 6.5

22. A building site of 10,000 square feet located in a C-4-7 zone is worth $500,000. All other things being equal, a zoning change to C-6-7 would make this plot worth

22.____

A. $250,000   B. $750,000   C. $1,000,000   D. $600,000

Question 23.

DIRECTIONS: Answer Question 23 on the basis of the following information.

23. Suppose that you are appraising a rent-controlled apartment house which has the following income and expenses as submitted by the owner (you have no reason to question the accuracy of the statement):

23.____

Gross Income		$89,030
Expenses		
Payroll	$7,865	
Fuel	3,680	
Light & Power	2,042	
Painting	4,500	
Plumbing	1,030	
Repairs	4,232	
Supplies	2,785	
Elevator Maintenance	1,314	
Capital Improvements	1,860	
Legal & Audit	900	
Payroll Taxes	450	
Miscellaneous	770	
Mortgage Interest	11,320	
Real Estate Taxes	20,800	
Water & Sewer Tax	862	
Insurance	3,100	
Management	2.700	
Total	$70,210	70.210
Net Income		$18,820

A reconstruction of the above statement for assessing purposes would indicate a net income free and clear of

A. $33,860   B. $32,000   C. $50,000   D. $20,680

Questions 24-25.

DIRECTIONS: Answer Questions 24 and 25 SOLELY on the basis of the information in the paragraph below.

You are reassessing a parcel of property where the land area is 8,273 square feet, zoned C-6-6 and improved with a six-story and basement office building containing a gross area of 45,836 square feet above ground. (The land is currently assessed consistent with the existing zoning.) Seven years after construction of the building, the owners entered into a 75-year net lease with the owner of an adjacent parcel to permit the lessee to utilize the unused development rights inherent in the parcel improved with the six-story office building. The lease called for an annual net rental of $33,000 per annum for the excess development rights.

24. Based on the information in the above paragraph, and disregarding any bonus for plaza, the MAXIMUM number of above-ground development rights that could be transferred is, most nearly, 24.____

   A. 37,200 square feet   B.   53,400 square feet
   C. 78,300 square feet   D.   103,500 square feet

25. Based on the information in the above paragraph, the MOST appropriate conclusion regarding the land value of the "granting" parcel is that the 25.____

   A. land value should be reduced to conform with the actual use and area of the improvement
   B. land value should remain at its present level because it is assessed in conformity with other parcels on the block which are also zoned C-6-6
   C. land value should be increased because of the net rental being received for the development rights transfer
   D. net-lease rentals should be added to the residual net income of the land, developed by the land residual technique, using the current income and expenses applicable to the six-story office building, and a revaluation of the land should be calculated

KEY (CORRECT ANSWERS)

1.	D	11.	C
2.	A	12.	D
3.	C	13.	A
4.	C	14.	A
5.	A	15.	B
6.	C	16.	A
7.	C	17.	D
8.	C	18.	A
9.	A	19.	D
10.	C	20.	B

21. B
22. B
23. B
24. C
25. D

TEST 2

DIRECTIONS: Each question or incomplete statement is followed by several suggested answers or completions. Select the one that BEST answers the question or completes the statement. PRINT THE LETTER OF THE CORRECT ANSWER IN THE SPACE AT THE RIGHT.

1. In selecting a capitalization rate in today's market there are several factors which must be considered. Some of these factors are reasonably factual while others are judgmental. Of the following factors, which one should be considered *primarily* judgmental? 1.____

    A. Available ratio of mortgage money to fair market values
    B. The income projection term in years
    C. Interest rate that will attract mortgage money at the time of the appraisal
    D. Maximum full mortgage amortization term available at the time of appraisal

2. You are assessing a parcel of land which has been inadequately improved and the net income from the property is insufficient to yield an adequate return on the market value of the land. 2.____
Of the following, the MOST appropriate method of estimating a market value for this parcel of land, assuming redevelopment is 5 years away, is to

    A. appraise the land for its highest and best use and then add a minimal amount for the improvement and adjust this value by a time discount factor
    B. appraise the land for the highest and best use and then deduct the cost of demolishing the improvement and then add the increased value of the land 5 years hence
    C. appraise the property on the basis of its current income and attribute all the value to the land, adjusting the value by taking a 5-year time discount
    D. appraise the land for its highest and best use, then apply a 5-year time discount for the cost of demolition and another 5-year time discount for the resulting land value

3. On a street in a district zoned R-2, 40x100 lots have a value of $20,000 and are so assessed based on a front foot value of $500. A vacant parcel on this street has a dimension of 60 feet by 100 feet deep. It has been assessed for $30,000 (600 front feet x $500). The owner argues that he can only build one house on this plot and, therefore, he should be assessed only for $20,000. 3.____
Of the following, the MOST appropriate response to the owner is:

    A. The 60x100 plot is sufficient for the construction of 2 houses on the plot and hence is more valuable
    B. The owner can build a 2 family house on this size plot and, therefore, it is worth more than a 40x100 plot, and the 2-family house can be easily converted to a 3-family house
    C. The 60x100 plot is worth more than a 40x100 plot although probably not in proportion to their areas, and a modification of the assessed value will be made to reflect a reasonable increment for size
    D. A zoning variance can be obtained which will justify the difference in assessed value

4. The one of the following statements about the "principle of substitution" which is MOST accurate is that it

   A. is given little weight by the courts
   B. affirms that a builder may depart from building specifications when specified materials are not easily obtainable
   C. has application to the three approaches to value
   D. relates to the alternate choices in selecting the proper approach to value

5. As applied to the appraisal of real property, the *one* of the following statements which is MOST valid about the "principle of anticipation" is that it

   A. provides the basis for the "percentage" clauses in leases
   B. affirms that change is ever present especially with regard to taxes and utility charges
   C. affirms that value is the present worth of future benefits
   D. states that excess profits breed ruinous competition

Questions 6-8.

DIRECTIONS: Answer Questions 6 through 8 on the basis of the information in the following passage.

You are responsible for reviewing, in 2008, the assessment of an office building with 100,000 square feet rentable area. This building rents to several major tenants on 10-year leases and is 100% rented. Based on 1990 figures, the rent is $7.00 per square foot. There are escalation clauses built into the leases for tax increases and operating costs over the 1990 figures. The assessment in 1990 was $3,500,000. The tax rate in 1990 was $60 per thousand assessed, and operating expenses were $1.75 per square foot. The tax rate in 1997 was $87.50 per thousand assessed and operating costs were $2.00 per square foot.

6. Based on the information in the above passage, the tenants' share of the operating costs in 2007 was

   A. 17.5%   B. 50%   C. 25%   D. 12.5%

7. Based on the information in the above passage, the net return to capital in 2007, excluding all operating costs and taxes, was

   A. $821,250   B. $315,000   C. $525,000   D. $725,000

8. Based on the information in the above passage, and assuming you considered a 9% capitalization rate as an appropriate return on capital, how would the rate be reflected in the assessed value in 2008 as opposed to 2000? The assessed value would

   A. *increase,* because gross income is higher
   B. *decrease* to reflect higher operating expenses and taxes
   C. *increase* to offset the tax rate increase
   D. *remain the same*

9. Assume that when you attempt to measure the size of apartments in a recently renovated apartment building, the superintendent of the building denies you access to the premises despite all your efforts.
Of the following, the BEST action to take in this situation is to

    A. call the police and ask them to force entry
    B. enter when the superintendent is not there
    C. call your supervisor to assist you in gaining entry
    D. obtain the measurements from the building plans

10. Assessors and appraisers interview property owners and builders in order to gather data affecting property value. You are *most likely* to encourage those being interviewed to cooperate with you by

    A. limiting the interview only to those areas you wish to discuss
    B. impressing those being interviewed that you are acting as a representative of the government, and, as such, if they fail to cooperate, they are violating the law
    C. explaining procedures and answering questions, when appropriate
    D. letting the person being interviewed initiate the discussion

11. Assume that you are interviewing a veteran for a veteran's exemption under Section 458 of the tax law. You find that he is not qualified to receive an exemption. Of the following, the BEST course of action to take in this situation is to

    A. tell him that he will receive formal written notification of your decision and that you can tell him nothing at present
    B. have your supervisor inform him of the decision not to grant him the exemption
    C. inform him that he is not eligible for the exemption, and if he appeals, his assessment may increase
    D. tell him that he is not eligible for the exemption and explain the reasons why

12. Suppose that you have asked an assistant to gather some data which you need immediately for an important assignment. The assistant tells you that he has a lot of other work to do, and will obtain the information for you when he has the time.
In this situation, the action which would be BEST for you to take first is to

    A. point out that since you are an employee with higher rank, the assistant has to follow your orders
    B. report the assistant's lack of cooperation to your supervisor
    C. ask a more cooperative employee to get the data for you
    D. ask the assistant what work he has to do and why it is needed

13. In carrying out the duties of the job, you may sometimes have to interview people in the field who are uncooperative and even, in extreme cases, verbally abusive. Of the following, the BEST way to *initially* deal with a person who is verbally abusive is to

    A. remain calm and try to find out whether he has a legitimate complaint
    B. end the interview and leave the premises
    C. tell him that you agree with some of his complaints but you have to follow orders
    D. respond in a similar manner until he calms down

14. Suppose that a property owner is reluctant to provide information concerning certain renovations he has made. Of the following, it would be BEST to tell the property owner that

    A. you will send your supervisor to obtain the information
    B. it is important that he give you the information himself, in order for an accurate assessment to be made
    C. if he refuses to provide the information, you will make an overly-high assessment, thus forcing him to reveal the information
    D. the renovations probably will not warrant an increase in his assessment, so he should not be reluctant to give you the information

15. Suppose that while you are in the field, you are approached by a property owner who complains that the amount of the previous year's assessed valuation of his property is higher than that of his neighbor although he claims that there is no difference in the properties. You made both assessments, and have data indicating that the properties are not, in fact, identical.
    Of the following, it would be BEST for you to tell this person that

    A. there is a difference in the properties, and explain the basis on which you ascribed his assessment
    B. you cannot discuss the assessment with him; he should file an appeal during the appeal period
    C. if a mistake were made, you will see that it is corrected, but you cannot reveal any information
    D. assessments are based solely on established guidelines; you cannot give him details about his assessment

16. Assume that you are to recommend whether to grant tax exempt status to a non-profit foundation incorporated in the State for the study of Tibetan Buddhist Doctrines, whose charter provides that the corporation is organized solely for the religious purpose of instructing members in the use of Tibetan Buddhism.
    Of the following, the MOST important factor in making your recommendation is

    A. your investigations of the actual use of the property to determine that it is being used for its charter purposes
    B. your determination, based on research, whether Tibetan Buddhism is an established religion eligible for tax exempt status
    C. whether or not tax exempt status has been granted to other similar foundations
    D. the number of existing tax exempt properties in your district

17. Assume that you are called upon to assist a senior citizen submit an application for a Senior Citizen exemption on a two-family house he owns. He lives in one apartment and his son lives in the rental apartment. The son pays no rent but pays most of the father's expenses.
    The *appropriate* action to take is to

    A. refuse to initiate the application on the ground of ineligibility since the son pays most of the father's expenses
    B. ascribe a rental estimate to the son's apartment, which is then listed as income, and submit the application for determination

C. make a ruling on the applicant's eligibility for the tax exemption based on the percentage of income contributed by the son
D. ascribe a rental estimate to the son's apartment, which is then listed as income, and make a determination on the applicant's eligibility

18. Suppose that a landlord has altered an existing rooming house, converting it to class A apartments.
    Under the law, the tax exemption to which he is entitled is:

    A. Full exemption of the increase in building value, exempt for 12 years
    B. Fifty percent of the increase in building value, exempt for 12 years
    C. Full exemption of the increase in building value, decreasing every two years by 20% over a 10-year period
    D. Fifty percent of the increase in building value, decreasing by 5% every year over a 10-year period

18.____

19. Which one of the following is NOT considered taxable real property?

    A. Gas ranges and stoves B. Safe deposit vaults
    C. Gasoline tanks   D. Window air conditioners

19.____

20. Which of the following items is NOT allowed as eligible funds on which tax exemptions are granted for veterans?

    A. A bonus granted by the State   B. G.I interest refund
    C. Refunds on G.I. insurance   D. National Guard drill pay

20.____

KEY (CORRECT ANSWERS)

1. B   11. D
2. D   12. D
3. C   13. A
4. C   14. B
5. C   15. A

6. D   16. A
7. B   17. B
8. D   18. A
9. D   19. D
10. C   20. D

EXAMINATION SECTION
TEST 1

DIRECTIONS: Each question or incomplete statement is followed by several suggested answers or completions. Select the one that BEST answers the question or completes the statement. *PRINT THE LETTER OF THE CORRECT ANSWER IN THE SPACE AT THE RIGHT.*

1. Real property, as legally defined, includes 1._____

    A. gas ranges
    B. refrigerators
    C. furniture
    D. heating systems

2. Ownership of real estate includes the exclusive right, in every instance, to 2._____

    A. take minerals from the sub-surface portions
    B. receive unobstructed light and air from adjacent parcels
    C. use adjacent parcels for access if the property is land-locked
    D. perpetuate a non-conforming use

3. The *Bundle of Rights* refers to the 3._____

    A. constitutional authority to appropriate property
    B. various rights attached to ownership of real estate
    C. rights of tenants under net lease arrangements
    D. sheaf of papers in a real estate transaction

4. Cost equals value when 4._____

    A. construction cost indices are stable
    B. national conditions are normal
    C. a new building improves a site most profitably
    D. depreciation is not excessive

5. Market value is BEST defined as the 5._____

    A. highest price, expressed in dollars, that a property would sell for under the most favorable market conditions
    B. difference between the Cost Approach and Income Approach
    C. average of the three approaches to Value
    D. highest price, expressed in dollars, that a willing, well-informed buyer would pay and a willing, well-informed seller would accept

6. In order for an object to have value in an economic sense, it MUST have 6._____

    A. an attractive appearance
    B. practical utility
    C. a clear title
    D. tangible materials

7. *Highest and Best Use* means 7._____

    A. most profitable use
    B. most intensive use
    C. the use which produces the largest dollar income
    D. the largest structure

49

8. The PROPER point in the appraisal process at which the highest and best use analysis should be made is

   A. correlation of the three approaches
   B. definition of the appraisal problem
   C. final valuation estimate
   D. preliminary survey of the appraisal task

9. The *principle of change* is evidenced in

   A. restrictive covenants running with the land
   B. the evolutionary stages in the life of a neighborhood
   C. the land residual technique
   D. the Sheridan-Karkow formula

10. The *principle of balance* is exhibited in the

    A. process of making adjustments in a market data analysis
    B. refining of the capitalization rate through the utilization of quality considerations on a relative basis
    C. agents in production in a property existing in such relative proportions that they produce the maximum residual net income to land
    D. number of apartments and rooms in an apartment house

11. The *principle of contribution states* that

    A. all three approaches to value contribute equally to the final valuation estimate
    B. land and buildings contribute to the creation of economic rents
    C. the value of an agent in production depends upon how much it adds to net income
    D. only business enterprise makes a real contribution

12. In the cost approach to value, under ideal conditions, land value is estimated by the

    A. analysis of market data on a comparative basis
    B. analysis of local tax assessment records
    C. land residual technique
    D. property residual technique

13. In estimating Replacement Cost, the majority of appraisers use the

    A. quantity survey method
    B. unit cost in place method
    C. ENGINEERING NEWS RECORD
    D. unit cost per cubic or square foot method

14. In the Cost Approach of an appraisal of a parcel of real property, the Replacement Cost estimate should include cost of

    A. wall-to-wall carpeting
    B. insurance during construction of improvements
    C. agent's management fees
    D. washing machines

15. *Accrued Depreciation* is BEST defined as the 15.____

    A. provision for recapture of capital invested in improvements on the land
    B. measures taken to guard against excessive decay and physical deterioration
    C. difference between the cost of replacement, new, and the present appraised market value
    D. loss in value resulting from any and all causes

16. In estimating accrued depreciation, it is considered the BEST practice to use 16.____

    A. the *observed condition* technique
    B. Age-Life tables
    C. Bureau of Internal Revenue tables
    D. Real Estate Board statistics

17. Only one of the three major components of accrued depreciation is said to result from causes extrinsic to the property being appraised. 17.____
    This component is

    A. curable functional obsolescence
    B. physical deterioration
    C. economic obsolescence
    D. incurable functional obsolescence

18. The test to determine whether an item of functional obsolescence is curable or incurable is 18.____

    A. the consensus of opinion among real estate brokers
    B. the expenditure required to cure it, an item requiring an expenditure of more than $100,000 being incurable
    C. whether the cost of effecting the cure can be recouped in equivalent or greater value
    D. whether the item is mechanical or structural, the former being curable, the latter incurable

19. A cause of economic obsolescence is 19.____

    A. utilization of sub-standard specifications in construction of improvements under appraisal
    B. inadequate electric wiring
    C. poor architectural planning for improvements under appraisal
    D. rent control legislation

20. For purposes of capitalization, net income is USUALLY computed before the expense of 20.____

    A. debt service charges   B. property taxes
    C. replacement reserve   D. management

21. Capitalization may be described as 21.____

    A. establishing the income to be received
    B. converting the net income into value
    C. computing the amortization on the investment
    D. taking an interest and depreciation return on the building value

22. The estimate of economic life is based PRIMARILY on the _____ of the improvement.   22._____

    A. physical durability
    B. age
    C. size
    D. relative competitive utility

23. Net income imputable to land is capitalized in perpetuity because   23._____

    A. the entire investment is amortized out of the building income
    B. the land returns are presumed to last forever since urban land does not physically depreciate and land may thus be successively utilized
    C. investors capitalize land income in this manner since they cannot take depreciation on the land for tax purposes
    D. land represents a reversionary interest

24. The capitalization process must provide for recovery of the building investment over the economic life of the building because   24._____

    A. the investment should be recovered at the same approximate rate as the building is anticipated to decline in value from depreciation
    B. it is customary to recover every asset out of income, regardless of whether it is depreciable or not
    C. the investor always believes the amortization on the mortgage is designed to achieve the recovery of his capital for him
    D. amortization may not be equal to depreciation

25. The capitalization process referred to as *direct capitalization plus straight line depreciation* is based on an assumption that the   25._____

    A. income stream will remain level
    B. building has suffered a substantial amount of functional obsolescence
    C. income stream will decline over the years
    D. curing of most accrued depreciation is possible

26. In capitalization techniques, the method of providing for future depreciation that generally permits highest valuation is the   26._____

    A. annuity system   B. quantity survey
    C. sinking fund   D. straight line method

27. The building residual technique is applicable when   27._____

    A. accurate building cost data is available
    B. the building improves the site to its highest and best use
    C. land is in short supply in the market
    D. there is an abundance of market data relating to comparable sites

28. A capitalization rate is the   28._____

    A. amount of taxes levied upon a capital gain
    B. equalization rate for property taxes
    C. rate of return necessary to attract capital
    D. rate of capital depreciation

29. The *Band of Investment* method of selecting a capitalization rate is   29.____

    A. built up on the *safe rate*
    B. applicable only when land residual technique will be used
    C. based on analysis of sales
    D. based on weighted average of mortgage and equity rates

30. Since the use of the Inwood (annuity) factor provides for complete depreciation of a real   30.____
    estate investment over its assumed economic life, the use of such technique in the
    appraisal of improved real property necessitates

    A. provision for substantial tax levies
    B. an estimate of the value of the land reversion
    C. an especially careful neighborhood analysis
    D. a very thorough inspection of improvements

31. In the land residual technique, the appraiser   31.____

    A. bases his opinion on careful analysis of market data
    B. need not inspect the building unless there are building violations on it
    C. sometimes bases his estimates on a hypothetical structure representing highest
       and best use
    D. is concerned only with raw land costs

32. The so-called *overall* capitalization rate is BEST arrived at by   32.____

    A. obtaining the ratio of net income to selling price of comparable properties
    B. consulting the Dow Service for the standard capitalization rates most frequently
       used
    C. examination of Census Statistics
    D. employing the summation or *build-up* technique

33. In real estate appraisal work, the market data approach should particularly be used   33.____

    A. when the sales market has experienced substantial activity
    B. when cost information is too difficult to obtain
    C. when the subject property is new
    D. only when a residential property is being appraised

34. The market data approach is used for direct valuation of properties and it is also useful in   34.____

    A. making quantity surveys
    B. making insurance appraisals
    C. establishing capitalization rates
    D. controlling depreciation

35. The heart of the market data approach is   35.____

    A. thorough checking of deed registration
    B. careful averaging of sales statistics
    C. thorough-going analysis of the records of the Building Department
    D. careful comparisons between comparables and property being appraised

KEY (CORRECT ANSWERS)

1. D
2. A
3. B
4. C
5. D

6. B
7. A
8. D
9. B
10. C

11. C
12. A
13. D
14. B
15. C

16. A
17. C
18. C
19. D
20. A

21. B
22. D
23. B
24. A
25. C

26. A
27. D
28. C
29. D
30. B

31. C
32. A
33. A
34. C
35. D

TEST 2

DIRECTIONS: Each question or incomplete statement is followed by several suggested answers or completions. Select the one that BEST answers the question or completes the statement. *PRINT THE LETTER OF THE CORRECT ANSWER IN THE SPACE AT THE RIGHT.*

1. Appraisals for any purpose in the real estate field, in an economic sense, are required because 1.____

    A. a high unit cost is involved
    B. realty is a non-standardized commodity
    C. it is a customary practice
    D. brokers are usually uninformed

2. The legal basis for the estimation of full value in real estate tax assessment appraisals is 2.____

    A. stabilized market value, without regard to cyclical extremes
    B. a combination of the market comparison and income approaches
    C. cost for improvements, less any depreciation, plus land value estimated by comparison
    D. capitalized value of the residual net income

3. In a purely objective sense, no matter what the purpose of the appraisal may be, the market value of the real estate at a given moment is ALWAYS 3.____

    A. identical
    B. varied
    C. mixed
    D. dependent on the approach

4. Certiorari appraisals are unique in technique because 4.____

    A. they frequently result in court actions
    B. the tax rate is incorporated in the capitalization rate
    C. all three value approaches are used
    D. they are used in no other state except New York

5. There is an effective limitation on the height of reinforced concrete structures because 5.____

    A. the large columns required take up too much floor space and impair floor layouts
    B. the structural framework is too rigid for climatic changes
    C. the building code limits the height of reinforced concrete structures
    D. it is expensive to haul concrete to excessive heights

6. Aside from zoning restrictions, the height of a steel skeleton frame building is limited by the 6.____

    A. cost of the steel framing
    B. labor cost involved at great heights resulting from labor scarcity
    C. cost of utility installations
    D. adequacy of the net rent received on the construction cost of the last floor

7. A typical semi-fireproof apartment house has 7.____

    A. all wood floors but masonry walls
    B. concrete first floor arch, wood upper floors, load bearing masonry walls
    C. light steel bar joists, 2" poured concrete floors, load bearing masonry walls
    D. all concrete floors and load bearing masonry walls

8. Continual flaking of paint on the inner surface of an outer masonry wall PROBABLY indicates

   A. a poor paint job caused by adulterating the paint with a chemical
   B. shoddy construction permissible under an inadequate building code
   C. driving rains from the east
   D. a need for pointing up the loose and dislodged mortar in the joints

9. The appraiser makes an inspection of the realty under appraisal because

   A. it keeps him informed on building construction
   B. he must be an engineer to be qualified
   C. the results of the inspection have a direct bearing on the value
   D. a very detailed description of the realty is expected of him

10. The LEAST costly heating system to install and service, which takes the least amount of space and costs the most for fuel, is

    A. coal stoker   B. oil burner
    C. gas-fired hot water   D. utility steam

11. The type of material used for plumbing risers, branches, and crotons has a direct bearing on value because

    A. the better the quality and the more durable the material, the higher the anticipated net income
    B. superintendents are prohibited by union rules from making repairs to the plumbing system
    C. the mechanical equipment depreciates in the same manner as the building shell
    D. some types of material become functionally obsolete faster than others

12. An inspection of the rentable space is as important as an inspection of the building shell and equipment because

    A. the appraiser can determine if there are any furnished units
    B. it establishes the basis for a comparable rent analysis
    C. the occupancy must be checked against the leases
    D. it makes the report look more impressive

13. Which one of the following is GENERALLY found in an unaltered old law tenement?

    A. Combination washtub and bathtub
    B. Dumbwaiters
    C. Central heat
    D. Off-foyer layouts

14. Which one of the following is MOST generally found in a new law tenement?

    A. A standpipe system   B. Dumbwaiters
    C. Colored tile baths   D. Windowless rooms

15. If an inspection revealed that an apartment house was dangerously underwired, the appraiser should PRIMARILY solve this in his appraisal report by

    A. advising the owner to correct the condition forthwith
    B. advising the client to notify the Building Department immediately
    C. subtracting the capital cost of re-wiring from the market value, after reflecting the rent increases permitted by the Rent Commission in the net income
    D. ignoring the condition on the assumption that the owner will eventually replace the wiring

16. If a building is of competitive, that is, average construction quality, and if it has been well maintained to the date of the appraisal, the LEAST significant type of depreciation is probably

    A. super session
    B. physical deterioration
    C. functional obsolescence
    D. inadequacy

17. The type of air conditioning system installed in most new apartment houses is

    A. air-cooled central system with adequate ducts
    B. peripheral system circulating chilled water
    C. heavy duty fan system
    D. unit in wall sleeve

18. Land use is usually the MOST intensive in _____ districts.

    A. apartment   B. hotel   C. loft   D. office

19. A significant decline in employment in a city may affect real estate market values through

    A. economic obsolescence
    B. neighborhood decay
    C. removal of middle class to the suburbs
    D. the aging process

20. The removal of some of the middle income class from the core of the city to the suburbs has resulted in a(n)

    A. increase in the available supply of dwelling units
    B. decline in controlled rents
    C. acceleration of physical deterioration and economic obsolescence in those central residential neighborhoods
    D. opportunity to modernize controlled rent apartments

21. Downtown major retail sections have been adversely affected PRIMARILY by

    A. obsolete buildings
    B. too many taxicabs and too few buses
    C. poor planning of merchant associations
    D. outlying shopping center competition

22. If published material were not available, the BEST source for obtaining the net annual addition to the housing stock would be

    A. condemnation records

B. tax and assessment records
C. the Register's Office
D. building and demolition permits

23. The trend referred to as *decentralization* is caused LARGELY by

    A. encroachment of industry into residential areas in outlying cities throughout the country
    B. rent control legislation
    C. removal of commerce, industry, and people from the heart of the city to outlying cities or to the periphery
    D. inequitable tax assessment policies

24. The cubical content of an office building was 2,100,000 cubic feet. The Dow Service Valuation Calculator gave $1.10 as the net field reproduction cost. The appraiser added 20% to cover all miscellaneous costs and excavation. Depreciation was estimated at 2 1/2% per annum. The building was 25 years old on the appraisal date. Land value was estimated at $15,000 a front foot for the 200' x 100' plot.
    The total value by the cost approach is MOST NEARLY

    A. $4,039,500   B. $4,762,000
    C. $5,191,300   D. $6,244,000

25. The quantity survey method of cost estimation is not used by most market value appraisers because

    A. appraisal groups oppose it
    B. they are not qualified to use it
    C. cost has no importance in valuation
    D. the unit-in-place method is better

26. An over-calculation or over-estimation of building cost, assuming a particular level of rent is obtainable, will

    A. influence lenders on the mortgage to require less amortization
    B. penalize the land value by the approximate amount of the over-calculation of the building cost
    C. result in a faulty depreciation allowance for income tax purposes
    D. make necessary the engagement of a cost expert on a sub-contract basis

27. The construction cost of a six-story semi-fireproof apartment house is less than that of a fireproof reinforced concrete apartment house of similar size by APPROXIMATELY

    A. 40%   B. 30%   C. 15%   D. 10%

28. The cost approach can ALWAYS be used in any appraisal because

    A. it can be used as a ceiling of possible market value for the real estate
    B. no appraisal can be made without it
    C. the physical components of realty are the primary bases for market value
    D. it makes the appraisal report more convincing as a result of the cost figures

29. The assessor was assigned to re-appraise for property tax purposes a 60-year-old loft-type structure that was 50% vacant. Many similar structures in the same district had been demolished, and the plots improved with new commercial buildings.
Under the circumstances, which appraisal approach, of the following, would BEST be utilized?

    A. Reproduction cost, less depreciation, plus land value
    B. Replacement cost, plus land value
    C. Market comparison, treating the improvement as almost fully depreciated
    D. the building residual method of capitalization

30. The assessor was assigned to re-appraise for property tax purposes a privately-owned, specially designed and constructed art gallery with high ceilings and ornate construction, for which there was no market in its present use. He concluded that it would not be practical to convert the structure to another use should the art gallery use terminate. He decided to use the cost approach and worked out a reproduction cost for the structure.
In the absence of a market for similar structures, the depreciation computation should MOST probably be based on

    A. May's quantity survey method of computing depreciation
    B. a sinking fund technique
    C. an age-life method based on a straight-line depreciation allowance
    D. an observation derived from personal experience

31. In comparing the results of the cost approach and the income approach when assessing a new building on a given plot, the assessor noted that the income approach yielded a greater total value, despite the use of a high capitalization rate.
Assuming the assessor's cost calculations to be accurate, the differential can BEST be attributed to the fact that

    A. there is always a higher total value when the income approach is used rather than the cost approach
    B. there is usually an increment in value attributable to the land over its acquisition cost, underlying a successfully rented and completed building in a market of equilibrium
    C. the cost approach never reflects the value obtained from the income approach because the former is independent of the rents obtained in the property
    D. the law does not permit equipment in the realty to be treated as real fixtures subject to real estate taxation

32. The assessor was asked to estimate the market land value underlying a one-story store building. The property had recently sold for $1,200,000. The land assessment was $400,000, and the total assessment was $800,000.
Using the assessment ratio extraction process, the assessor should estimate the land value at

    A. $300,000   B. $500,000   C. $600,000   D. $800,000

33. The assessor's unit lot value for a typical side street had been established at $500,000. A vacant corner plot 100' x 75' on the same street sold for $3,000,000. The Hoffman-Neill rule depth factor for 75 feet was 84.49. Assuming standard corner and key lot increments, the unit lot value indicated by the sale is MOST NEARLY

    A. $625,000   B. $700,000   C. $800,000   D. $890,000

34. One of the BEST means of finding the appropriate overall capitalization rate for income property on a market comparison basis is the

   A. earnings price ratio of similar properties
   B. long-term government bond rate in the money market
   C. risk rates in the market
   D. mortgage interest rates

34.____

35. You are asked to assess a six-story apartment house on a 100' x 100' plot. You find records of four sales of similar properties.
Which one has no applicability?

   A. R.S. $.55 mortgage $125,000
   B. R.S. $77. mortgage $80,000 P.M.M. $30,000
   C. R.S. $110. mortgage $65,000
   D. Stated consideration: $1,800,000

35.____

KEY (CORRECT ANSWERS)

1. B		16. B	
2. C		17. A	
3. A		18. D	
4. B		19. A	
5. A		20. C	
6. D		21. D	
7. B		22. B	
8. D		23. C	
9. C		24. A	
10. C		25. B	
11. A		26. B	
12. B		27. C	
13. A		28. A	
14. B		29. C	
15. C		30. C	

31. B
32. C
33. B
34. A
35. A

TEST 3

DIRECTIONS: Each question or incomplete statement is followed several suggested answers or completions. Select one that BEST answers the question or completes the statement. *PRINT THE LETTER OF THE CORRECT ANSWER IN THE SPACE AT THE RIGHT.*

1. Which one of the following is an INCORRECT technique for analyzing comparable sales?

   A. Ratio of selling price to assessed valuation
   B. Applying locational differential rating factor
   C. Selling price per unit of measurement
   D. Going back fifteen years in checking sales

   1.____

2. The appraiser employed in a certiorari proceeding submitted twenty-five sales, eighteen of which were made prior to the appraisal date, three within six months after the appraisal date, and the balance two and one-half years after the appraisal date. The MAXIMUM number of sales which the trial justice could admit as evidence of value was

   A. 23   B. 21   C. 19   D. 17

   2.____

3. The market comparison approach is frequently considered the primary or best approach, provided the

   A. income approach is used as a check
   B. subject property is a standardized type and recent comparable market sales are numerous
   C. reproduction cost, less age-life depreciation, plus land value, yields the same result
   D. appraiser subscribes to a sales service

   3.____

4. The assessor was appraising a newly completed apartment house which, in his judgement, was worth less than its replacement cost because of some serious deficiencies in design, layout, and equipment.
   In capitalizing the net income, the CORRECT capitalization method to apply to this new building is the _____ method.

   A. building residual   B. land residual
   C. property residual   D. land reversion

   4.____

5. You wish to establish a capitalization rate for the capitalization of net income, before any deduction for depreciation. You decide the Band of Investment Theory is best for this purpose. Debt service charges for similar property is running 8% on a 60% mortgage. Equity returns currently are 10%.
   The MOST appropriate capitalization rate is

   A. 7.60%   B. 8.80%   C. 8.90%   D. 9.10%

   5.____

6. Of the following, the BEST mathematical means of capitalizing a net rental from property occupied by an AAA-1 tenant under a thirty year net lease is

   A. annuity table, as Inwood's Premise
   B. interest plus sinking fund
   C. interest plus straight-line depreciation
   D. interest rate, after subtracting depreciation

   6.____

7. The land residual method of capitalization must be used with great caution, particularly when the building has not yet been constructed, because

   A. it requires exceptional technical competence
   B. the leverage factor can produce gross distortions in the residual land return
   C. construction costs are difficult to estimate
   D. it is unethical to capitalize income attributable to a building not yet constructed

8. The method of capitalization which recognizes the valuation principle that land value should never be penalized or discounted merely because of the inadequacy of a depreciated structure is the _____ method.

   A. gross multiplier
   B. net multiplier
   C. building residual
   D. Kniskern-Schmutz

9. Land value under a rent-controlled apartment house was estimated by comparison at $1,000,000. Net income after all expenses except debt service charges was $120,000. The building's economic life was estimated at 25 years and the interest rate at 6%. The annuity factor for 25 years at 6% was 12.78.
   The total value of land and improvements was

   A. $1,766,800
   B. $1,873,600
   C. $2,056,530
   D. $2,593,600

10. The equity return was $4,000. Debt service charges were $6,000. The property sold for $150,000.
    The overall rate of return, free of mortgage debt, was MOST NEARLY

    A. 5.8%   B. 6.2%   C. 6.7%   D. 7.5%

11. The assessor was asked to appraise, for property tax purposes by the property residual method, a department store property under a 40-year lease at $1,000,000 a year. Building life and the lease term are considered coincident. Land value at lease expiration was estimated at $10,000,000. The annuity factor for 40 years at 7% interest was 13.3. The deferment factor for 40 years at 7% interest was .07.
    The present value is MOST NEARLY

    A. $9,800,000
    B. $12,500,000
    C. $13,300,000
    D. $14,000,000

12. A new retail shopping center was considered to represent the highest utilization of the site. It produced a total net income of $1,000,000. The building cost was $8,000,000. Economic life was 40 years. Interest rate was 7%. Assuming straight-line depreciation and employing the most appropriate capitalization methods, the total value is MOST NEARLY

    A. $32,650,000
    B. $26,300,000
    C. $21,250,000
    D. $11,430,000

13. For the property in the preceding question, the ratio of land to total appraised value is MOST NEARLY

    A. 20%   B. 30%   C. 40%   D. 50%

14. You are appraising a vacant lot 25' x 75', 25' from the corner. 14._____
    Which of the following would you consider in estimating the size of the unit lot?

    A. Corner influence, plus Hoffman-Neill factor
    B. Corner and key influence
    C. Key influence, plus Hoffman-Neill factor
    D. Key influence

15. The RECORD AND GUIDE reported the following sale: Park Ave., 908-910 (5:149-37 15._____
    swc, 80th (Nos. 70-76) 81.2 x 80.6, 14 sty. apt; Harry and Jane Fischel Foundation
    (Albert Wald, v.pres.) 960 Park Ave. to 910 Park Ave., Inc. 910 Park Ave.; B&S; 1st mtg.
    $165,734.19; PM mtge. $489,151.08; Apr. 30; May 2 '57; A $235,000. $470,000 (RS
    $725.45).
    What is the selling price and cash payment, respectively?

    A. $825,234.19; $170,348.12
    B. $1,413,583.72; $569,250.00
    C. $319,681.41; $320,281.00
    D. $975,432.00; $251,684.44

16. Using the sales figures given in the preceding question and assuming the depth factor for 16._____
    80' is 87.73, the number of unit lots and the unit lot value, respectively, are MOST
    NEARLY _____ unit lots and _____.

    A. 3.27; $78,904.00   B. 3.69; $91,283.00
    C. 3.92; $69,524.00   D. 3.72; $111,130.00

17. According to the Tax Department, the assessor's field book must contain 17._____

    A. notations on national real estate conditions for each tax year
    B. annuity tables pasted on the inside fold
    C. the actual condition of all buildings in course of construction as of taxable status
       date
    D. the telephone numbers of taxpayers

18. The CHIEF function of the Tax Department's Research Bureau is to 18._____

    A. engage in primary research in real estate, economics, and valuation techniques
    B. prepare research reports for the City Planning Commission
    C. tabulate the ratio of selling prices to assessed values in various cities throughout
       the country
    D. act as an adjunct of the Certiorari Bureau

19. The property cards furnished each assessor do NOT contain 19._____

    A. sales and leases
    B. court decisions
    C. construction costs
    D. national real estate market index

20. Which one of the following is NOT entitled to partial or complete tax exemption? 20._____

    A. Medical society   B. Parsonages
    C. Trade association   D. Veterans' organization

21. In New York City, exempt property is MOST NEARLY what percent of the total of all property?

    A. 15%   B. 25%   C. 30%   D. 35%

22. The *Assessor's Report for Certiorari Hearing,* in addition to providing a detailed physical description, also computes

    A. the capitalization of the income
    B. the percent of net on the assessed value
    C. the operating costs per cubic foot
    D. a quantity survey cost estimate

23. An example of a typical expense usually listed under Item 9, OTHER EXPENSES, in an Application for Correction of Assessed Valuation of Real Estate is

    A. hall and corridor painting
    B. plumbing repairs
    C. liability insurance
    D. management fees

24. In connection with an Application for Additional Veteran Exemption, the item of information which the assessor must obtain is the

    A. cost of capital improvements to property since purchase
    B. quantity survey cost estimates from reliable contractors
    C. type of veteran's discharge
    D. date on which the veteran purchased the property

25. A remission of real estate from taxation occasionally occurs when

    A. a corporation has a foreign charter
    B. taxes have been in arrears for three or more years
    C. an *in rem* proceeding is pending
    D. a corporation qualifies for tax exemption

KEY (CORRECT ANSWERS)

1. D
2. B
3. B
4. A
5. B

6. A
7. B
8. C
9. A
10. C

11. D
12. D
13. B
14. C
15. A

16. D
17. C
18. A
19. D
20. C

21. C
22. B
23. D
24. A
25. D

66

EXAMINATION SECTION
TEST 1

DIRECTIONS: Each question or incomplete statement is followed by several suggested answers or completions. Select the one that BEST answers the question or completes the statement. *PRINT THE LETTER OF THE CORRECT ANSWER IN THE SPACE AT THE RIGHT.*

1. In the assessment of a single-family attached home, seven sales of similar property at the following prices are noted: $231,000, $234,000, $232,000, $232,500, $228,700, $230,500, and $228,000.
   The MEDIAN sales price of these properties is

   A. $231,500   B. $230,750   C. $239,951   D. $231,000

2. A study of sales trends in a neighborhood indicates the following data on average prices (2010 - base year):

Year	Price Index
2010	1.00
2011	1.10
2012	1.32
2013	1.20
2014	1.15

   All other things being equal, if a parcel sold for $100,000 in 2011, it would have an EQUIVALENT price in 2014 of
   A. $115,000   B. $104,545   C. $104,498   D. $101,500

3. For an object to have value in an economic sense, it must

   A. be visually attractive
   B. have utility and relative scarcity
   C. have a clear title
   D. be scarce and be transferrable

4. The *principle of change* is evidenced in the

   A. use of one interest rate for mortgage and a different one for equity
   B. building residual technique
   C. various forms of land ownership
   D. evolutionary stages in the life of a neighborhood

5. In determining whether property is personal rather than real, the one of the following factors which is NOT pertinent is the

   A. relative cost of the property as compared to value of land on which it is located
   B. use and occupancy of the premises
   C. manner in which the property is attached to the land
   D. intention of the party who installed the property in the premises

6. The one of the following statements about the *principle of substitution* which is MOST accurate is that it

   A. has application to the three approaches to value
   B. is no longer accepted by the courts
   C. affirms that when a builder cannot get specified material, he may substitute other material reasonably similar
   D. relates to the alternate choices in capitalization rate selection

7. The one of the following statements which is MOST valid about the *principle of anticipation* in its application to the appraisal of real property is that it

   A. affirms that change is ever present, especially with regard to rental projections
   B. states that excess profits breed ruinous competition
   C. affirms that value is the present worth of future benefits
   D. provides the basis for the use of escalator clauses in leases

8. Sales assessment ratios, compiled from a statistical analysis of sales data, are LEAST likely to reveal the validity of the

   A. level or levels of assessed valuations
   B. equality of assessments in various areas of the assessing district
   C. sales data itself to sale/purchase motivations
   D. cost and depreciation factors used in assessing property

9. The *purpose* of an appraisal should be included as a section in the final report CHIEFLY to

   A. give a short summary of the approach used to determine value
   B. provide the basis for fixing the appraiser's compensation
   C. indicate the destination of the report
   D. set forth the reason for making the appraisal

10. The income capitalization evaluation approach is MOST valid when applied to a

    A. taxpayer   B. townhouse
    C. two-family dwelling   D. condominium unit

11. Which of the following is the BEST source of demographic data?

    A. Chamber of Commerce reports
    B. F.H.A. Rental Surveys
    C. U.S. Census Tract Studies
    D. Real Estate Board Tracts

12. In general, the one of the following statements about rental conditions in city neighborhoods which is MOST valid is that they

    A. follow national trends
    B. may indicate trends which do not necessarily correspond to regional and national trends
    C. may lag behind national trends but will eventually coincide with them
    D. do not always follow national trends but follow regional trends

13. *Highest and best use* of land can be defined as the   13.____

    A. most intensive use under urban renewal plans
    B. use which produces the largest gross income
    C. use which permits the largest building compatible with zoning provisions
    D. most profitable use

14. The *Bundle of Rights* relates to   14.____

    A. rights of tenants under rent laws
    B. constitutional authority to appropriate real property
    C. various rights attached to ownership of real estate
    D. four rights which state governments possess with regard to real estate

15. *Plottage* is GENERALLY considered an incremental influence in the appraisal of   15.____

    A. a 40-by-100-foot parcel in a single-family home area
    B. a 30-foot corner parcel at the intersection of two major retail streets
    C. two or more contiguous lots held under single ownership and utility
    D. a corner lot with a depth of 118 feet

16. If an independent appraiser in need of sales information does not have access to the   16.____
    published sales data, he can BEST obtain the information he needs by

    A. securing sales data from assessors' cards in the finance administration
    B. consulting sales data in the county clerk's register's office
    C. reviewing the newspaper accounts of sales
    D. examining the city sales tax records

17. *Appraisal area,* as used in local courts, might BEST be defined as the actual area   17.____

    A. computed by the appraiser
    B. adjusted for various increments and depth factors
    C. adjusted for locational amenities
    D. stipulated by both sides in litigation

18. The term *trending* means adjusting sales data for the   18.____

    A. time of sale
    B. physical characteristics of the building
    C. locational factors involved
    D. shape and depth of the lot

19. When sales data is exchanged prior to a trial on assessment appeal, it MUST include   19.____

    A. name of the grantor's attorney
    B. date sale was confirmed
    C. appraiser's rating of *comparable* as compared to *subject*
    D. date and page of recorded instrument

20. Confirmation of sales information as evidence of value is accomplished when   20.____

    A. a copy of the closing statement is obtained
    B. title actually passes

C. ownership changes appear on the assessment roll
D. revenue stamps affixed to the deed agree with *reported* price

21. The *vesting* date in condemnation cases is the date on which

    A. a case goes to trial
    B. the owner first makes a claim for his money
    C. the payment of the award is designated by the court
    D. the taking order is signed by the court

22. Depreciation, as the term is used in appraisal literature, USUALLY means a loss in value

    A. from all causes
    B. from physical deterioration only
    C. from physical deterioration and economic factors only
    D. as certified by a qualified insurance adjuster

23. *Economic Tent* is that rental which is

    A. reserved in a lease agreement
    B. derived from market data
    C. the average of yearly rentals received during past years
    D. the projected rental expectancy

24. *Effective* rental refers to the

    A. annualized montly rental now being collected
    B. gross rental expectancy less vacancy allowance
    C. rental stipulated in a lease
    D. base rental plus *overage*

25. The amount of rental income expected to be collected over economic rental is designated as

    A. overage   B. percentage rental
    C. reserve rental   D. excess rental

26. Office building operational costs are USUALLY expressed in terms of cost per _____ foot.

    A. gross square   B. cubic
    C. net usable   D. net rentable square

27. The LARGEST single item of operating expense in a modern office building is, generally,

    A. contractual cleaning
    B. wages (exclusive of cleaning)
    C. oil for heating and cooling
    D. electricity for tenants and buildings

28. The present worth of a net income stream for a period of 15 years deferred five years is the net income multiplied by the _____ factor.

    A. 20-year   B. 15-year
    C. 20-year factor less the 15-year D. 20-year factor less the 5-year

29. The following formula can be used to develop overall capitalization rate:
R = Y - MC + Depreciation X sinking fund factor
In this formula, the symbol M stands for

   A. money
   B. mortgage amount
   C. mortgage ratio
   D. mortgage rate

30. The leased fee position is valued by

   A. discounting reserved rentals and adding value of reversion
   B. discounting the contract rental stream and adding the present worth of reversion
   C. subtracting the present worth of the rental stream from the free-and-clear value of property
   D. adding the future value of property to the future value of rental income

31. A title of the administrative code imposes a tax on each deed at the time of delivery of the deed from the grantor to the grantee when the consideration exceeds $250,000. The LEAST valid of the following statements regarding the payment of this transfer tax is that

   A. the tax shall be at one-half of one percent of the net consideration
   B. a return must be filed either by the grantor or grantee
   C. the tax is paid by the grantor but the grantee is liable if the grantor does not pay
   D. the grantee, if not otherwise exempt, must pay the tax, if the grantor is exempt

32. Real property owned by senior citizens may be eligible for partial exemption from real estate taxation pursuant to the state real property tax law and the city charter. The one of the following situations which will preclude the granting of the exemption is that the

   A. property is owned by husband and wife who are aged 66 and 60 years, respectively
   B. combined income of the owners is $24,000 per annum
   C. property consists of an owner-occupied legal residence above a grocery store
   D. property was acquired less than ten years prior to the date of making application for exemption

33. Pursuant to a section of the real property tax law, new construction deemed eligible for tax exemption benefits by the city during construction and the following four years shall be _____ exempt during the period of construction, followed by _____ of the full assessed valuation.

   A. *fully*; two years of exemption at 100% and then two years of exemption at 80%
   B. *partially*; two years of exemption at 80% of the full assessed valuation, and an additional two years at 60%
   C. *fully*; exemptions of one year at 80%, one year at 60%, one year at 40%, and one year at 20%
   D. *fully*; exemptions of one year at 90%, one year at 80%, and two years at 60%

34. An honorably discharged Army Chaplain who is currently ministering to a congregation has applied for a clergyman's exemption and a veteran's exemption on his home. According to the state tax law, this chaplain

    A. cannot get both exemptions on a single piece of property
    B. may be able to get both exemptions but the total exemption is limited to $60,000
    C. may obtain both exemptions if he proves that he resides at the property for which he is claiming exemption
    D. may get both exemptions only if his equity in the house is greater than 30% of its market value

35. The one of the following statements that is VALID with respect to the tax commission is that

    A. the tax commission may place upon the books of the annual record of assessed valuations any omitted parcels prior to the date for public inspection thereof
    B. at least three of the members of the commission must be of a political party different from that of the president of the commission
    C. members of the tax commission have the right of entry upon real property at all reasonable times to ascertain the character of the property
    D. the tax commission may remit or reduce a tax is such tax is found excessive or erroneous within two years after delivery of the assessment rolls to the finance administration for the collection of such tax

36. After a certiorari report has been prepared by an assessor and submitted to the certiorari bureau, he learns that the property has been refinanced.
    The one of the following which is the PROPER course of action for an assessor to take in this situation is to

    A. notify the certiorari bureau immediately
    B. note the fact in the field book for future consideration
    C. notify the assessor-in-charge of the county in which the property is located
    D. ignore it as properties are assessed on a free-and-clear basis

37. In order to equalize the tax roll, the finance administrator decides to decrease the assessed value of a parcel of real estate on March 1. The owner has never filed for correction of the valuation.
    The finance administrator

    A. must direct the owner to file an application prior to March 15
    B. may make the change on the assessment rolls immediately without notice to the owner
    C. may make the change on the assessment rolls immediately but must give the owner notice prior to March 15
    D. must give the owner ten days' notice prior to making the change

38. An assessor is required to enter certain relevant appraisal data in his field book.
    Of the following types of data, the one which he is NOT required to enter in the field book is

    A. zoning designations for each block
    B. gross square foot area and, where appropriate, the cubic content of each building

C. information contained in permits issued by the department of marine and aviation concerning physical improvements to city-owned properties
D. information contained in the city planning commission calendars

39. The one of the following statements that is LEAST valid with regard to property exempted from real property taxes is that

    A. assessors, upon finding a change in either ownership or use for which the exemption was granted, may restore the property to the assessable tax rolls
    B. assessors, upon finding a new improvement on exempt property, must report this fact on a query sheet for referral to the tax commission
    C. if construction has not started on vacant land previously granted tax exemption because of an expressed intention to build upon or develop, the assessor must submit a query sheet for each year that the property remains unimproved
    D. exempt properties of any nature, if wholly exempt, must be assessed on the same basis as taxable realty

40. The landlord's information return, filed with the finance administration, is a(n)

    A. certification of the actual consideration paid for the property by the grantee
    B. valuable source for rental data for commercial properties
    C. statement by the owner of a commercial property that he is not using the structure in violation of zoning use
    D. an architectural computation of the gross square foot area and, where appropriate, the cubic content of a building other than one-family dwellings

KEY (CORRECT ANSWERS)

1. D	11. C	21. D	31. B
2. B	12. B	22. A	32. C
3. B	13. D	23. B	33. A
4. D	14. C	24. B	34. C
5. A	15. C	25. D	35. C
6. A	16. B	26. D	36. C
7. C	17. B	27. A	37. B
8. C	18. A	28. D	38. D
9. D	19. B	29. C	39. A
10. A	20. A	30. B	40. B

EXAMINATION SECTION
TEST 1

DIRECTIONS: Each question or incomplete statement is followed by several suggested answers or completions. Select the one that BEST answers the question or completes the statement. *PRINT THE LETTER OF THE CORRECT ANSWER IN THE SPACE AT THE RIGHT.*

1. Deed restrictions imposed by sellers of real property are very effective devices for maintaining the character of real estate developments and for protecting property values. A restriction which has been OUTLAWED by recent Supreme Court decisions is that which

   A. controls the architectural style of improvements since the court believed this would result in stereotyped neighborhoods and prevent modern styles from emerging
   B. limits lands and other site improvements such as fences, washlines, and TV antennae since owners of properties not having such restriction enjoy these benefits
   C. is contrary to the public interest or is based on race, creed, or color
   D. defines the size and qualities of buildings to be constructed since this prevents an owner from improving his property to its highest and best use

   1._____

2. Transferrability is a legal concept which has an effect on the determination of property value. In order to have value, property must be transferrable.
   The concept of transferrability necessarily implies all of the following EXCEPT

   A. control of the use of the property
   B. physical mobility of the property
   C. ownership
   D. control of the right to give the property away

   2._____

3. Equality and uniformity of assessment requires that all types of properties be assessed at the relative values of one type to the other and that all individual properties be valued relatively one to the other. Assume that the relationship of assessment to full value is 50%.
   Which one of the following is overassessed in terms of equality and uniformity?

   A. A home with a full value of $500,000 is assessed for $150,000.
   B. A vacant lot whose full value is $200,000 is assessed at $100,000.
   C. A warehouse whose full value is $1,000,000 is assessed at $600,000.
   D. An office building with a full value of $10,000,000 is assessed at $4,000,000.

   3._____

4. Property subject to taxation under State statutes is termed real estate, real property, or, in some instances, simply land. Included is the land itself, all buildings, articles, and structures erected upon the land or affixed to the land.
   In assessing a bowling alley for real property tax purposes, which of the following should NOT be assessed? The

   A. land on which the bowling alley is situated
   B. foundation, walls, and roof of the building
   C. central air conditioning system which cools the building
   D. actual bowling alleys which are removable

   4._____

5. Listed below are three statements relating to characteristics of the real estate market:
   I. The real estate market in the United States lacks centralized governmental control
   II. Bid and price offerings of buyer and seller are NOT generally publicized
   III. Real estate parcels are not standardized in respect to size or shape

   Of the three statements presented above, the ones which represent ACCURATE statements about the real estate market are

   A. I, II, III
   B. I and II, but not III
   C. II and III, but not I
   D. none of the above

6. A property owner is dissatisfied with his assessment and his application for correction is denied by the Tax Commission and tri-board hearings.
   The one of the following which is the CORRECT procedure for the property owner to follow is to

   A. petition the Commissioner of the City Department of Real Estate to overrule the decision
   B. request the state real estate board to review the assessing authorities' decision
   C. initiate legal proceedings within the provisions of the state and local statutes
   D. apply for a hearing before the City Planning Commission

7. One of the tests that distinguishes trade fixtures from real property is the

   A. size of the item in question
   B. value of the item
   C. manner in which the item is installed
   D. estimated useful life of the item

8. The *present worth of future benefits arising out of ownership* is known as

   A. value
   B. capital asset
   C. annuity
   D. increment

9. The borrower of a mortgage loan is primarily liable for the payment of the mortgage debt and signs a pledge as the promise to pay.
   In the event that there are several borrowers, the term which should be used to describe their obligation is

   A. jointly
   B. severally
   C. jointly and severally
   D. in common

10. As a characteristic of value, scarcity is a relative term.
    In determining the value of land, scarcity must be considered in relation to all of the following EXCEPT

    A. demand
    B. supply
    C. possible alternate uses of the land
    D. economic encumbrances of developers and investors

11. Of the following, the statement MOST likely to be considered accurate about building cost estimates is that such estimates

    A. should not vary, as the exact price of materials and labor can be determined at any given date
    B. are not subject to wide variations since a building is merely the combination of materials and labor brought together in accordance with specifications
    C. can vary considerably because of the nature of the contracting business and the fluctuations in labor and materials costs at different times and places
    D. are extremely accurate as builders are able to use cost services that are developed from experience, surveys, and statistical evidence

12. In a realty investment, there are various charges which absorb the gross income produced by the investment. The gross income itself represents a percentage of the value of the investment. Assume that mortgage charges, owner's equity interest, real estate taxes, and operating expenses absorb the gross income completely and that the gross income represents 18.18 percent of value.
    The gross income multiplier that could be used to arrive at the value is

    A. 5.5   B. 6.0   C. 6.5   D. 7.0

13. One method of estimating reproduction cost is unit-in-place analysis.
    If, under this method, it is determined that the cost of one square foot of a brick wall is $37.50, the TOTAL cost of the four walls of a one-story, 18-foot-high building containing 4,000 square feet, built on the front 2/3 of a 40 x 150 foot lot is

    A. $94,500   B. $189,000   C. $270,000   D. $540,000

14. A religious organization is entitled to a real property tax exemption where such organization is non-profit, organized for its exempt purpose, and used exclusively for such exempt purpose.
    Which one of the following properties owned by a religious organization most probably would NOT be exempt from taxation? A

    A. building housing a religious school
    B. playground adjacent to a religious school
    C. parking lot used by a religious school
    D. building leased by a religious school to a caterer

15. A veteran's exemption assumes that a veteran has received certain funds related to his military service used in the purchase or improvement of his home. Assume that John Doe owns a home on Smith Street in which he has used all of his eligible funds and has received a $2,000 veteran's exemption. He decides to sell this home and purchase a larger home on Jones Street.
    Which one of the following actions by John Doe would MOST likely enable him to transfer his $2,000 veteran's exemption to his new home on Jones Street?

    A. He buys the home on Jones Street while waiting for a purchaser for his Smith Street home.
    B. He rents his home on Smith Street and purchases the home on Jones Street.
    C. He purchases the home on Jones Street, and then on the very next day he sells his home on Smith Street.
    D. He first sells his home on Smith Street and then the very next day purchases the home on Jones Street.

16. Assume that an assessor is capitalizing the net income of a parcel of property for assessment purposes.
Of the following, the information of LEAST concern to the assessor would be that the

    A. fire insurance on the building indicated a value far exceeding the value produced by capitalizing the income
    B. actual rent was considerably lower than rent being paid for similar properties
    C. lessee of the property contracted to pay all increases in taxes above a certain base period
    D. lessee had an option to buy at a certain fixed price

17. Land has physical and economic characteristics.
The physical characteristics of land which has caused it to be classified as real estate is its

    A. availability for different uses
    B. return on investment
    C. use as collateral in securing loans
    D. immobility

18. In considering comparable sales as a method of valuing property for assessment purposes, two main factors arise. One is the distance between the site being assessed and the comparable property. The other is the recency of the comparable sale.
Which one of the following sales is most likely to be considered unreasonable for use as a comparable sale? In valuing

    A. a golf course, the only golf course sale available was made five years ago, and the course was located 50 miles away
    B. an industrial building, a similar building in the same industrial park sold two years ago is used as a comparable sale
    C. an office building, the recent sale of a large store located immediately adjacent to the office building is used as in comparable sale
    D. a one family home, the recent sale of an identical home situated in a similar community two miles away is considered a comparable sale

19. The taxpayer has the burden of proving that the assessed value on his property is excessive. The valuation established by the assessor is presumed correct. However, the presumption of correctness disappears in the face of contradictory evidence.
Of the following, the LEAST convincing evidence provided by the taxpayer to support his contention of an excessive assessment is that

    A. in a recent sale of comparable property, the sales price was lower than his assessment
    B. twenty years ago, he purchased the subject property at a price considerably lower than the assessment
    C. the replacement costs of subject property less depreciation produce a value less than the assessment
    D. the capitalization of the net income of the property produces a value considerably less than the assessment

20. A real property tax assessment case is being heard by the court. Which one of the following statements represents **pertinent evidence for the court to consider** in rendering its decision? The

 A. full value of the property in question
 B. owner's inability to pay the real property taxes
 C. local assessor's lack of sufficient experience to render a just decision
 D. doubling of real property taxes on this property over the last ten years

21. The principle that value at a given location is proportionate to street frontage receives added import at corner lots. The highest lot values in business areas will almost always be the corner lots.
 This statement MOST accurately defines the term

 A. corner influence B. increment
 C. intangible asset D. key influence

22. That use of the land which will provide the greatest net return to the land over a reasonable period of time is a definition of the term

 A. reversion B. valuation
 C. highest and best use D. capitalization

23. An agreement whereby the owner of a property holds it off the market in return for a consideration is called a(n)

 A. sales agreement B. binder
 C. escrow D. option

24. The upright side of a doorway, window, or fireplace is called the

 A. buttress B. apron C. jamb D. cantilever

25. An ornamental railing or parapet made of coping or a hand rail and balusters is called a(n)

 A. kerf B. balustrade C. batten D. ashlar

26. A hinged window frame, commonly made so the window will open outward is called a

 A. casement B. double-hung C. bay D. sash

27. *Purchasing power, utility,* and *supply* are terms generally associated with

 A. value B. cost C. price D. capital

28. In most real estate transactions, a buyer finances the major portion of the purchase price by borrowing and pledging to assure the repayment of the purchase loan with interest over a specific period of time.
 The one of the following which does NOT represent a method of financing commonly used in the purchase of realty is a

 A. mortgage B. promissory note
 C. bond D. stock option

29. Assume that, as an assessor, you are busily working in your office when you are interrupted by a telephone call. The caller requests information which you do not have. The PROPER action for you to take is to tell the caller

    A. you are sorry but you don't have that information
    B. that you would like to help him, but you are just too busy
    C. to hold on while you find out who can give him the correct information, and then transfer his call.
    D. what you guess might be the correct answer to his question

30. Assume that you are an assessor. A property owner comes into your office to check the assessment on his property. In the course of the discussion, he becomes angry and abusive.
    Of the following, the MOST effective action you can take is to

    A. tell the person that you will not tolerate that kind of behavior and will have him removed from the office if he doesn't stop
    B. display your irritation at his behavior so that he will know he has not intimidated you
    C. call the building security office immediately
    D. keep your self-control and try to calm the person

31. Assume that you are an assessor. You receive a phone call in the office from an agitated property owner. The information you give him is not what he had hoped to hear, and he asks you to give him your name.
    Of the following, the MOST appropriate action for you to take is to

    A. give the property owner your name
    B. ask your supervisor to speak to the caller
    C. tell him that you are not required to give your name
    D. find out why he wants to know your name

32. Following are four steps that should be taken to solve a problem involving public relations:
    I. Weigh and decide; consider possible actions
    II. Follow-up; check the results of your actions
    III. Get the facts; determine the exact nature of the problem
    IV. Take action; implement your plan
    Which of the following choices shows the PROPER sequence of the above steps an assessor should take?

    A. IV, II, III, I   B. III, I, IV, II
    C. I, IV, II, III   D. II, III, IV, I

33. As an assessor, you may be required to answer letters from the public.
    Which of the following techniques SHOULD be used in such correspondence?

    A. Try to make the public feel grateful to your agency for the services it receives from the agency.
    B. Do not volunteer information other than that requested.
    C. Be as clear as possible, but avoid verbosity.
    D. Try to use as much technical language as possible to impress the public with your knowledge.

34. In which section of his appraisal report would an appraiser include detailed maps, floor plans, and blue prints?

    A. Introduction
    B. Analysis and conclusions
    C. Appendix
    D. Preface

35. The one of the following items which would NOT generally be included in the *Summary of Important Conclusions* section of an appraisal report is

    A. net income expectancy
    B. the estimate of land value and highest and best use
    C. capitalized value estimate
    D. population trends

36. In addition to the basic information contained in an appraisal report, certain auxiliary documents must accompany a complete narrative report.
    The one of the following NOT required to be included in this report is

    A. a letter of transmittal relating to the narrative report
    B. a statement of qualifications of the appraiser
    C. disclosure of the appraiser's personal finances and business interests unrelated to the specific property
    D. the certificate of the appraiser

37. Public recording of instruments relating to property rights is used to notify third parties of the existence of rights in property and to establish the priority of rights or claims to property.
    Since some instruments merge with a subsequently executed instrument, the one instrument which is very SELDOM publicly recorded is the

    A. ownership deed
    B. mortgage
    C. mechanic's lien
    D. contract of sale

38. Zoning is the device by which planning is expressed in concrete terms and consists of ordinances and maps defining the geographic areas within which various types of land use limitations are enforced.
    In light of this definition,

    A. zoning is limited to the geographic area over which the municipal authorities have jurisdiction and may not be extended beyond those limits
    B. zoning generates city growth and insures the development of a particular land use in a given area
    C. an area zoned for commercial use will insure the success of any such use in that area
    D. zoning controls automatically coincide with those uses dictated by market trends

39. The demand for single family homes is a composite of price, income, and subjective interests or desires in which investments in homes are determined in some degree by attempts to benefit from speculation in a rising market. This anticipation of rising markets serves to intensify increased real estate activity. Conversely, these same subjective elements which serve to reinforce a rising market may disappear in a declining market and so hasten the decrease in real estate investments.
This statement indicates that

    A. home ownership is so dependent on family whims that price is not a determinant of the decision to purchase a house
    B. there is a direct relationship between business conditions and the rates of increase and decrease in the demand for single family homes
    C. home purchasing activity remains on a constant level because of the compelling desires of most families to own their own home
    D. most families are so possessed of the desire to have a home of their own that demand offsets any other factors against purchase

40. A borrower obtained an $80,000 mortgage loan under the level-or-constant payment plan for 20 years at 7 percent interest. His monthly payments amount to $775.30. Which of the following represent the CORRECT amounts for interest and for payment on principal for each of the first two monthly payments?

A.	1st month	Interest	$560.00	Principal	$215.30
	2nd month	Interest	$558.50	Principal	$216.80
B.	1st month	Interest	$466.70	Principal	$308.60
	2nd month	Interest	$464.90	Principal	$310.40
C.	1st month	Interest	$672.00	Principal	$103.30
	2nd month	Interest	$671.10	Principal	$104.20
D.	1st month	Interest	$466.70	Principal	$308.60
	2nd month	Interest	$433.10	Principal	$342.20

KEY (CORRECT ANSWERS)

1. C		11. C		21. A		31. A
2. B		12. A		22. C		32. B
3. C		13. B		23. D		33. C
4. D		14. D		24. C		34. C
5. A		15. D		25. B		35. D
6. C		16. A		26. A		36. C
7. C		17. D		27. D		37. D
8. A		18. C		28. D		38. A
9. C		19. B		29. C		39. B
10. D		20. A		30. D		40. B

TEST 2

DIRECTIONS: Each question or incomplete statement is followed by several suggested answers or completions. Select the one that BEST answers the question or completes the statement. *PRINT THE LETTER OF THE CORRECT ANSWER IN THE SPACE AT THE RIGHT.*

Questions 1-3.

DIRECTIONS: Answer Questions 1 through 3 according to the information given in the following passage.

Section 502 of the State Real Property Tax Law – Form of Assessment Roll – states in Subdivision 2 that when a tax map has been approved by the State Board, reference to the lot, block and section number or other identification numbers of any parcel on such map should be deemed as sufficient description of such parcel. Otherwise, the name of the owner, last known or abutting owners and a description sufficient to identify the parcel must be listed.

Subdivision 3 states that the assessment roll shall contain a column for the entry for the assessed value of land exclusive of improvements for each separately assessed parcel followed by a column for the entry of the total assessed valuation. It then states that only the total assessed valuation shall be subject to judicial review.

1. A city in the state has a tax map describing real property by section, block and lot, and this map has been approved by the state board. Robert Roberts purchased a one-family home from William Williams at 777 Seventh Street, Woodside, described as Section 22, Block 222, Lot 2 on the tax map.
   According to the above passage, which description on the Assessment Roll is legally INCORRECT?

   A. William Williams, 333 Third Street, Woodside, Section 22, Block 222, Lot 2
   B. Robert Roberts, 777 Seventh Street, Woodside, Section 22, Block 222, Lot 2
   C. William Williams, 777 Seventh Street, Woodside, Section 22, Block 222, Lot 2
   D. Robert Roberts, 777 Seventh Street, Woodside, Section 22, Block 222, Lot 3

   1.____

2. An assessing district in the city has a tax map describing real property by section, block and lot. This map has not as yet been approved by the state board.
   According to the passage, which one of the following descriptions would NOT be correct?

   A. Amos Jones, 999 Smith Boulevard, Elmhurst
   B. Section 37, Block 750, Lot 9
   C. Property located at 999 Smith Boulevard, Elmhurst, surrounded by properties owned by John Doe, Richard Roe, Sam Samuels, and Alvin Abrams
   D. Property on Smith Boulevard, Elmhurst, bounded on the East by John Doe, on the West by Richard Roe, on the South by Sam Samuels, and on the North by Alvin Abrams

   2.____

3. According to the passage, which of the following entries of assessed valuations would be PROPER under the provisions of Subdivision 3?

    A. Land - $500,000; Total - $1,000,000
    B. Improvement - $500,000; Total - $1,000,000
    C. Total - $1,000,000; Improvement plus land - $1,000,000
    D. Land - $500,000; Improvement - $500,000

Questions 4-6.

DIRECTIONS: In each of Questions 4 through 6, four sentences are given. For each question, choose as your answer the group of numbers that would represent the MOST logical order of these sentences if they were arranged in paragraph form.

4.
    I. However, a photograph or a map of a city at a given moment of time fails to show the dynamic character of the city's growth.
    II. Thus, if the location of a certain type of area has changed from one period to another, it is possible to determine the direction and speed with which such movements have occurred by using devices of this kind.
    III. One method for collecting the necessary information is by the use of time interval maps.
    IV. Several photographs taken at different time intervals or several maps for different periods reveal the processes of change.

    A. I, IV, II, III   B. III, I, II, IV
    C. III, I, IV, II   D. I, III, IV, II

5.
    I. In small towns, all neighborhoods may be within easy walking distance of schools, shopping centers, places of employment, and amusement parks.
    II. Adequacy of transportation, like so many other factors involved in neighborhood analysis, is a relative matter.
    III. In most larger cities, however, transportation has a vital bearing on neighborhood stability since neighborhoods which do not have access to desirable transportation facilities at reasonable cost suffer from the competition of those which are more favorably located.
    IV. In such cases, transportation is of no significance in determining neighborhood stability.

    A. II, I, IV, III   B. III, I, II, IV
    C. III, IV, I, II   D. II, IV, III, I

6.
    I. If he plans to sell lots, he needs to know something of the demand for lots of the type and price range he is considering.
    II. In addition, the subdivider or developer needs information about the potential market for the specific types of products which he intends to sell.
    III. Prior to undertaking a new land development project, it is essential that the general conditions of the market be understood.
    IV. If he intends to subdivide and completely develop a tract of land, constructing homes, apartments, a shopping center, or other buildings on the lots, he will need information about their salability or rentability.

    A. IV, III, I, II   B. III, II, I, IV
    C. I, III, II, IV   D. I, II, IV, III

Questions 7-10.

DIRECTIONS: Answer Questions 7 through 10 according to the information given in the following passage.

In capitalizing the net income of property to produce a value, certain expenses are permitted to be deducted from gross income. Even though the premises may be fully rented, it is proper to deduct from the gross income an allowance for vacancy. All expenses attributable to the maintenance and upkeep of the premises are deductible. These include heat, light and power, water and sewers, wages or employees and expenses attributable to wages, insurance, repairs, and maintenance, supplies and materials, legal and accounting fees, telephone, rental commission, advertising, and so forth. If the premises are furnished, a reserve for the depreciation of personal property is deductible. A capital improvement to the building is not a deductible expense. Real estate taxes should not be deducted as an expense. Instead, taxes should be factored as part of the overall capitalization rate.

It is proper to allow an expense for management of the building even in cases where the owner himself is manager. But, payments of interest and principal of the mortgage are not a properly deductible expense. Real property is appraised free and clear of all encumbrances. Otherwise, two identical buildings located next to each other might be valued differently because one has a greater mortgage than the other.

7. According to the above passage, the one of the following which is NOT a proper deductible expense during the year in which the expense is incurred is the cost for

    A. advertising to rent the premises
    B. accounting fees
    C. utilities
    D. putting in central air conditioning

8. According to the above passage, the one of the following statements concerning deductible expenses which is CORRECT is that

    A. a vacancy allowance is a proper deductible expense even though the premises may be fully rented
    B. real estate taxes are a proper deductible expense
    C. if the owner manages his own property, he cannot charge a management fee as a deductible expense
    D. payments for interest and principal of the mortgage are proper deductible expenses

9. According to the passage, two identical adjacent buildings CANNOT receive different valuations because of differences in their

    A. mortgages   B. net income
    C. leases   D. management fees

10. According to the passage, an owner of furnished premises may set aside a reserve as a deductible expense for all of the following EXCEPT

    A. refrigerators   B. carpeting
    C. bookcases   D. walls

Questions 11-13.

DIRECTIONS: Answer Questions 11 through 13 according to the information given in the following passage.

The standard for assessment in the State is contained in Section 306 of the Real Property Tax Law. It states that all real property in each assessing unit shall be assessed at the full value thereof. However, the Courts of the State have not required assessors to assess at 100% of full value. Assessments of property for real estate tax purposes at less than full value are not invalid if they are made at a uniform percentage of full value throughout the assessing district. In assessing real property, full value is equivalent to market value.

In determining market value of real property for tax purposes, every element which can reasonably affect value of property ought to be considered, and the main considerations should be given to actual sales of the subject or similar property, cost to produce or reproduce the property, capitalization of income therefrom, and the combination of these factors.

11. According to the above passage, the one of the following statements which is INCORRECT is that all real property in each assessing unit

    A. must be assessed at full value
    B. shall be assessed at full value or at a uniform percentage of full value
    C. may be assessed at 50% of full value
    D. may be assessed at 100% of full value

12. According to the above passage, the one of the following elements of value which should be given the LEAST consideration in determining market value is

    A. actual or comparable sales
    B. reproduction cost
    C. amount of mortgage
    D. capitalization of income

13. According to the passage, the basis for the legality of assessing units making assessments at a uniform percentage of full value rather than at full value is

    A. Section 306 of the Real Property Tax Law
    B. decisions of the State Courts
    C. judgments of individual assessors
    D. decisions of municipal executives

Questions 14-17.

DIRECTIONS: Answer Questions 14 through 17 according to the information given in the following passage.

Depreciation – Any reduction from the upper limit of value. An effect caused by deterioration and/or obsolescence. Deterioration is evidenced by wear and tear, decay, dry rot, cracks, encrustations, or structural defects. Obsolescence is divisible into two parts, functional, or economic. Functional obsolescence may be due to poor planning, mechanical inadequacy or overadequacy, functional inadequacy or overadequacy due to size, style, or age. It is evidenced by conditions within the property. Economic obsolescence is caused by changes external to the property, such as neighborhood infiltrations of inharmonious groups or property uses, legislation, etc. It is also the actual decline in market value of the improvement to land from the time of purchase to the time of sale.

14. According to the above passage, a form of physical deterioration can be caused by   14._____

    A. termite infestation
    B. zoning regulations
    C. inadequate wiring
    D. extra high ceilings

15. According to the passage, a form of economic obsolescence may be caused by   15._____

    A. structural defects
    B. poor architectural design
    C. changes in zoning regulations
    D. chemical reactions

16. According to the passage, the statement which BEST explains the meaning of depreciation is that it is a loss in value   16._____

    A. caused only by economic obsolescence
    B. resulting from any cause
    C. caused only by wear and tear
    D. resulting from conditions of changes external to the property

17. According to the passage, the lack of air conditioning in warm climates is   17._____

    A. a form of physical deterioration
    B. a form of functional obsolescence
    C. a form of economic obsolescence
    D. not a form of depreciation

Questions 18-21.

DIRECTIONS: Answer Questions 18 through 21 according to the information given in the following passage.

In determining the valuation of income producing property, the capitalisation of income is accepted as a proper approach to value. Income producing property is bought and sold for the purpose of making money. How much an investor would pay would, of course, depend on how much he could earn on his investment. The amount he would earn on his investment is called a return. The amount of return depends on the degree of risk involved.

If one has $1,000,000 to invest, it can be put in a bank account at perhaps a 5 percent return. In the bank, the money is relatively safe so the return is lower. If the money were invested by purchasing a block of stores in a depressed area, of course, one would not be satisfied with a 5 percent return. This is what the capitalization of income comes down to — the better the return, the higher the risk. This is the approach an experienced real estate investor uses in determining what he would pay for property.

18. According to the above passage, which one of the following investments would an experienced real estate investor with $1,000,000 MOST likely choose? A(n)   18.___

    A. apartment building in a slum area yielding a 6 percent return
    B. office building rented to professionals yielding a 6 percent return
    C. shopping center in a depressed area yielding a 10 percent return
    D. warehouse rented on a long-term lease to a major corporation yielding a 10 percent return

19. According to the passage, in the capitalization of income, the relationship between the degree of risk and the rate of return GENERALLY is expected to be   19.___

    A. indeterminate   B. variable   C. inverse   D. direct

20. According to the passage, in purchasing income producing property, the one of the following which would NOT be a factor influencing an experienced real estate investor is the   20.___

    A. socio-economic characteristics of the area in which the property is located
    B. rate of return on investment
    C. original cost of the property
    D. degree of risk involved

21. According to the above passage, the property listed below which would be LEAST likely to be valued by the capitalization of income is a(n)   21.___

    A. apartment house with no vacancies
    B. office building rented to 70 percent of capacity
    C. shopping center with several new tenants
    D. vacant lot located next to a factory

Questions 22-25.

DIRECTIONS: Answer Questions 22 through 25 according to the information contained in the following passage.

The cost approach is used by assessors mainly in valuing one family homes and properties of a special nature which are not commonly bought and sold and do not produce an income.

There are three aspects to the cost approach to valuation. The first is the actual cost of construction. Where the property has recently been built, the cost of constructing the property is relevant. It, however, may not be a true test as to its value. The building may have been constructed so as to serve the special needs of the owner. What it costs to construct may not truly reflect its value; it may be worth more or less. If it is income producing property, the income may be more or less than expected. It may be sold for more or less than it cost to build.

The second aspect is replacement cost and applies to older structures. It involves the construction of a similar type of building with the same purpose. It does not require the use of the same materials or design.

Reproduction cost is the third aspect, and it also applies to older structures. It involves construction with the exact same materials and design. The cost in the two latter aspects is construction at today's prices with an allowance made for depreciation from the day the original building was constructed.

22. According to the above passage, which one of the following is a CORRECT statement concerning the cost approach to valuation?

   A. In determining value by the replacement and reproduction cost methods, an allowance must be made for depreciation from the day the building was originally constructed.
   B. The cost approach method is the best method to apply in valuing an office building.
   C. When a structure has been recently built, its actual cost is the best method of determining its value.
   D. The fact that a structure has been built to meet the special needs of the occupant is a relevant factor in valuation.

23. An assessor, in valuing a ten-year-old apartment house, finds that its original construction cost was $12,000,000. In capitalizing its net income, he realizes a valuation of $8,000,000. In using the replacement cost method and allowing for depreciation, the assessor arrives at a valuation of $9,000,000.
   According to the above passage, which one of the following valuations is LEAST acceptable for this apartment house?

   A. $12,000,000   B. $8,000,000   C. $9,000,000   D. $8,500,000

24. The construction cost of a recently built structure is relevant to value, but may not be a true test of value. According to the passage, which one of the following statements CORRECTLY explains why this is true?

   A. The builder may not know how to construct economically.
   B. A building can depreciate very quickly.
   C. The building may have been built to satisfy certain unique specifications.
   D. Cost-of-construction is not an accepted method of valuation.

25. According to the passage, which one of the following statements CORRECTLY defines the essential difference between the replacement cost and reproduction cost aspects of the cost approach?

   A. Replacement cost is used only in assessing older buildings; reproduction cost is used only when the building has been recently constructed.
   B. Reproduction cost does not include any allowance for depreciation; replacement cost allows for depreciation from the date of construction of the original building.
   C. Replacement cost involves construction with the same exact materials; reproduction cost does not require the use of the same materials.
   D. Reproduction cost involves construction with the exact same materials and design; replacement cost does not require the use of the same materials and design.

Questions 26-31.

DIRECTIONS: Answer Questions 26 through 31 on the basis of the information given in the following passage.

Realty, because of fixity in investment, immobility in location, and necessity for shelter purposes, lends itself readily to economic controls when such are deemed essential to serve social or political ends, or where the interest of health, safety, and morality of community pop-

ulation or the nation at large warrants it. Realty has consistently been recognized as a form of private property which is sufficiently invested with public interest to warrant its control either under the police power of a sovereign state and its branches of government or by direct and statutory legislation enacted within the framework of the governmental constitution.

Whenever war or catastrophe causes a sudden shifting of population or suspension of building operations, or both, an imbalance is brought about in the supply and demand for housing. This imbalance in housing demand and supply creates conditions of insecurity and instability among the tenants who fear indiscriminate eviction or unwarranted upward rental adjustments. It is this background of possible exploitation during times of economic stress and strain that underlies the enactment of emergency rent control legislation.

Although rent control has been in effect in many communities, particularly the larger metropolitan communities, since the end of World War II, the attitude of all levels of government is to view this form of legislation as temporary and to hasten, as far as their power permits, a return to normal relations between landlords and tenants.

26. According to the passage, the reason that realty can conveniently be subjected to controls is due to

    A. public interest
    B. site immobility
    C. population shifts
    D. moral considerations

27. The above passage includes as a justification for the imposition of economic controls all of the following EXCEPT

    A. threats to physical safety
    B. socio-politico considerations
    C. dangers to health in the community
    D. requirements of police powers

28. According to the passage, a LIKELY cause for a cessation of construction might be a

    A. natural disaster
    B. change in the demand for housing
    C. change in the supply of housing
    D. demographic fluctuation

29. According to the passage, of the following, a tenant's insecurity would MOST likely result in his fear of

    A. reduction in necessary services
    B. loss in equity
    C. rent increases
    D. condemnation proceedings

30. According to the passage, indiscriminate evictions by landlords during periods of economic difficulties constitute

    A. unlawful acts
    B. justifiable measures
    C. desirable actions
    D. exploitation of tenants

31. According to the above passage, economic controls of realty have been in effect on a widespread basis since

    A. 1918 B. 1945 C. 1953 D. 1964

Questions 32-35.

DIRECTIONS: Answer Questions 32 through 35 on the basis of the following passage.

Although zoning is a phase of city planning and is concerned with land use control of private property, zoning powers are better known and more generally applied than most city planning powers. Zoning powers predate the formulation of a master plan and even the formation of the planning commission itself. The widespread application of zoning powers is evident from a survey conducted by the International City Managers' Association. As reported in the Municipal Yearbook, 98 percent of all cities in excess of ten thousand population had enacted comprehensive zoning ordinances governing the utilization of privately owned land. Since 60 percent of all urban land is generally held under private ownership, the impact of zoning laws upon income and value of real property is most significant.

32. Of the following, the one whose land use is MOST likely to be affected by zoning controls, according to the passage, is

    A. Gimbel's Department Store
    B. the Port Authority terminal
    C. the New York Public Library at 42nd Street
    D. the Federal Building

33. According to the passage, in relation to the powers of city planning, zoning powers are

    A. not as familiar to the general public
    B. formulated subsequent to the establishment of the powers of the planning commission
    C. more general in their application
    D. likely to develop as a result of the community's master plan

34. According to the passage, if there are 200 cities in the United States with a population exceeding 10,000 persons, the number of such cities LIKELY to have enacted comprehensive zoning laws is

    A. 190 B. 192 C. 194 D. 196

35. According to the passage, for each 400 acres of urban land, it is LIKELY that the amount of land which would be privately owned would be _____ acres.

    A. 220 B. 240 C. 260 D. 280

KEY (CORRECT ANSWERS)

1.	D	16.	B
2.	B	17.	B
3.	A	18.	D
4.	C	19.	D
5.	A	20.	C
6.	B	21.	D
7.	D	22.	A
8.	A	23.	A
9.	A	24.	C
10.	D	25.	D
11.	A	26.	B
12.	C	27.	D
13.	B	28.	A
14.	A	29.	C
15.	C	30.	D

31. B
32. A
33. C
34. D
35. B

TEST 3

DIRECTIONS: Each question or incomplete statement is followed by several suggested answers or completions. Select the one that BEST answers the question or completes the statement. *PRINT THE LETTER OF THE CORRECT ANSWER IN THE SPACE AT THE RIGHT.*

1. A property decreases in value from $450,000 to $350,000. The percent of decrease is MOST NEARLY

   A. 20.5% B. 22.2% C. 25.0% D. 28.6%

   1.____

2. The fraction $\frac{487}{101326}$, expressed as a decimal, is MOST NEARLY

   A. .0482 B. .00481 C. .0049 D. .00392

   2.____

3. The reciprocal of the sum of 2/3 and 1/6 can be expressed as

   A. 0.83 B. 1.20 C. 1.25 D. 1.50

   3.____

4. Total land and building costs for a new commercial property equal $250.00 per square foot.
   If the investors expect a 10 percent return on their costs, and if total operating expenses average 5 percent of total costs, annual gross rentals per square foot must be AT LEAST

   A. $37.50 B. $42.50 C. $50.00 D. $60.00

   4.____

5. The formula for computing the amount of annual deposit in a compound interest-bearing account to provide a lump sum at the end of a period of years is $X = \frac{r}{(1+r)^{n-1}}$ (X is the amount of annual deposit, r is the rate of interest, and n is the number of years). Using the formula, the annual amount of the deposit at the end of each year to accumulate to $200,000 at the end of 3 years with interest at 2 percent on annual balances is

   A. $61,200.00 B. $62,033.30 C. $65,359.00 D. $66,666.60

   5.____

6. An investor sold two properties at $1,500,000 each. On one, he made a 25 percent profit. On the other, he suffered a 25 percent loss.
   The NET result of his sales was

   A. neither a gain nor a loss   B. a $200,000 loss
   C. a $750,000 gain   D. a $750,000 loss

   6.____

7. A contractor decides to install a chain fence covering the perimeter of a parcel 75 feet wide and 112 feet in depth. Which one of the following represents the number of feet to be covered? _____ feet.

   A. 187 B. 364 C. 374 D. 8,400

   7.____

93

8. A builder estimates he can build an average of 4-1/2 one-family homes to an acre. There are 640 acres to one square mile.
Which one of the following CORRECTLY represents the number of one family homes the builder would estimate he can build on one square mile?

   A. 1,280   B. 1,920   C. 2,560   D. 2,880

9. $.01059 deposited at 7 percent interest will yield $1.00 in 30 years. If a person deposited $1,059 at 7 percent interest on April 1, 2004, which one of the following amounts would represent the worth of this deposit on March 31, 2034?

   A. $100   B. $1,000   C. $10,000   D. $100,000

10. A building has an economic life of forty years.
Assuming the building depreciates at a constant annual rate, which one of the following CORRECTLY represents the yearly percentage of depreciation?

    A. 2.0%   B. 2.5%   C. 5.0%   D. 7.0%

11. A building produces a gross income of $2,000,000 with a net income of $200,000, before mortgage charges and capital re-capture. The owner is able to increase the gross income 5 percent without a corresponding increase in operating costs.
The effect upon the net income will be an INCREASE of

    A. 5%   B. 10%   C. 12.5%   D. 50%

12. The present value of $1.00 not payable for 8 years, and at 10 percent interest, is $.4665.
Which of the following amounts represents the PRESENT value of $1,000 payable 8 years hence at 10 percent interest?

    A. $46.65   B. $466.50   C. $4,665.00   D. $46,650.00

13. The amount of real property taxes to be levied by a city is $100 million. The assessment roll subject to taxation shows an assessed valuation of $2 billion.
Which one of the following tax rates CORRECTLY represents the tax rate to be levied per $100 of assessed valuation?

    A. $.50   B. $5.00   C. $50.00   D. $500.00

Questions 14-19.

   DIRECTIONS: The graph below presents data on two demographic characteristics and the rate of new home construction in Empire State during the period 1995 through 2006. Answer Questions 14 through 19 on the basis of the graph alone.

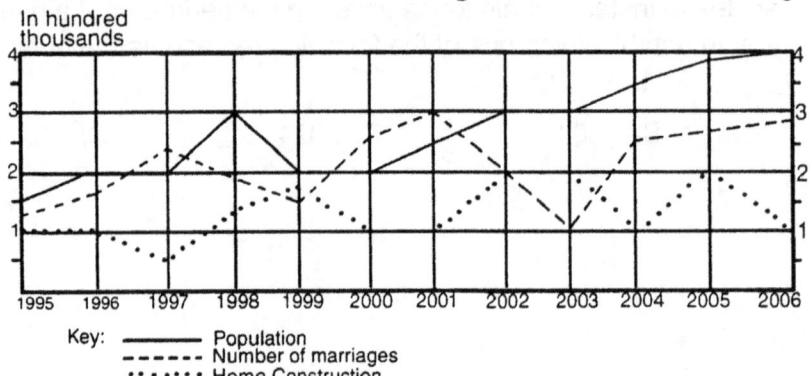

Key: ——— Population
   - - - - - Number of marriages
   · · · · · Home Construction

14. The increase in population in Empire State from 2000 to 2003 was approximately 14._____

    A. 50,000   B. 100,000   C. 150,000   D. 200,000

15. The year with the greatest increase in population was 15._____

    A. 1998   B. 1999   C. 2002   D. 2004

16. The greatest overall increase in the number of marriages occurred during the period 16._____

    A. 1997-1999   B. 1998-2000   C. 2000-2002   D. 2004-2006

17. In the period from 1995 through 2002, the trend in home construction could BEST be described as 17._____

    A. increasing steadily throughout the period
    B. remaining relatively stable
    C. overall increasing with periods of decline
    D. overall decreasing with fluctuations

18. If the rate of population increase that occurred between 1997 and 1998 occurs between 2006 and 2007, the population of Empire State in 2007 would be 18._____

    A. 400,000   B. 500,000   C. 600,000   D. 800,000

19. The period when there was no change in the number of homes constructed and no change in population was 19._____

    A. 1996-1997   B. 1999-2000   C. 2000-2001   D. 2002-2003

Questions 20-25.

DIRECTIONS: The graph below presents data on the rate of new office construction in the uptown, midtown, and downtown areas of Gotham City for the period from 1987 through 2001. Answer Questions 20 through 25 on the basis of the information provided in the graph.

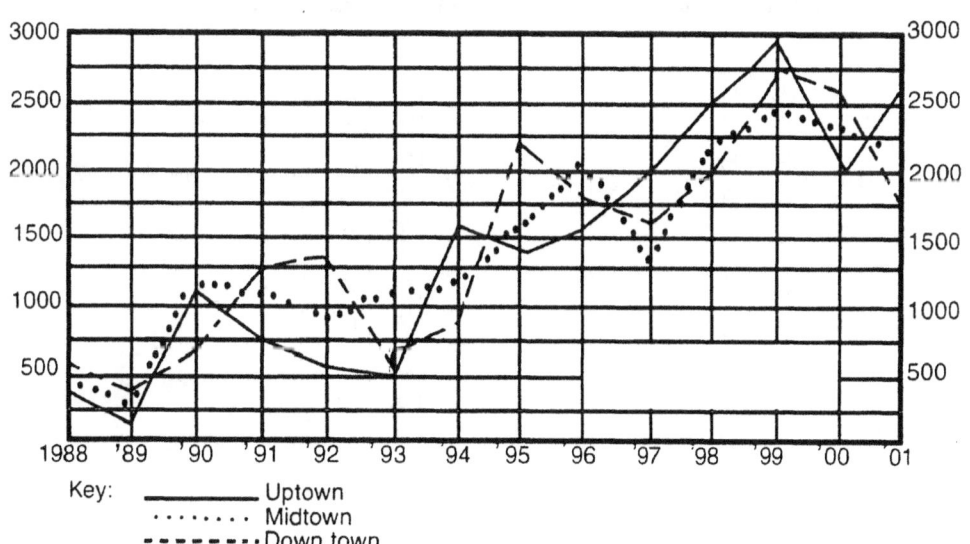

20. The amount of office space which was constructed in Gotham City in the year 1997 is MOST NEARLY _____ square feet.   20._____

    A. 2,100,000   B. 3,500,000   C. 4,900,000   D. 5,700,000

21. In which of the following years was the LEAST amount of office space constructed in the downtown area?   21._____

    A. 1988   B. 1991   C. 1993   D. 1995

22. The year with the GREATEST amount of new office construction was   22._____

    A. 1990   B. 1994   C. 1999   D. 2001

23. In the years 1995 through 1999, the overall trend in new uptown office space construction could BEST be described as   23._____

    A. generally stable
    B. steadily increasing with small annual fluctuations
    C. generally increasing with large annual fluctuations
    D. steadily decreasing with major annual fluctuations

24. The GREATEST increase in percentage of new office space construction occurred in the year   24._____

    A. 1998   B. 1995   C. 1992   D. 1990

25. Consider the relationship between the amount of midtown office construction in 1990 and 1994.   25._____
    If the same relationship would exist in 2001 and 2005, the amount of midtown office construction in 2005 would be _____ square feet.

    A. 1,300,000   B. 1,600,000   C. G. 2,100,000   D. 2,500,000

KEY (CORRECT ANSWERS)

1. B
2. B
3. B
4. A
5. C

6. B
7. C
8. D
9. D
10. B

11. D
12. B
13. B
14. B
15. A

16. B
17. C
18. C
19. D
20. C

21. A
22. C
23. B
24. D
25. C

GRAPHS, MAPS, SKETCHES

EXAMINATION SECTION
TEST 1

DIRECTIONS: Each question or incomplete statement is followed by several suggested answers or completions. Select the one that BEST answers the question or completes the statement. *PRINT THE LETTER OF THE CORRECT ANSWER IN THE SPACE AT THE RIGHT.*

Questions 1-7.

DIRECTIONS: Questions 1 to 7, inclusive, are based on information contained on Chart A.

1. Puerto Ricans were the LARGEST number of people in

    A. 1975   B. 1973   C. 1979   D. 1971

2. At some time between 1974 and 1975, two groups had the same number of persons. These two groups were

    A. Puerto Rican and Black
    B. Caucasian and Black
    C. Oriental and Black
    D. Puerto Rican and Caucasian

3. In the same year that the Black population reached its GREATEST peak, the LOWEST number of people residing in Revere were of the following group or groups:

    A. Puerto Rican and Caucasian
    B. Oriental
    C. Puerto Rican
    D. Puerto Rican and Oriental

4. The group which showed the GREATEST increase in population from 1970 to 1979 is

    A. Puerto Rican
    B. Caucasian
    C. Oriental
    D. not determinable from the graph

5. In 1977, the Black population was higher by APPROXIMATELY 20% over

    A. 1972   B. 1976   C. 1974   D. 1978

6. The SMALLEST number of people in 1973 were

    A. Puerto Rican and Black
    B. Oriental and Black
    C. Puerto Rican and Caucasian
    D. Puerto Rican and Oriental

1.____

2.____

3.____

4.____

5.____

6.____

97

7. The percent increase in population of Puerto Ricans from 1971 to 1978 is *most nearly* 7.____
   A. 34%   B. 18%   C. 62%   D. 80%

CHART A

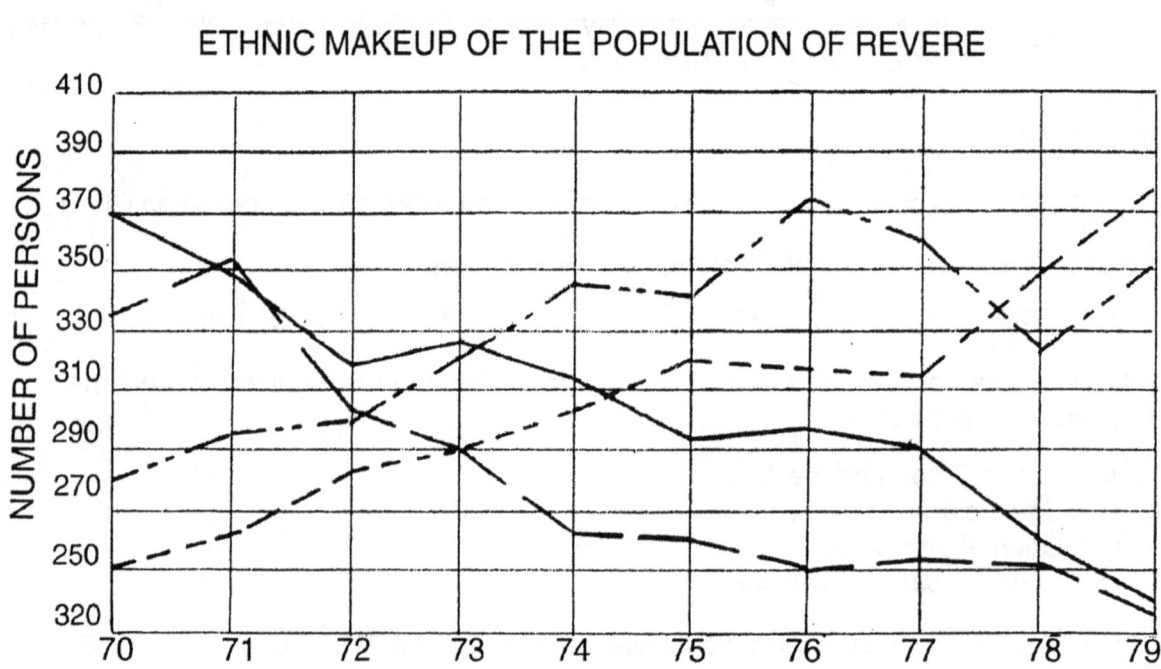

KEY (CORRECT ANSWERS)

1. C
2. D
3. B
4. A
5. A
6. D
7. A

TEST 2

DIRECTIONS: Each question or incomplete statement is followed by several suggested answers or completions. Select the one that BEST answers the question or completes the statement. *PRINT THE LETTER OF THE CORRECT ANSWER IN THE SPACE AT THE RIGHT.*

Questions 1-2.

DIRECTIONS: Questions 1 and 2 are based on information contained on Chart B.

1. The percent of Black middle students attending overcrowded schools in the period 1967 to 1968 is *most nearly*

    A. 34.6   B. 37.6   C. 44.0   D. 47.5

    1.____

2. The percent growth in total school enrollment between 1960-61 and 1967-68 is *most nearly*

    A. 37.6
    B. 45.7
    C. 35.8
    D. cannot be determined from data given

    2.____

2 (#2)

CHART B

Summary: School Utilization and Enrollment

PRIMARY SCHOOLS	1960-61	1967-68
NUMBER OF SCHOOLS	20/105	20/102
ENROLLMENT/CAPACITY	16685/15842	18204/17813
UTILIZATION: OVER/UNDER	NET +1942/-1099	NET +2045/-1654
	NO. +843	NO. +391
WHITE ENROLLMENT	3645 21.8	3146 17.2
NEGRO ENROLLMENT	12691 76.1	14304 78.5
PUERTO RICAN ENROLLMENT	349 2.1	754 4.1

MIDDLE SCHOOLS	1960-61	1967-68
NUMBER OF SCHOOLS	3/101	5/96
ENROLLMENT/CAPACITY	4869/4808	7502/7811
UTILIZATION: OVER/UNDER	NET +235/-174	NET +276/-585
	NO. +61	NO. -309
WHITE ENROLLMENT	1478 30.4	1717 22.8
NEGRO ENROLLMENT	3279 67.3	5228 69.6
PUERTO RICAN ENROLLMENT	112 2.3	557 7.4

HIGH SCHOOLS	1960-61	1967-68
NUMBER OF SCHOOLS	2/78	3/107
ENROLLMENT/CAPACITY	1791/2300	6003/5847
UTILIZATION: OVER/UNDER	NET +15/-224	NET +985/-829
	NO. -509	NO. +156
WHITE ENROLLMENT	1106 61.8	3266 54.4
NEGRO ENROLLMENT	650 35.3	2561 42.6
PUERTO RICAN ENROLLMENT	35 2.0	176 2.9

Detail: School Utilization and Enrollment 1967-1968

PRIMARY SCHOOLS	CONSTRUCTION—DATES AND TYPE*	GRADES	AVERAGE YRS OVER OR UNDER GRADE	SPECIAL PROGRAMS	ENROLLMENT TOTAL	WHITE NO	WHITE %	NEGRO NO	NEGRO %	PUERTO RICAN NO	PUERTO RICAN %	CAPACITY TOTAL	AVAIL-SHORT	% UTIL	# OF OTHER UTIL ROOMS
PS 15	1939	K-6	-.1	T,AS	565	2	.3	523	92.5	40	7.0	669	- 104	84.4	
PS 30	1965	K-6	+1.2	T,AS	1605	854	53.2	748	46.6	3	.1	1099	+ 506	146.0	18 (NOTE M)
PS 35	1931	K-6	+.6	AS	640	345	53.9	259	40.4	36	5.6	702	- 62	91.1	6 PORTABLES
PS 36	1924,63	K-6	+.3	SS	703	9	1.2	684	97.2	10	1.4	509	+ 194	138.1	6 PORTABLES
PS 37	1928	K-6	+.7	MES,AS	615	61	9.9	544	88.4	10	1.6	419	+ 196	146.7	
PS 40	1912,42,64	K-6	-.8	SS,MES	1058	7	.7	994	93.9	55	5.1	869	+ 189	121.7	
PS 45	1914,28,63	K-6	+.1	SP	986	9	.8	949	96.2	30	3.0	856	+ 130	115.1	6 (NOTE H) 4 PORTABLES
PS 48	1936	K-6	-.2	SS	495	10	2.0	482	97.3	3	.6	632	- 137	78.3	
PS 50	1922	K-6	-1.2	SS	772	116	15.0	593	76.8	63	8.1	833	- 61	92.6	2 (NOTE O)
PS 80	1964	K-6	+.5	T,AS	1052	421	40.0	574	54.5	57	5.4	1197	- 145	87.8	
PS 82	1906	K-6	-1.5		440	375	85.2	21	4.7	44	10.0	378	+ 62	116.4	
PS 95	1915,25	K-6	-.3	SS	1274	489	38.3	647	50.7	138	10.8	1320	- 46	96.5	2 (NOTE P)
PS 116	1923,64	K-6	-.4	SS	914	2	.2	902	98.6	10	1.0	1067	- 153	85.6	
PS 118	1923,32	K-6	-.0	T	887	28	3.1	832	93.7	27	3.0	1089	- 202	81.4	
PS 123	1928,32,64	K-6	-1.2	SS	1565	41	2.6	1448	92.5	76	4.8	1103	+ 462	141.8	17 PORTABLES
PS 134	1928,38	K-6	-.3	T	1067	42	3.9	959	89.8	66	6.1	761	+ 306	140.2	
PS 136	1928,38	K-6	-.9	T	987	10	1.0	950	96.2	27	2.7	1301	- 314	75.8	1 (NOTE Q)
PS 140	1929,38,63	K-6	-.8	SS	1160	46	3.9	1098	94.6	16	1.3	1241	- 81	93.4	
PS 160	1939	K-6	-.6	SS	1019	11	1.0	1006	98.7	2	.1	1030	- 11	98.9	
PS 178	1951	K-6	+1.8		400	268	67.0	91	22.7	41	10.2	738	- 338	54.2	
TOTAL PRIMARY SCHOOLS— 20					18204	3146	17.2	14304	78.5	754	4.1	17813	+ 2045 / - 1654	102.1	

MIDDLE SCHOOLS															
IS 8	1963	6-8	-.5	SS,PI	1562	325	20.8	1124	71.9	113	7.2	1523	+ 39	102.5	
IS 59	1956	6-8	-.1	PI,T,AS	1633	621	38.0	846	51.8	166	10.1	1396	+ 237	116.9	
IS 72	1967	6-7	*	T,AS	1396	210	15.0	1171	83.8	15	1.0	1647	- 251	84.7	
JS 192	1930,38	6-8	-1.5	SS	1096	21	1.9	1004	91.6	71	6.4	1333	- 237	82.2	
	1963	7-9	-.8		1815	540	29.7	1083	59.6	192	10.5	1912	- 97	94.9	
TOTAL MIDDLE SCHOOLS— 5					7502	1717	22.8	5228	69.6	557	7.4	7811	+ 276 / - 585	96.0	

HIGH SCHOOLS															
SPRINGFLD GDNS	1965	9-12	-.3		4277	2758	64.4	1462	34.1	57	1.3	3292	+ 985	129.9	
JAMAICA VOC	1896-C	9-12	-2.9		644	382	59.3	235	36.4	27	4.1	895	- 251	71.9	
W WILSON VOC	1942	9-12	-3.7		1082	126	11.6	864	79.8	92	8.5	1660	- 578	65.1	
TOTAL HIGH SCHOOLS— 3					6003	3266	54.4	2561	42.6	176	2.9	5847	+ 985 / - 829	102.6	

NOTES

1 INCLUDES ENROLLMENT AND CAPACITY AT ANNEX (PS 170) IN QUEENS PLANNING DISTRICT 8
* EXCEPT WHERE NOTED ALL SCHOOLS ARE OF FIREPROOF CONSTRUCTION
C NOT FIREPROOF
X NOT AVAILABLE

CODE
T: TRANSITIONAL SCHOOL
AS: AFTER SCHOOL STUDY CENTER
SS: SPECIAL SERVICE SCHOOL
MES: MORE EFFECTIVE SCHOOL
SP: SPECIAL PRIMARY SCHOOL
PI: PILOT INTERMEDIATE SCHOOL

NOTES
M IN ROCHDALE VILLAGE
N 4 PORTABLES, 2 IN UNION METHODIST CHURCH
O IN BROOKS MEMORIAL METHODIST CHURCH
P AT 139-35 88TH STREET
Q IN GRACE METHODIST EPISCOPAL CHURCH

KEY (CORRECT ANSWERS)

1. B
2. C

TEST 3

DIRECTIONS: Each question or incomplete statement is followed by several suggested answers or completions. Select the one that BEST answers the question or completes the statement. *PRINT THE LETTER OF THE CORRECT ANSWER IN THE SPACE AT THE RIGHT.*

Questions 1-4.

DIRECTIONS: Questions 1 to 4, inclusive, are based on the information contained on Chart C.

1. What percent of all households in 1960 are Puerto Rican households with incomes of $6,000 or more per year? 1.___

   A. 38% B. 57% C. 6% D. 0.6%

2. The median income in all households in 1960 is in the range of 2.___

   A. $3,000 - $5,999
   B. $6,000 - $9,999
   C. $10,000 - $14,999
   D. cannot be determined from data given

3. The total number of white persons living in one or two person households in 1960 is 3.___

   A. 13,126 B. 28,884 C. 24,704 D. 46.5

4. Which of the following statements is MOST likely to be true? 4.___

   A. In 1970, the majority of the population in the above data is white.
   B. The majority of households in 1960 have incomes under $6,000.
   C. There are 8668 people in 1960 in households with incomes under $3,000.
   D. The majority of households in 1960 with incomes under $2,000 are white.

CHART C

Population and Housing Data

Housing Units

	TOTAL	1 ROOM	2 ROOMS	3 ROOMS	4 ROOMS	5 ROOMS	6+ ROOMS
TOTAL HOUSING UNITS - 1960	57611	1484	2492	10491	9074	8409	25661
TOTAL OCCUPIED HOUSING UNITS	56187						
RENTER OCCUPIED - TOTAL	23040						
PUBLIC	1048	–	44	240	553	199	12
PUBLICLY AIDED	–	–	–	–	–	–	–
OWNER OCCUPIED - TOTAL	33147						
PUBLICLY AIDED	–						
PUBLIC HOUSING - 1970							
PUBLIC RENTER	1434	–	44	321	736	300	33
PUBLICLY AIDED RENTER	65	–	–	22	26	17	–
PUBLICLY AIDED OWNER	6075	–	3	2770	2214	568	520

Population Growth

(Line graph showing population declining from ~200,000 in 1950 to ~150,000 in 1960 to lower in 1970)

Ethnic Make-up (in percent)

	1950	1960	1970
White ○			
Black ●			
Puerto Rican *			

Households 1960 (in percent)

	% OF ALL HOUSEHOLDS	PERSONS IN HOUSEHOLDS					
		1	2	3	4	5	6+
White	56	14	33	21	17	9	7
Black	43	7	23	20	19	13	18
Puerto Rican	1	4	13	17	18	21	27
All Households	100%	12	23	20	17	12	12

Income 1960

	PERSONS IN HOUSEHOLD						TOTAL NUMBER OF HOUSEHOLDS
	1	2	3	4	5	6+	
WHITE HOUSEHOLDS							
UNDER $ 2000	1652	1153	276	143	122	1	3346
$ 2000 - $ 2999	459	717	176	67	58	–	1477
$ 3000 - $ 5999	1472	3018	1688	1290	944	–	8412
$ 6000 - $ 9999	501	3520	2649	2936	1900	–	10566
$ 10000 - $ 14999	79	1378	1255	1069	1144	–	4925
$ 15000 AND OVER	17	476	535	637	680	–	2345
NEGRO AND OTHER NON-WHITE HOUSEHOLDS							
UNDER $ 2000	494	664	386	303	444	–	2291
$ 2000 - $ 2999	237	453	315	192	280	–	1477
$ 3000 - $ 5999	587	2368	1721	1304	2313	–	8293
$ 6000 - $ 9999	98	1735	1984	1650	2465	–	7932
$ 10000 - $ 14999	13	380	547	679	1370	–	3025
$ 15000 AND OVER	–	23	82	116	435	–	656
PUERTO RICAN HOUSEHOLDS							
UNDER $ 2000	9	7	7	11	11	–	45
$ 2000 - $ 2999	4	2	2	14	12	–	32
$ 3000 - $ 5999	10	17	45	26	71	–	169
$ 6000 - $ 9999	–	42	35	30	112	–	219
$ 10000 - $ 14999	–	8	5	21	53	–	87
$ 15000 AND OVER	–	1	4	2	19	–	26
ALL HOUSEHOLDS							
UNDER $ 2000	2155	1824	669	457	577	–	5682
$ 2000 - $ 2999	700	1170	493	273	350	–	2986
$ 3000 - $ 5999	2069	5403	3454	2620	3328	–	16874
$ 6000 - $ 9999	599	5297	4668	4616	4477	–	18657
$ 10000 - $ 14999	92	1766	1807	1769	2567	–	8041
$ 15000 AND OVER	17	499	621	756	1134	–	3027

KEY (CORRECT ANSWERS)

1. D
2. B
3. C
4. D

TEST 4

DIRECTIONS: Each question or incomplete statement is followed by several suggested answers or completions. Select the one that BEST answers the question or completes the statement. *PRINT THE LETTER OF THE CORRECT ANSWER IN THE SPACE AT THE RIGHT.*

Questions 1-4.

DIRECTIONS: Questions 1 through 4, inclusive, are based on information contained on Chart D.

1. The percentage of households by ethnic make-up in 1960 was *most nearly* 1.____

   A. 16% white, 12% Black and other non-white, 16% Puerto Rican, and 56% not reported
   B. 39% white, 26% Black and other non-white, and 35% Puerto Rican
   C. 95% white, 3% Black and 2% Puerto Rican
   D. 99% white, 1% Black and other non-white, and 0% Puerto Rican

2. In 1960, the predominant age group was in the age range of 2.____

   A. 5-15   B. 25-44   C. 45-64   D. 0-15

3. In 1960, the LARGEST singular and discrete income group consisted of households with the following characteristics: 3.____

   A. Black and other non-white households of 3 persons with total earnings of between $6,000 and $9,999
   B. White households with 3 persons with total earnings from under $2,000 to $5,999
   C. White households of 2 persons with total earnings between $6,000 and $9,999
   D. White households with total earnings under $2,000

4. The percent population increase between 1950 and 1970 was most nearly 4.____

   A. 56%   B. 30%   C. 25%   D. 33%

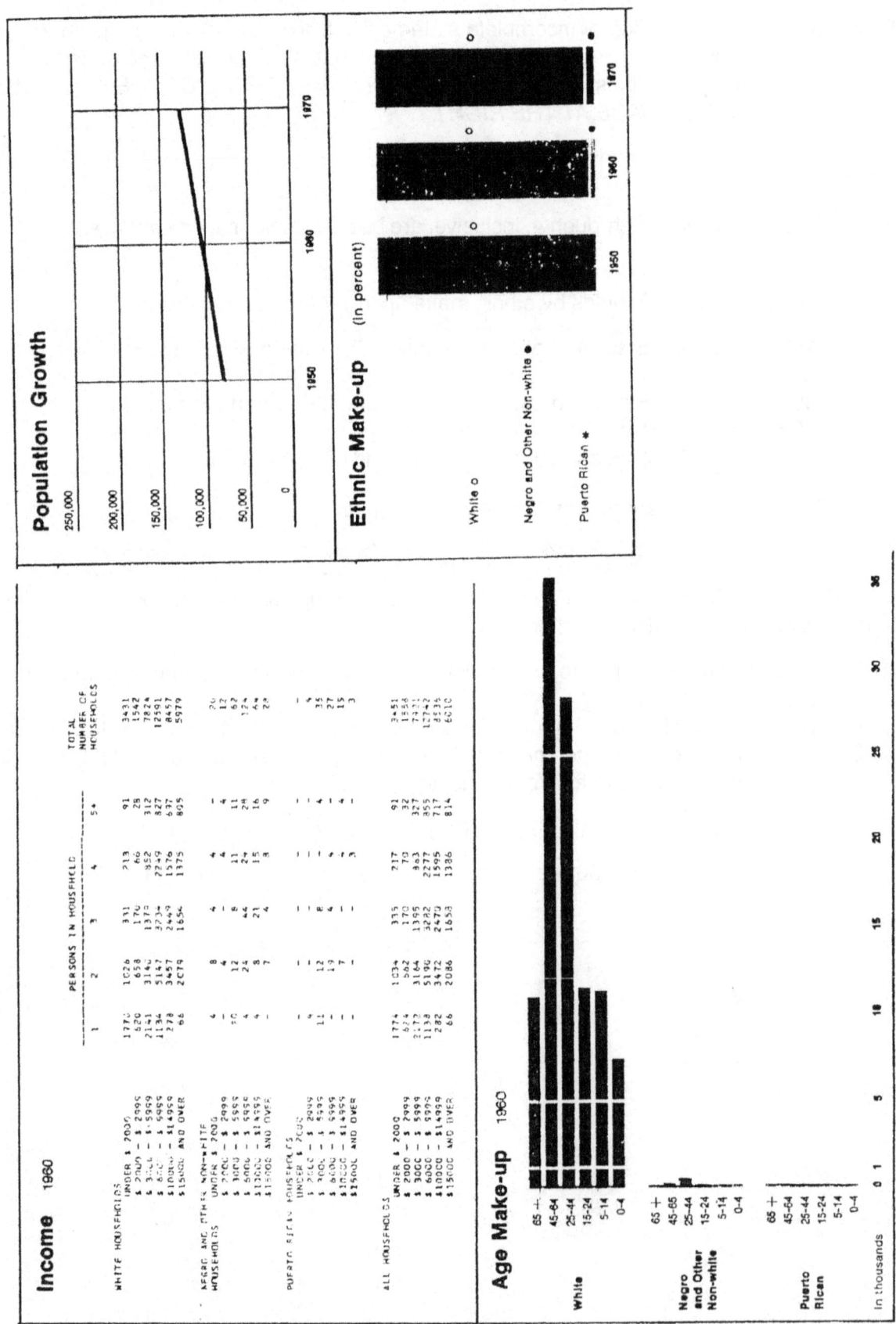

CHART D

KEY (CORRECT ANSWERS)

1. D
2. C
3. C
4. A

TEST 5

DIRECTIONS: Each question or incomplete statement is followed by several suggested answers or completions. Select the one that BEST answers the question or completes the statement. *PRINT THE LETTER OF THE CORRECT ANSWER IN THE SPACE AT THE RIGHT.*

Questions 1-3.

DIRECTIONS: Questions 1 through 3, inclusive, are based on information contained on Zoning Map E. Zoning Map E is drawn to scale. Candidates are to scale off measurements.

1. One-third of Block A (shaded area) has already been developed as a public housing project. It is proposed that a second development be built on the remainder of the site. The approximate size of the proposed site, in acres, is *most nearly* (43,650 sq.ft. = 1 acre)

    A. 5.9 B. 55 C. 1.8 D. 10.3

2. If Site B were developed for housing and 40% of the site was covered by buildings, the amount of open space would be *most nearly* _____ acres.

    A. 2.5 B. 6.3 C. 3.8 D. 2.7

3. A new elementary school will have to be built to accommodate the children from the two proposed projects at A and B.
If the new school must be within 1/2 mile walk of any point in either project, which would be the *most likely* site?

    A. 1 B. 2 C. 3 D. 4

ZONING MAP E

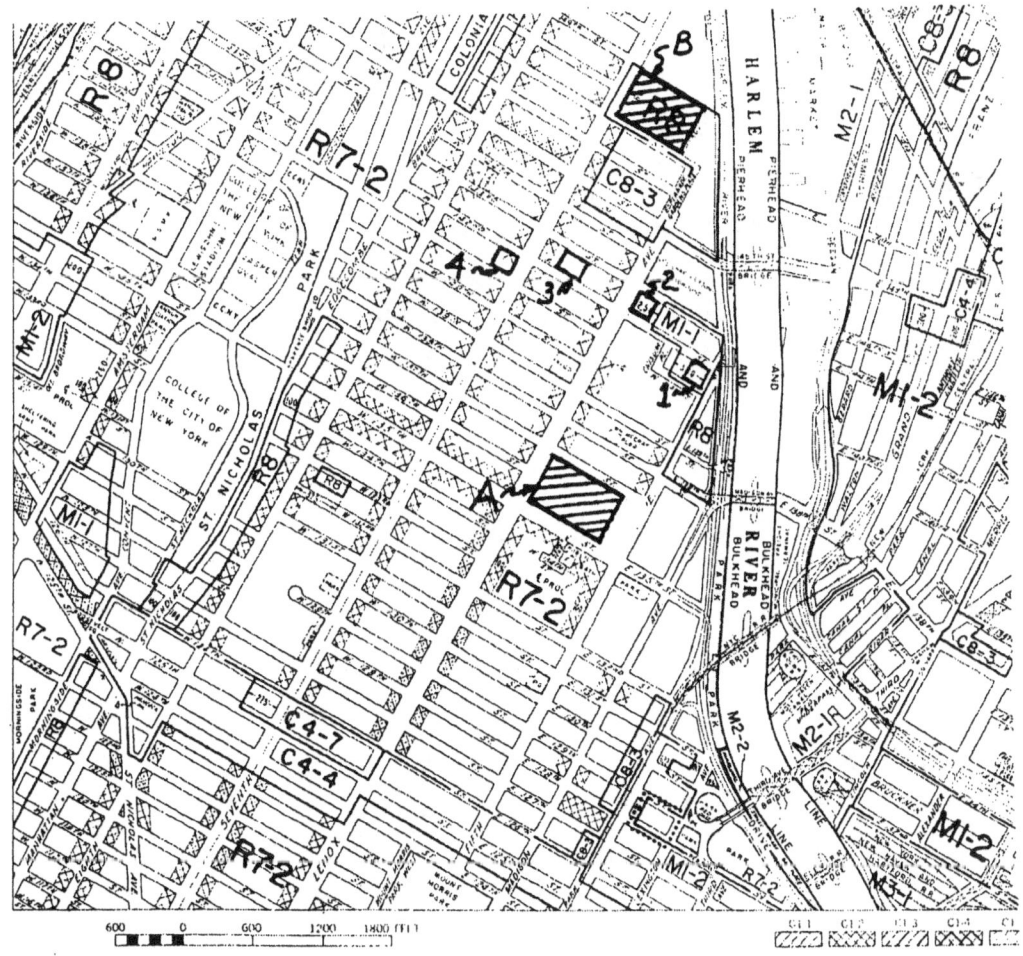

KEY (CORRECT ANSWERS)

1. A
2. C
3. B

TEST 6

DIRECTIONS: Each question or incomplete statement is followed by several suggested answers or completions. Select the one that BEST answers the question or completes the statement. *PRINT THE LETTER OF THE CORRECT ANSWER IN THE SPACE AT THE RIGHT.*

Questions 1-2.

DIRECTIONS: Questions 1 and 2 are to be answered in accordance with the Coast and Geodetic Map F.

1. The difference in elevation between the lowest and highest point of Ewen Park is *most nearly* _____ feet.   1._____

   A. 100 B. 25 C. 200 D. 50

2. Given: The scale of the map is as shown.   2._____
   The distance between the College of Mt. St. Vincent and Ewen Park is *most nearly* _____ feet.

   A. 2,000 B. 6,000 C. 24,000 D. 12,000

COAST & GEODETIC MAP F

CONTOUR INTERVAL 10 FEET

KEY (CORRECT ANSWERS)

1. A
2. D

TEST 7

DIRECTIONS: Each question or incomplete statement is followed by several suggested answers or completions. Select the one that BEST answers the question or completes the statement. *PRINT THE LETTER OF THE CORRECT ANSWER IN THE SPACE AT THE RIGHT.*

Questions 1-3.

DIRECTIONS: Questions 1 to 3, inclusive, are based on information contained on Sketch G, a birds-eye view of a proposed development.

NOTE: The attached single family homes in the periphery are one-story high and contain 1,000 square feet. They are square buildings.

1. The dimension A of this single family attached home is *most nearly* _____ feet. 1.____
   A. 20   B. 32   C. 50   D. 100

2. The dimension B of the road is *most nearly* _____ feet. 2.____
   A. 25   B. 48   C. 75   D. 100

3. The dimension C of the courtyard is *most nearly* _____ feet. 3.____
   A. 40   B. 85   C. 57   D. 150

2 (#7)

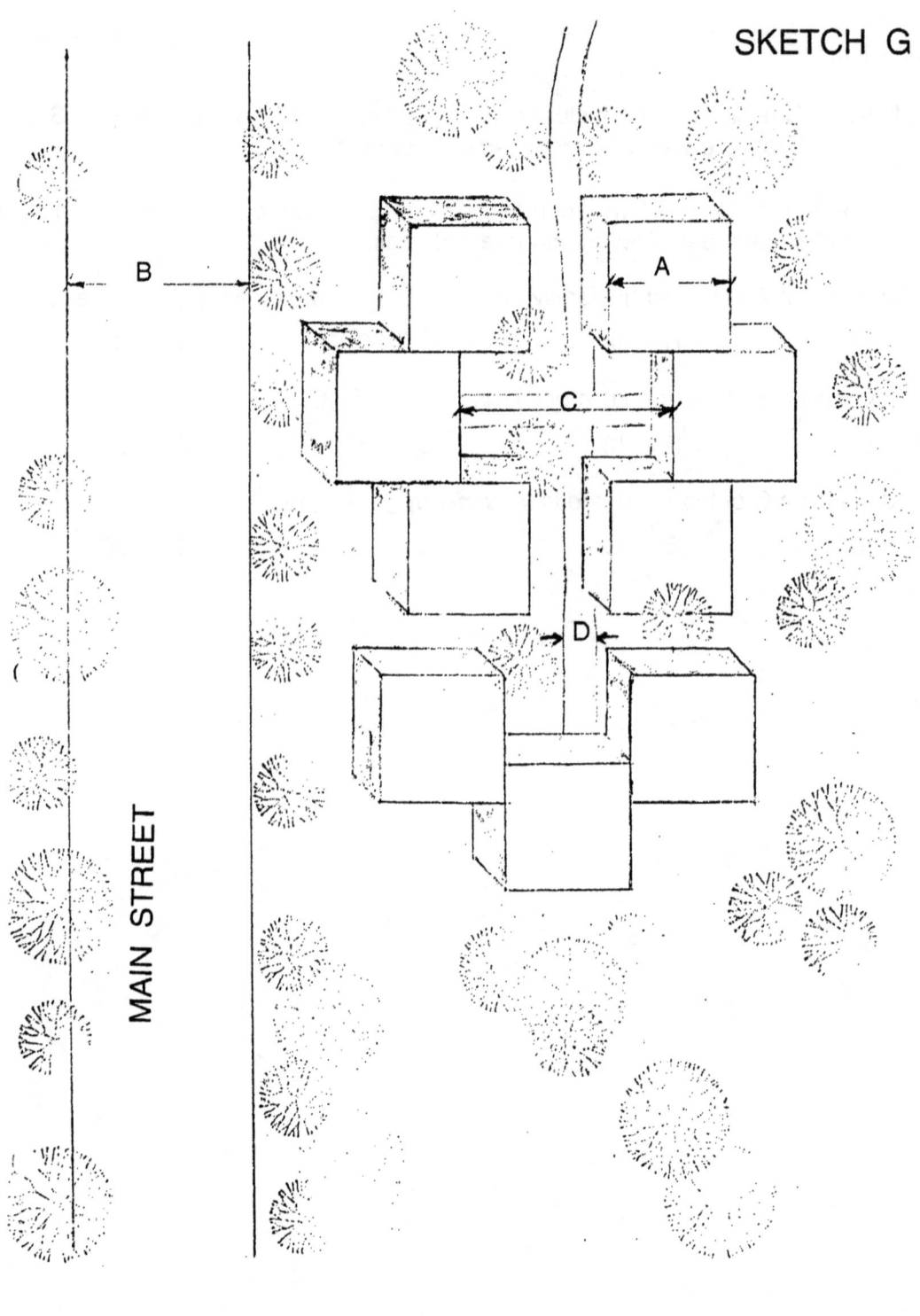

SKETCH G

MAIN STREET

KEY (CORRECT ANSWERS)

1. B
2. B
3. C

EXAMINATION SECTION
TEST 1

DIRECTIONS: Each question or incomplete statement is followed by several suggested answers or completions. Select the one that BEST answers the question or completes the statement. *PRINT THE LETTER OF THE CORRECT ANSWER IN THE SPACE AT THE RIGHT.*

1. When a supervisor requests a subordinate to prepare a report, he should not only indicate the areas to be covered in the report but should also indicate to the subordinate

    A. for whom it is intended and its purpose
    B. the conclusions he expects to reach
    C. the decision that he will make based on the facts presented
    D. why that subordinate was chosen to prepare it

1.____

2. The MOST accurate of the following principles of education and learning for a supervisor to keep in mind when planning a training program for the assistant supervisors under her supervision is that

    A. assistant supervisors, like all other individuals, vary in the rate at which they learn new material and in the degree to which they can retain what they do learn
    B. experienced assistant supervisors who have the same basic college education and agency experience will be able to learn new material at approximately the same rate of speed
    C. the speed with which assistant supervisors can learn new material after the age of forty is half as rapid as at ages twenty to thirty
    D. with regard to any specific task, it is easier and takes less time to break an experienced assistant supervisor of old, unsatisfactory work habits than it is to teach him new, acceptable ones

2.____

3. Assume that you are a supervisor and that you are planning to train a group of experienced investigators in certain specific skills which they need in their daily work.
The one of the following methods which may *generally* be expected to be MOST valuable in ascertaining the effectiveness of the training program is to

    A. administer an objective examination to these investigators prior to conducting the training program and an equivalent form of the examination after the program and compare the results
    B. evaluate and compare the work records of these investigators with regard to these skills prior to and after completion of the training program
    C. hold a staff meeting with the investigators after the training program is completed and allow them to discuss frankly their opinions of the values they derived from the various parts of the training
    D. prepare an objective and detailed questionnaire covering the program, have the investigators answer without identifying themselves, and analyze the answers given

3.____

4. A supervisor has received orders for a work assignment to be carried out by his unit. He has firmly decided on methods for carrying out this assignment which he believes will lead to its completion both properly and expeditiously. He has no intention whatsoever of changing his mind. After he has reached his decision, he calls a staff conference to discuss various alternative methods of carrying out the assignments without making clear that he has already decided upon the method to be used.
To hold a conference of this type would GENERALLY be a

   A. *good* idea, ecause his subordinates are likely to carry the assignment through better if they believe that they devised the methods used
   B. *good* idea, because the staff will have the opportunity and be properly motivated to gain knowledge and experience in methodology without endangering staff performance
   C. *poor* idea, because it would be a failure on the part of the supervisor to show the firm leadership which his unit has a right to expect
   D. *poor* idea, because the discovery by the staff that they had not actually participated in deciding upon methods to be used would have an adverse effect upon their morale

5. Supervisors are frequently faced with the necessity of training old employees in new tasks. An employee inexperienced in a task is much more likely to make a mistake than one who is experienced in it.
In delegating authority to an old employee to perform a new task, a supervisor should GENERALLY

   A. delegate the authority as soon as the subordinate gains minimum competence, allowing him to make mistakes which will not do major damage to the client or to the agency program
   B. delegate the authority as soon as the subordinate gains minimum competence but supervise him closely, enough so that he will not have the opportunity to make even minor mistakes
   C. make the delegation of authority dependent upon the importance which the client places upon the problems involved
   D. withhold the authority until the employee has become experienced in performing the task

6. A supervisor has been transferred from supervision of one group of units to another group of units. She spends the first three weeks in her new assignment in getting acquainted with her new subordinates, their problems, and their work. In this process, she notices that some of the records and forms which are submitted to her by two of the assistant supervisors are carelessly or improperly prepared.
The BEST of the following actions for the supervisor to take in this situation is to

   A. carefully check the work submitted by these assistant supervisors during an additional three weeks before taking any more positive action
   B. confer with these offending workers and show each one where her work needs improvement and how to go about achieving it
   C. institute an in-service training program specifically designed to solve such a problem and instruct the entire subordinate staff in proper work methods
   D. make a note of these errors for documentary use in preparing the annual service rating reports and advise the workers involved to prepare their work more carefully

7. A supervisor, who was promoted to this position a year ago, has supervised a certain assistant supervisor for this one year. The work of the assistant supervisor has been very poor because he has done a minimum of work, refused to take sufficient responsibility, been difficult to handle, and required very close supervision. Apparently due to the increasing insistence by his supervisor that he improve the caliber of his work, the assistant supervisor tenders his resignation, stating that the demands of the job are too much for him. The opinion of the previous supervisor, who had supervised this assistant supervisor for two years, agrees substantially with that of the new supervisor. Under such circumstances, the BEST of the following actions the supervisor can take in general is to

   A. recommend that the resignation be accepted and that he be rehired should he later apply when he feels able to do the job
   B. recommend that the resignation be accepted and that he not be rehired should he later so apply
   C. refuse to accept the resignation but try to persuade the assistant supervisor to accept psychiatric help
   D. refuse to accept the resignation, promising the assistant supervisor that he will be less closely supervised in the future since he is now so experienced

8. After completing a conference with a supervisor concerning the ramifications of a complex problem, an employee informs the supervisor that she feels that her assistant supervisor is too strict in her handling of all the workers under her supervision, especially in comparison with the other assistant supervisors.
   The one of the following actions which is *generally* BEST for the supervisor to take is to

   A. advise the worker in a friendly fashion to apply for a transfer to a unit which has a more lenient supervisor
   B. caution the employee that complaining about a fellow employee behind her back is frowned upon by higher authority as it is a sign of disloyalty
   C. inform the employee that she, the supervisor, will investigate the complaint to determine whether or not it has any validity
   D. tell the worker that the closer and stricter a supervisor is, the better and more completely trained will be her subordinate staff

9. Rumors have arisen to the effect that one of the investigators under your supervision has been attending classes at a local university during afternoon hours when he is supposed to be making field visits.
   The BEST of the following ways for you to approach this problem is to

   A. disregard the rumors since, like most rumors, they probably have no actual foundation in fact
   B. have a discreet investigation made in order to determine the actual facts prior to taking any other action
   C. inform the investigator that you know what he has been doing and that such behavior is overt dereliction of duty and is punishable by dismissal
   D. review the investigator's work record, spot check his performance, and take no further action unless the quality of his work is below average for the unit

10. A supervisor must consider many factors in evaluating a worker whom he has supervised for a considerable time. In evaluating the capacity of such a worker to use independent judgment, the one of the following to which the supervisor should *generally* give MOST consideration is the worker's

A. capacity to establish good relationships with people (clients, colleagues)
B. educational background
C. emotional stability
D. the quality and judgment shown by the worker in previous work situations known to the supervisor

11. A supervisor is conducting a special meeting with the assistant supervisors under her supervision to read and discuss some major complex changes in the rules and procedures. She notices that one of the assistant supervisors who is normally attentive at meetings seems to be paying no attention to what is being said. The supervisor stops reading the rules and asks the assistant supervisor a couple of questions about the changed procedure, to which she gets satisfactory answers.
The BEST action of the following for the supervisor to take at the meeting is to

A. advise the assistant supervisor gently but firmly that these changes are complex and that her undivided attention is required in order to fully comprehend them
B. avoid further embarrassment to the assistant supervisor by asking the group as a whole to pay more attention to what is being read
C. discontinue the questioning and resume reading the procedure
D. politely request the assistant supervisor to stop giving those present the impression that she is uninterested in what goes on about her

12. A supervisor becomes aware that one of her very competent experienced workers never takes notes during an interview with a client except to note an occasional name, address, or date. When asked about this practice by the supervisor, the worker states that she has a good memory for important details and has always been able to satisfactorily record an interview after the client has left.
It would *generally* be BEST for the supervisor to handle this situation by

A. discussing with her that more extensive note-taking may sometimes be desirable with a client who believes note-taking to be evidence that his problem will receive serious consideration
B. agreeing with this practice since note-taking interferes with the establishment of a proper worker-client relationship
C. explaining that, since interviewing is an art form rather than an exact science, a good worker must devise her own personal rules for interviewing and not be bound by general principles
D. warning the worker that memory is too uncertain a thing to be relied upon and, therefore, notes should be taken during an interview of all matters

13. When an experienced subordinate who has the authority and information necessary to make a decision on a certain difficult matter brings the matter to his supervisor without having made the decision, it would *generally* be BEST for the supervisor to

A. agree to make the decision for the subordinate after the subordinate has explained why he finds it difficult to make the decision and after he has made a recommendation
B. make the decision for the subordinate, explaining to him the reasons for arriving at the decision
C. refuse to make the decision, but discuss the various alternatives with the subordinate in order to clarify the issues involved
D. refuse to make the decision, explaining to the subordinate that he is deemed to be fully qualified and competent to make the decision

14. The one of the following instances when it is MOST important for an upper-level supervisor to follow the chain of command is when he is

    A. communicating decisions
    B. communicating information
    C. receiving suggestions
    D. seeking information

15. Experts in the field of personnel relations feel that it is generally a bad practice for subordinate employees to become aware of pending or contemplated changes in policy or organizational set-up via the *grapevine* CHIEFLY because

    A. evidence that one or more responsible officials have proved untrustworthy will undermine confidence in the agency
    B. the information disseminated by this method is seldom entirely accurate and generally spreads needless unrest among the subordinate staff
    C. the subordinate staff may conclude that the administration feels the staff cannot be trusted with the true information
    D. the subordinate staff may conclude that the administration lacks the courage to make an unpopular announcement through official channels

16. In order to maintain a proper relationship with a worker who is assigned to staff rather than line functions, a line supervisor should

    A. accept all recommendations of the staff worker
    B. include the staff worker in the conferences called by the supervisor for his subordinates
    C. keep the staff worker informed of developments in the area of his staff assignment
    D. require that the staff worker's recommendations be communicated to the supervisor through the supervisor's own superior

17. Of the following, the GREATEST disadvantage of placing a worker in a staff position under the direct supervision of the supervisor whom he advises is the possibility that the

    A. staff worker will tend to be insubordinate because of a feeling of superiority over the supervisor
    B. staff worker will tend to give advice of the type which the supervisor wants to hear or finds acceptable
    C. supervisor will tend to be mistrustful of the advice of a worker of subordinate rank
    D. supervisor will tend to derive little benefit from the advice because to supervise properly he should know at least as much as his subordinate

18. One factor which might be given consideration in deciding upon the optimum span of control of a supervisor over his immediate subordinates is the position of the supervisor in the hierarchy of the organization.
    It is GENERALLY considered proper that the number of subordinates immediately supervised by a higher, upper echelon supervisor

    A. is unrelated to and tends to form no pattern with the number supervised by lower-level supervisors
    B. should be about the same as the number supervised by a lower-level supervisor
    C. should be larger than the number supervised by a lower-level supervisor
    D. should be smaller than the number supervised by a lower-level supervisor

19. An important administrative problem is how precisely to define the limits on authority that is delegated to subordinate supervisors.
Such definition of limits of authority should be

   A. as precise as possible and practicable in all areas
   B. as precise as possible and practicable in areas of function, but should allow considerable flexibility in the area of personnel management
   C. as precise as possible and practicable in the area of personnel management, but should allow considerable flexibility in the areas of function
   D. in general terms so as to allow considerable flexibility both in the areas of function and in the areas of personnel management

20. The LEAST important of the following reasons why a particular activity should be assigned to a unit which performs activities dissimilar to it is that

   A. close coordination is needed between the particular activity and other activities performed by the unit
   B. it will enhance the reputation and prestige of the unit supervisor
   C. the unit makes frequent use of the results of this particular activity
   D. the unit supervisor has a sound knowledge and understanding of the particular activity

21. In a conference on difficult cases between a recently appointed supervisor and an experienced, above-average employee, the MOST valuable of the following services that the supervisor can offer the employee is a

   A. detached point of view
   B. knowledge of human needs
   C. knowledge of the agency's basic rules and regulations
   D. willingness to make decisions

22. A supervisor is put in charge of a special unit. She is exceptionally well qualified for this assignment by her training and experience. One of her very close personal friends has been working for some time in this unit. Both the supervisor and worker are certain that the rest of the employees in the unit, many of whom have been in the bureau for a long time, know of this close relationship.
Under these circumstances, the MOST advisable action for the supervisor to take is to

   A. ask that either she be allowed to return to her old assignment or, if that cannot be arranged, that her friend be transferred to another unit in the center
   B. avoid any overt sign of favoritism by acting impartiall and with greater reserve when dealing with this employee than with the rest of the staff
   C. discontinue any socializing with this employee either inside or outside the office so as to eliminate any gossip or dissatisfaction
   D. talk the situation over with the employee and arrive at a mutually acceptable plan of proper office decorum

23. A supervisor who wishes to attain established objectives should concentrate on

   A. determining whether management is operating at maximum effectiveness
   B. making suggestions for improving the organization
   C. planning work assignments
   D. securing salary increases for needy employees

24. A usually competent employee complains that he does not understand the procedures to be followed in performing a certain task although the supervisor has explained them twice and has demonstrated them.
Of the following, the BEST course of action for the supervisor to take is to

    A. ask the employee whether he has any problems which are bothering him
    B. assign someone else to the job
    C. explain the procedures again and demonstrate at the same time
    D. have the employee perform the job while he watches and gives additional instructions

25. GENERALLY, in order to be completely qualified as a supervisor, a person

    A. should be able to perform exceptionally well at least one of the jobs he supervises and have some knowledge of the others
    B. must have an intimate working knowledge of all facets of the jobs which he supervises
    C. should know the basic principles and procedures of the jobs he supervises
    D. need know little or nothing of the jobs which he supervises as long as he knows the principles of supervision

KEY (CORRECT ANSWERS)

1. A	11. C
2. A	12. A
3. B	13. C
4. D	14. A
5. A	15. B
6. B	16. C
7. B	17. B
8. C	18. D
9. B	19. A
10. D	20. B

21. A
22. A
23. C
24. D
25. C

TEST 2

DIRECTIONS: Each question or incomplete statement is followed by several suggested answers or completions. Select the one that BEST answers the question or completes the statement. *PRINT THE LETTER OF THE CORRECT ANSWER IN THE SPACE AT THE RIGHT.*

1. Your superior has asked you to notify employees of an important change in one of the operating procedures described in the manual. Every employee presently has a copy of this manual.
   Which of the following is *normally* the MOST practical way to get the employees to understand such a change?

   A. Notify each employee individually of the change and answer any questions he might have
   B. Send a written notice to key personnel, directing them to inform the people under them
   C. Call a general meeting, distribute a corrected page for the manual, and discuss the change
   D. Send a memo to employees describing the change in general terms and asking them to make the necessary corrections in their copies of the manual

2. A supervisor was directed by the head of his division to report figures for overtime wages. The supervisor asked a clerk under his supervision to give him the figures, and he passed the clerk's figures along to his superior without questioning them. It was then discovered that the clerk had carelessly supplied the wrong information. Who can PROPERLY be held responsible for the mistake, the supervisor or the payroll clerk?

   A. Only the supervisor because he should have known that the clerk would be careless
   B. Only the clerk because it should be unnecessary for supervisors to check the work of their subordinates except for work which is unusually complex or important
   C. Neither of them because it is perfectly understandable that such mistakes will occur from time to time
   D. Both of them because the person to whom a task is delegated is responsible to the supervisor who delegated the task, and the supervisor is responsible to his superior

3. As a supervisor, it is necessary for you to show a new employee how to enter information on standard forms that he will have to prepare. These forms have a number of blanks to be filled in, but the job is fairly simple once a person becomes familiar with it.
   The BEST way to show the new employee how to do the job is to

   A. explain how to do it and have him fill out a few forms, helping him with any difficulties
   B. give him a completed form to use as a model and tell him to do all the others exactly the same way
   C. put him on his own immediately and assume that he will learn for himself through trial and error
   D. give him several dozen completed forms to read and ask him to check back with you in a few hours when he feels ready to start work

4. Suppose that a usually competent employee whom you supervise has suddenly begun having difficulty completing his assignments. You ask the employee to speak to you privately about this situation, and he agrees that he would appreciate this opportunity because of a problem he is having.
Of the following, which one would be the BEST technique for you to use in speaking with him?

   A. Criticize the employee's performance as soon as he mentions his difficulty in completing his assignments
   B. Listen patiently to what the employee has to say before making any comments on your own
   C. Refuse to discuss any personal factors which the employee mentions when he tries to explain his recent work difficulty
   D. Allow the employee to argue with you but plan your attack and defense carefully

4.____

5. A certain supervisor does not compliment members of his staff when they come up with good ideas. He feels that coming up with good ideas is part of the job and does not merit special attention.
This supervisor's practice is

   A. *poor,* because recognition for good ideas is a good motivator
   B. *poor,* because the staff will suspect that the supervisor has no good ideas of his own
   C. *good,* because it is reasonable to assume that employees will tell their supervisor of ways to improve office practice
   D. *good,* because the other members of the staff are not made to seem inferior by comparison

5.____

6. An employee under your supervision complains about a decision you have made in assigning work in the office. You consider the matter to be unimportant, but it seems to be very important to him. He is excited and very angry. Of the following, the MOST appropriate action for you to take FIRST is to

   A. listen to the details of his complaint
   B. refer him to your superior
   C. tell him to *cool off* before discussing the matter
   D. tell him to settle it with the other employees

6.____

7. An experienced employee complains to his unit supervisor that the latter's continual, very close supervision of his work is unnecessary and annoying. The unit supervisor has been recently appointed.
Of the following, it would *generally* be BEST for the unit supervisor to

   A. agree to discontinue all supervision if the employee will agree, if he has any problems, to consult the supervisor
   B. assure the employee that close supervision is necessary but should not be taken personally
   C. consider with the employee what aspects of the supervision could be reduced
   D. explain that he is supervising closely only until he learns what the job is all about

7.____

8. A supervisor had a clerk assigned to help him review records. One day the supervisor asked the clerk to continue checking the records, and the clerk said, *No, I'm not doing any more of that today.*
   In this instance, the supervisor should IMMEDIATELY

   A. ask the clerk why he will not check the records
   B. ask another clerk to do the job
   C. tell the clerk he must do it or be transferred
   D. contact his own supervisor

9. Assume that you have been assigned to supervise other employees. You find that one of your subordinates makes many mistakes whenever he prepares a particular report. Of the following, the MOST desirable course of action for you to follow FIRST in such a situation is to

   A. retrain the subordinate in the preparation of the report
   B. transfer the subordinate to another unit
   C. tell the subordinate to improve or resign
   D. give the employee different duties

10. Some employees of a department have sent an anonymous letter containing many complaints to the department head. Of the following, what is this MOST likely to show about the department?

    A. It is probably a good place to work.
    B. Communications are probably poor.
    C. The complaints are probably unjustified.
    D. These employees are probably untrustworthy.

11. Of the following, the BEST reason for rotating employee work assignments is that such rotation

    A. challenges the ingenuity of supervisors in making assignments
    B. gives each employee a chance at both desirable and undesirable assignments
    C. creates specialists among all employees
    D. increases the competitive spirit among employees

12. Although an employee under your supervision frequently protests when receiving a monotonous assignment, he nevertheless performs the assigned task efficiently. His protests, however, disturb the other employees and interfere with their work.
    Of the following actions you may take in handling this employee, the MOST desirable one is for you to

    A. point out to him the effect of his conduct on the staff's work and request his cooperation in accepting such assignments
    B. arrange to issue such assignments to him when the other members of the staff are not present
    C. inform him that you will request his transfer to another unit unless he puts a halt to his unjustifiable protests
    D. ask other members of the staff to tell him that he is disturbing them by his protests

13. A supervisor has had several problems with a clerk who assists him. He calls the clerk in for a discussion of the matters.
    Which of the following should comprise the MAJOR part of the discussion?

    A. All the things the clerk has done wrong
    B. The most recent things the clerk has done wrong
    C. The things the clerk has done well in addition to the things he has done wrong
    D. The clerk's previous experience and personal problems

14. Assume that certain work processed in your office is then sent to another office for further processing. One of the employees in your office tells you that the supervisor in the other office has been complaining about your office's method of handling the work.
    Of the following, the MOST appropriate action for you to take is to

    A. get all the details from the employee and then speak to the other supervisor
    B. ignore the situation and continue to do the best you can
    C. remind the supervisor that it is not his function to evaluate your work
    D. refrain from reporting the matter to your superior

15. It is the practice in your department to make objective evaluations of the performance of different units. This requires looking at the results achieved by a particular unit during a specified period of time; for instance, the number of applications processed, the number of inquiries answered, the number of inspections made, and so forth.
    Of the following, the BEST method of evaluating the performance of each unit is to compare its results with the

    A. results achieved by all units of the same size that are performing other kinds of work
    B. goals that the unit was reasonably expected to meet during the specified period
    C. performance of the same unit during a similar period of time four or five years earlier
    D. amount of money spent to achieve these results

16. It is possible that you may be asked to submit a brief written evaluation of the work of several employees under your supervision.
    Such an evaluation should *normally* give LEAST emphasis to an employee's

    A. attendance record, including tardiness and absence
    B. ability to grasp new assignments and carry them out effectively
    C. educational background and previous employment experience
    D. ability to get along with co-workers

17. Of the following leadership characteristics, the one that is *generally* considered PRIMARY for a supervisor is the ability to

    A. achieve good working relations with fellow supervisors
    B. get subordinates to air their personal problems
    C. take action to get the job done
    D. plan his work efficiently

18. A recently appointed supervisor is placed in charge of a district which includes several senior employees. He finds that while these subordinates are able to learn new tasks and methods, some of them tend to take longer to learn procedural changes than newer, younger workers.
    Of the following, the MAIN reason for this is that senior workers

    A. are embarrassed by younger workers' intelligence
    B. have to *unlearn* what was taught them in the past
    C. form learning blocks when they are supervised by a younger person
    D. are more interested in doing the work than in academic discussions

19. Which of the following is *generally* considered to be the MOST desirable way for a supervisor to begin a discussion of an employee's performance with the employee?

    A. Accentuate the positive by giving credit where credit is due
    B. Encourage the employee to suggest ways in which he can improve
    C. Point out specific instances of poor performance
    D. Suggest training programs that the employee may be interested in

20. For a supervisor to use consultative supervision with his subordinates effectively, it is ESSENTIAL that he

    A. accept the fact that his formal authority will be weakened by the procedure
    B. admit that he does not know more than all his men together and that his ideas are not always best
    C. utilize a committee system so that the procedure is orderly
    D. make sure that all subordinates are consulted so that no one feels left out

21. During a conversation with his supervisor, a subordinate begins to discuss what appears to the supervisor to be a deep-seated personality problem that has been bothering the subordinate.
    For the supervisor to suggest to the subordinate the possibility of professional help would NORMALLY be

    A. *undesirable;* the necessity of requiring professional help would automatically disqualify the subordinate from being promoted in the future
    B. *desirable;* generally a supervisor can be of limited assistance in personally solving deep-seated personality problems
    C. *undesirable;* since the supervisor was approached by the employee, it is his responsibility as a supervisor to help the employee solve his problem
    D. *desirable;* in accordance with the Civil Service Commission regulations, a supervisor is not allowed to get involved in subordinates' personal problems

22. When a new method of performing a job operation is to be instituted, the one of the following approaches which will MOST generally gain acceptance of the change by subordinates is to

    A. hold a friendly, informal meeting after the change has been implemented to explain the advantages of the new method
    B. consult the subordinates involved in the change as early as possible in the planning stage
    C. work closely with just one of the subordinates who will be affected by the change so that others need not be taken off the job

D. implement the change, instruct employees fully in the new method, and then follow up on results

23. Of the following, the supervisory practice which is LEAST likely to produce a favorable work environment is that the supervisor

    A. takes an active interest in subordinates
    B. does not tolerate mistakes, regardless of who has made the mistake
    C. gives praise when justified
    D. disciplines individuals in accordance with their violation of the rules

24. When a supervisor finds it necessary to let a subordinate know that he is dissatisfied with the subordinate's level of performance, which of the following tactics would *usually* prove MOST effective in improving the subordinate's performance?

    A. The supervisor should be angry when criticizing in order to prevent the mistakes from recurring.
    B. Once criticism has been made, the supervisor should be sure to continuously impress the seriousness of the mistakes upon the subordinate.
    C. When making his criticism, the supervisor should guard against referring to any work that was well done since this would reduce the effect of his criticism.
    D. The supervisor should focus his criticism on the mistakes being made and should avoid downgrading the subordinate personally.

25. Of the following, the BEST descriptive statement of an effective supervisor is *generally* that he

    A. works alongside his subordinates on the same type of work
    B. catches all errors when they are made
    C. gives many specific work orders and few general work orders
    D. devotes much of his time to long-range activities, such as planning and improving human relations

7 (#2)

KEY (CORRECT ANSWERS)

1. C
2. D
3. A
4. B
5. A

6. A
7. C
8. A
9. A
10. B

11. B
12. A
13. C
14. A
15. B

16. C
17. C
18. B
19. A
20. D

21. B
22. B
23. B
24. D
25. D

———

PREPARING WRITTEN MATERIAL

EXAMINATION SECTION

TEST 1

DIRECTIONS: Each short paragraph below is followed by four restatements or summaries of the information contained within it. Select the one that most completely and accurately restates the information given in the paragraph. *PRINT THE LETTER OF THE CORRECT ANSWER IN THE SPACE AT THE RIGHT.*

1. India's night jasmine, or hurshinghar, is different from most flowering plants, in that its flowers are closed during the day, and open after dark. The scientific reason for this is probably that the plant has avoided competing with other flowers for pollinating insects and birds, and relies instead on the service of nocturnal bats that are drawn to the flower's nectar. According to an old Indian legend, however, the flowers sprouted from the funeral ashes of a beautiful young girl who had fallen hopelessly in love with the sun. 1.____
    A. Despite the Indian legend that explains why the hurshinghar's flowers open at dusk, scientists believe it has to do with competition for available pollinators.
    B. The Indian hurshinghar's closure of its flowers during the day is due to a lack of available pollinators.
    C. The hurshinghar of India has evolved an unhealthy dependency on nocturnal bats.
    D. Like most myths, the Indian legend of the hurshinghar's night-flowering has been disproved by science.

2. Charles Lindbergh's trans-Atlantic flight from New York to Paris made him an international hero in 1927, but he lived nearly another fifty years, and by most accounts they weren't terribly happy ones. The two greatest tragedies of his life—the 1932 kidnapping and murder of his oldest son, and an unshakeable reputation as a Nazi sympathizer during World War II—he blamed squarely on the rabid media hounds who stalked his every move. 2.____
    A. Despite the fact that Charles Lindbergh had a hand in the two greatest tragedies of his life, he insisted on blaming the media for his problems.
    B. Charles Lindbergh lived a largely unhappy life after the glory of his 1927 trans-Atlantic flight, and he blamed his unhappiness on media attention
    C. Charles Lindbergh's later life was marked by despair and disillusionment.
    D. Because of the rabid media attention sparked by Charles Lindbergh's 1927 trans-Atlantic flight, he would later consider it the last happy event of his life

3. The United States, one of the world's youngest nations in the early twentieth century, had yet to spread its wings in terms of foreign affairs, preferring to remain isolated and opposed to meddling in the affairs of others. But the fact remained that as a young nation situated on the opposite side of the globe from Europe, Africa, and Asia, the United States had much work to do in 3.____

establishing relations with the rest of the world. So, too, as the European colonial powers continued to battle for influence in North and South America, did the United States come to believe that it was proper for them to keep these nations from encroaching into their sphere of influence.
   A. The roots of the Monroe Doctrine can be traced to the foreign policy shift of the United States during the early nineteenth century.
   B. In the early nineteenth century, the United States shifted its foreign policy to reflect a growing desire to actively protect its interests in the Western Hemisphere.
   C. In the early nineteenth century, the United States was too young and undeveloped to have devised much in the way of foreign policy.
   D. The United States adopted a more aggressive foreign policy in the early nineteenth century in order to become a diplomatic player on the world stage.

4. Hertha Ayrton, a nineteenth-century Englishwoman, pursued a career in science during a time when most women were not given the opportunity to go to college. Her series of successes led to her induction into the Institution of Electrical Engineers in 1899, when she was the first woman to receive this professional honor. Her most noted accomplishment was the research and invention of an anti-gas fan that the British War Office used in the trench warfare of World War I.
   A. The British Army's success in World War I can be partly attributed to Hertha Ayrton, a groundbreaking British scientist.
   B. Hertha Ayrton was the first woman to be inducted into the Institution of Electrical Engineers.
   C. The injustices of nineteenth-century England were no match for the brilliant mind of Hertha Ayrton.
   D. Hertha Ayrton defied the restrictions of her society by building a successful scientific career.

5. Scientists studying hyenas in Tanzania's Ngorongoro Crater have observed that hyena clans have evolved a system of territoriality that allows each clan a certain space to hunt within the 100-square-mile area. These territories are not marked by natural boundaries, but by droppings and excretions from the hyenas' scent glands. Usually, the hyenas take these boundary lines very seriously; some hyena clans have been observed abandoning their pursuit of certain prey after the prey has crossed into another territory, even though no members of the neighboring clan are anywhere in sight.
   A. The hyenas of Ngorongoro Crater illustrate that the best way to peacefully co-exist within a limited territory is to strictly delineate and defend territorial borders.
   B. While most territorial boundaries are marked using geographical features, the hyenas of Ngorongoro Crater have devised another method.
   C. The hyena clans of Ngorongoro Crater, in order to co-exist within a limited hunting territory, have developed a method of marking strict territorial boundaries.
   D. As with most species, the hyenas of Ngorongoro Crater have proven the age-old motto: "To the victor go the spoils."

6. The flood control policy of the U.S. Army Corps of Engineers has long been an obvious feature of the American landscape—the Corps seeks to contain the nation's rivers with an enormous network of dams and levees, "channelizing" rivers into small, confined routes that will stay clear of settled flood-plains when rivers rise. As a command of the U.S. Army, the Corps seems to have long seen the nation's rivers as an enemy to be fought; one of the agency's early training films speaks of the Corps' "battle" with its adversary, Mother Nature.

   A. The dams and levees built by the U.S. Army Corps of Engineers have at least defeated their adversary, Mother Nature.
   B. The flood control policy of the U.S. Army Corps of Engineers has often reflected a military point of view, making the nation's rivers into enemies that must be defeated.
   C. When one realizes that the flood policy of the U.S. Army Corps of Engineers has always relied on a kind of military strategy, it is only possible to view the Corps' efforts as a failure.
   D. By damming and channelizing the nation's rivers, the U.S. Army Corps of Engineers have made America's flood plains safe for farming and development.

6.____

7. Frogs with extra legs or missing legs have been showing up with greater frequency over the past decade, and scientists have been baffled by the cause. Some researchers have concluded that pesticide runoff from farms is to blame; others say a common parasite, the trematode, is the culprit. Now, a new study suggests that both these factors in combination have disturbed normal development in many frogs, leading to the abnormalities.

   A. Despite several studies, scientists still have no idea what is causing the widespread incidence of deformities among aquatic frogs.
   B. In the debate over what is causing the increase in frog deformities, environmentalists tend to blame pesticide runoff, while others blame a common parasite, the trematode.
   C. A recent study suggests that both pesticide runoff and natural parasites have contributed to the increasing rate of deformities in frogs.
   D. Because of their aquatic habitat, frogs are among the most susceptible organisms to chemical ad environmental change, and this is illustrated by the increasing rate of physical deformities among frog populations.

7.____

8. The builders of the Egyptian pyramids, to insure that each massive structure was built on a completely flat surface, began by cutting a network of criss-crossing channels into the pyramid's mapped-out ground space and partly filling the channels with water. Because the channels were all interconnected, the water was distributed evenly throughout the channel system, and all the workers had to do to level their building surface was cut away any rock above the waterline.

   A. The modern carpenter's level uses a principle that was actually invented several centuries ago by the builders of the Egyptian pyramids.
   B. The discovery of the ancient Egyptians' sophisticated construction techniques is a quiet argument against the idea that they were built by slaves.

8.

C. The use of water to insure that the pyramids were level mark the Egyptians as one of the most scientifically advanced of the ancient civilizations.
D. The builders of the Egyptian pyramids used a simple but ingenious method for ensuring a level building surface with interconnected channels of water

9. Thunderhead Mountain, a six-hundred-foot-high formation of granite in the Black Hills of South Dakota, is slowly undergoing a transformation that will not be finished for more than a century, when what remains of the mountain will have become the largest sculpture in the world. The statue, begun in 1947 by a Boston Sculptor named Henry Ziolkowski, is still being carved and blasted by his wife and children into the likeness of Crazy Horse, the legendary chief of the Sioux tribe of American natives. The enormity of the sculpture—the planned length of one of the figure's arms is 263 feet—is understandable, given the historical greatness of Crazy Horse.   9.____
   A. Only a hero as great as Crazy Horse could warrant a sculpture so large that it will take morae than a century to complete.
   B. In 1947, sculptor Henry Ziolkowski began work on what he imagined would be the largest sculpture in the world—even though he knew he would not live to see it completed.
   C. The huge Black Hills sculpture of the great Sioux chief Crazy Horse, still being carried out by the family of Henry Ziolkowski, will some day be the largest sculpture in the world.
   D. South Dakota's Thunderhead Mountain will soon be the site of the world's largest sculpture, a statue of the Sioux chief Crazy Horse.

10. Because they were some of the first explorers to venture into the western frontier of North America, the French were responsible for the naming of several native tribes. Some of these names were poorly conceived—the worst of which was perhaps Eskimo, the name for the natives of the far North, which translates roughly as "eaters of raw flesh." The name is incorrect; these people have always cooked their fish and game, and they now call themselves the Inuit, a native term that means "the people."   10.____
   A. The first to explore much of North America's western frontier were the French, and they usually gave improper or poorly-informed names to the native tribes.
   B. The Eskimos of North America have never eaten raw flesh, so it is curious that the French would give them a name that means "eaters of raw flesh."
   C. The Inuit have fought for many years to overcome the impression that they eat raw flesh.
   D. Like many native tribes, the Inuit were once incorrectly named by French explorers, but they have since corrected the mistake themselves.

5 (#1)

11. Of the 30,000 species of spiders worldwide, only a handful are dangerous to human beings, but this doesn't prevent many people from having a powerful fear of all spiders, whether they are venomous or not. The leading scientific theory about arachnophobia, as this fear is known, is that far in our evolutionary past, some species of spider must have presented a serious enough threat to people that the sight of a star-shaped body or an eight-legged walk was coded into our genes as a danger signal. 11.____
    A. Scientists theorize that peoples' widespread fear of spiders can be traced to an ancient spider species that was dangerous enough to trigger this fearful reaction.
    B. The fear known as arachnophobia is triggered by the sight of a star-shaped body or an eight-legged walk.
    C. Because most spiders have a uniquely shaped body that triggers a human fear response, many humans are afflicted with the fear of spiders known as arachnophobia.
    D. Though only a few of the planet's 30,000 spider species are dangerous to people, many people have an unreasonable fear of them.

12. From the 1970s to the 1990s, the percentage of Americans living in the suburbs climbed from 37% to 47%. In the latter part of the 1990s, a movement emerged that questioned the good of such a population shift—or at least, the good of the speed and manner in which this suburban land was being developed. Often, people began to argue, the planning of such growth was flawed, resulting in a phenomenon that has become known as suburban "sprawl," or the growth of suburban orbits around cities at rates faster than infrastructures could support, and in ways that are damaging to the environment 12.____
    A. The term "urban sprawl" was coined in the 1990s, when the movement against unchecked suburban development began to gather momentum.
    B. In the 1980s and 1990s, home builders benefited from a boom in their most favored demographic segment, suburban new home buyers.
    C. Suburban development tends to suffer from poor planning, which can lead to a lower quality of life for residents
    D. The surge in suburban residences in the late twentieth century was criticized by many as "sprawl" that could not be supported by existing resources

13. Medicare, a $200 billion-a-year program, processes 1 billion claims annually, and in the year 2000, the computer system that handles these claims came under criticism. The General Accounting Office branded Medicare's financial management system as outdated and Inadequate—one in a series of studies and reports warning that the program is plagued with duplication, overcharges, double billings, and confusion among users. 13.____
    A. The General Accounting Office's 2000 report proves that Medicare is bloated bureaucracy in need of substantial reform.
    B. Medicare's confusing computer network is an example of how the federal government often neglects the programs that mean the most to average American citizens.

C. In the year 2000, the General Accounting Office criticized Medicare's financial accounting network as inefficient and outdated.
D. Because it has to handle so many claims each year, Medicare's financial accounting system often produces redundancies and errors.

14. The earliest known writing materials were thin clay tablets, used in Mesopotamia more than 5,000 years ago. Although the tablets were cheap and easy to produce, they had two major disadvantages: they were difficult to store, and once the clay had dried and hardened, a person could not write on them. The ancient Egyptians later discovered a better writing material—the thin bark of the papyrus reed, a plant that grew near the mouth of the Nile River, which could be peeled into long strips, woven into a mat-like layer, pounded flat with heavy mallets, and then dried in the sun.
    A. The Egyptians, after centuries of frustration with clay writing tablets, were finally forced to invent a better writing surface.
    B. With the bark of the papyrus reed, ancient Egyptians made a writing material that overcame the disadvantages of clay tablets.
    C. The Egyptian invention of the papyrus scroll was necessitated in part by a relative lack of available clay.
    D. The word "paper" can be traced to the innovations of the Egyptians, who made the first paper-like writing material from the bark of papyrus plant.

14.____

15. In 1850, the German pianomaker Heinrich Steinweg and his family stepped off an immigrant ship in New York City, threw themselves into competition with dozens of other established craftsmen, and defeated them all by reinventing the instrument. The company they created commanded the market for nearly the next century and a half, while their competitors—some of the most acclaimed pianomakers in the business—faded into obscurity. And all the while, Steinway & Sons, through their sponsorship and encouragement of the world's most distinguished pianists, helped define the cultural life of the young United States.
    A. The Steinways capitalized on weak competition during the mid-nineteenth century to capture the American piano market.
    B. Because of their technical and cultural innovations, the Steinways had an advantage over other American pianomakers.
    C. Heinrich Steinweg founded the Steinway piano empire in 1850.
    D. From humble immigrant origins, the Steinway family rose to dominate both the pianomaking industry and American musical culture.

15.____

16. Feng Shui, the ancient Chinese science of studying the natural environment's effect on a person's well-being, has gained new popularity in the design and decoration of buildings. Although a complex area of study, a basic premise of Feng Shui is that each building creates a unique field of energy which affects the inhabitants of that building or home. In recent years, decorators and realtors have begun to offer services which include a diagnosis of a building's Feng Shui, or energy.
    A. Feng Shui, the Chinese science of balancing environmental energies, has been given more aesthetic quality by recent practitioners.

16.____

B. Generally, practitioners of Feng Shui work to create balance within a room, carefully arranging sharp and soft surfaces to create a positive environment that suits the room's primary purpose.
C. The idea behind the Chinese "science" of Feng Sui objects give off certain energies that affect a building's inhabitants has been a difficult one for most Westerners to accept, but it is gaining in popularity.
D. The ancient Chinese science of Feng Shui, which studies the balance of energies in a person's environment, has become popular among those who design and decorate buildings.

17. Because the harsh seasonal variations of the Kansas plains make survival difficult for most plant life, the area is dominated by tall, sturdy grasses. The only tree that has been able to survive and prosper throughout the wide expanse of prairie is the cottonwood, which can take root and grow in the most extreme climatic conditions. Sometimes a storm will shear off a living branch and carry it downstream, where it may snag along a sandbar and take root. 17.____
    A. Among the plant life of the Kansas plains, the only tree is the cottonwood.
    B. The only prosperous tree on the Kansas plains is the cottonwood, which can take root and grow in a wide range of conditions.
    C. Only the cottonwood, whose branches can grow after being broken off and washed down a river, is capable of surviving the climatic extremes of the Kansas plains.
    D. Because it is the most widespread and hardiest tree on the Kansas plains, the cottonwood had become a symbol of pioneer grit and fortitude.

18. In the twenty-first century, it's easy to see the automobile as the keystone of American popular culture. Subtract linen dusters, driving goggles, and women's *crepe de chine* veils from our history, and you've taken the Roaring out of the Twenties. Take away the ducktail haircuts, pegged pants, and upturned collars from the teen Car Cult of the Fifties, and the decade isn't nearly as Fabulous. Were the chromed and tailfinned muscle cars of the automobile' Golden Age modeled after us, or were we mimicking them? 18.____
    A. Ever since its invention, the automobile has shaped American culture.
    B. Many of the familiar names we give historical era, such as "Roaring Twenties" and "Fabulous Fifties," were given because of the predominance of the automobile.
    C. Americans' tastes in clothing have been determined primarily by the cars they drive.
    D. Teenagers have had a fascination for automobiles ever since the motorcar was first invented.

19. Since the 1960s, an important issue for Canada has been the status of minority French-speaking Canadians, especially in the province of Quebec, whose inhabitants make up 30% of the Canadian population and trace their ancestry back to a Canada that preceded British influence. In response to pressure from Quebec nationalists, the government in 1982 added a Charter of Rights to the constitution, restoring important rights that dated back to the time of aboriginal treaties. Separatism is still a prominent issue, though successive 19.____

referendums and constitutional inquiries have not resulted in any realistic progress toward Quebec's independence.
- A. Despite the fact that Quebec's inhabitants have their roots in Canada's original settlers, they have been constantly oppressed by the descendants of those who came later, the British.
- B. It seems unavoidable that Quebec's linguistic and cultural differences with the rest of Canada will some day lead to its secession.
- C. French-speaking Quebec's activism over the last several decades has led to concessions by the Canadian government, but it seems that Quebec will remain a part of the country for some time.
- D. The inhabitants of Quebec are an aboriginal culture that has been exploited by the Canadian government for years, but they are gradually winning back their rights.

20. For years, musicians and scientists have tried to discover what it is about an eighteenth-century Stradivarius violin—which may sell for more than $1 million on today's market—that gives it its unique sound. In 1977, American scientist Joseph Nagyvary discovered that the Stradivarius is made of a spruce wood that came from Venice, where timber was stored beneath the sea, and unlike the dry-seasoned wood from which other violins were made, this spruce contains microscopic holes which add resonance to the violin's sound. Nagyvary also found the varnish used on the Stradivarius to be equally unique, containing tiny mineral crystals that appear to have come from ground-up gemstones, which would filter out high-pitched tones and give the violin a smoother sound.   20._____
- A. After carefully studying Stradivarius violins to discover the source of their unique sound, an American scientist discovered two qualities in the construction of them that set them apart from other instruments: the wood from which they were made, and the varnish used to coat the wood.
- B. The two qualities that give the Stradivarius violin such a unique sound are the wood, which adds resonance, and the finish, which filters out high-pitched tones.
- C. The Stradivarius violin, because of the unique wood and finish used in its construction, is widely regarded as the finest string instrument ever manufactured in the world.
- D. A close study of the Stradivarius violin has revealed that the best wood for making violins is Venetian spruce, stored underwater.

21. People who watch the display of fireflies on a clear summer evening are actually witnessing a complex chemical reaction called "bioluminescence," which turns certain organisms into living light bulbs. Organisms that produce this light undergo a reaction in which oxygen combines with a chemical called lucerfin and an enzyme called luciferase. Depending on the organism, the light produced from this reaction can range from the light green of the firefly to the bright red spots of a railroad worm.   21._____
- A. Although the function of most displays of bioluminescence is to attract mates, as is the case with fireflies, other species rely on bioluminescence for different purposes.

B. Bioluminescence, a phenomenon produced by several organisms, is the result of a chemical reaction that takes place within the body of the organism.
C. Of all the organisms in the world, only insects are capable of displaying bioluminescence.
D. Despite the fact that some organisms display bioluminescence, these reactions produce almost no heat, which is why the light they create is sometimes referred to as cold light.

22. The first of America's "log cabin" presidents, Andrew Jackson rose from humble backcountry origins to become a U.S. congressman and senator, a renowned military hero, and the seventh president of the United States. Among many Americans, especially those of the western frontier, he was acclaimed as a symbol of the "new" American: self-made, strong through closeness to nature, and endowed with a powerful moral courage.
    A. Andrew Jackson was the first American president to rise from modest origins.
    B. Because he was born poor, President Andrew Jackson was more popular among Americans of the western frontier.
    C. Andrew Jackson's humble background, along with his outstanding achievements, made him into a symbol of American strength and self-sufficiency.
    D. Andrew Jackson achieved success as a legislator, soldier, and president because he was born humbly and had to work for every honor he ever received.

23. In the past few decades, while much of the world's imagination has focused on the possibilities of outer space, some scientists have been exploring a different frontier—the ocean floor. Although ships have been sailing the oceans for centuries, only recently have scientists developed vehicles strong enough to sustain the pressure of deep-sea exploration and observation. These fiberglass vehicles, called submersibles, are usually just big enough to take two or three people to the deepest parts of the oceans' floors.
    A. Modern submersible vehicles, thanks to recent technological innovations, are now exploring underwater cliffs, crevices, and mountain ranges that were once unreachable.
    B. While most people tend to fantasize about exploring outer space, they should be turning toward a more accessible realm—the depths of the earth's oceans.
    C. Because of the necessarily small size of submersible vehicles, exploration of the deep ocean is not a widespread activity.
    D. Recent technological developments have helped scientists to turn their attention from deep space to the deep ocean.

24. The panda—a native of the remote mountainous regions of China—subsists almost entirely on the tender shoots of the bamboo plant. This restrictive diet has allowed the panda to evolve an anatomical structure that is completely different from that of other bears, whose paws are aligned for running, stabbing, and scratching. The panda's paw has an over-developed wrist bone that juts out below the other claws like a thumb, and the panda uses this "thumb" to grip bamboo shoots while it strips them of their leaves.

    A. The panda is the only bear-like animal that feeds on vegetation, and it has a kind of thumb to help it grip bamboo shoots.
    B. The panda's limited diet of bamboo has led it to evolve a thumb-like appendage for grasping bamboo shoots.
    C. The panda's thumb-like appendage is a factor that limits its diet to the shoots of the bamboo plant.
    D. Because bamboo shoots must be held tightly while eaten, the panda's thumb-like appendage ensure that it is the only bear-like animal that eats bamboo.

24.____

25. The stability and security of the Balkan region remains a primary concern for Greece in post-Cold War Europe, and Greece's active participation in peacekeeping and humanitarian operations in Georgia, Albania, and Bosnia are substantial examples of this commitment. Due to its geopolitical position, Greece believes it necessary to maintain, at least for now, a more nationalized defense force than other European nations. It is Greece's hope that the new spirit of integration and cooperation will help establish a common European foreign affairs and defense policy that might ease some of these regional tensions, and allow a greater level of Greek participation in NATO's integrated military structure.

    A. Greece's proximity to the unstable Balkan region has led it to keep a more nationalized military, though it hopes to become more involved in a common European defense force.
    B. The Balkan states present a greater threat to Greece than any other European nation, and Greece has adopted a highly nationalist military force as a result.
    C. Greece, the only Balkan state to belong to NATO, has an isolationist approach to defense, but hopes to achieve greater integration in the organization's combined forces.
    D. Greece's failure to become more militarily integrated with the rest of Europe can be attributed to the failure to establish a common European defense policy.

25.____

KEY (CORRECT ANSWERS)

1. A
2. B
3. B
4. D
5. C

6. B
7. C
8. D
9. C
10. D

11. A
12. D
13. C
14. B
15. D

16. D
17. B
18. A
19. C
20. A

21. B
22. C
23. D
24. B
25. A

PREPARING WRITTEN MATERIAL

PARAGRAPH REARRANGEMENT
COMMENTARY

The sentences that follow are in scrambled order. You are to rearrange them in proper order and indicate the letter choice containing the correct answer at the space at the right.

Each group of sentences in this section is actually a paragraph presented in scrambled order. Each sentence in the group has a place in that paragraph; no sentence is to be left out. You are to read each group of sentences and decide upon the best order in which to put the sentences so as to form a well-organized paragraph.

The questions in this section measure the ability to solve a problem when all the facts relevant to its solution are not given.

More specifically, certain positions of responsibility and authority require the employee to discover connection between events sometimes, apparently, unrelated. In order to do this, the employee will find it necessary to correctly infer that unspecified events have probably occurred or are likely to occur. This ability becomes especially important when action must be taken on incomplete information.

Accordingly, these questions require competitors to choose among several suggested alternatives, each of which presents a different sequential arrangement of the events. Competitors must choose the MOST logical of the suggested sequences.

In order to do so, they may be required to draw on general knowledge to infer missing concepts or events that are essential to sequencing the given events. Competitors should be careful to infer only what is essential to the sequence. The plausibility of the wrong alternatives will always require the inclusion of unlikely events or of additional chains of events which are NOT essential to sequencing the given events.

It's very important to remember that you are looking for the best of the four possible choices, and that the best choice of all may not even be one of the answers you're given to choose from.

There is no one right way to solve these problems. Many people have found it helpful to first write out the order of the sentences, as they would have arranged them, on their scrap paper before looking at the possible answers. If their optimum answer is there, this can save them some time. If it isn't, this method can still give insight into solving the problem. Others find it most helpful to just go through each of the possible choices, contrasting each as they go along. You should use whatever method feels comfortable and works for you.

While most of these types of questions are not that difficult, we've added a higher percentage of the difficult type, just to give you more practice. Usually there are only one or two questions on this section that contain such subtle distinctions that you're unable to answer confidently. And you then may find yourself stuck deciding between two possible choices, neither of which you're sure about.

PREPARING WRITTEN MATERIAL
EXAMINATION SECTION
TEST 1

DIRECTIONS: The following groups of sentences need to be arranged in an order that makes sense. Select the letter preceding the sequence that represents the BEST sentence order. *PRINT THE LETTER OF THE CORRECT ANSWER IN THE SPACE AT THE RIGHT.*

1. I. A large Naval station on Alameda Island, near Oakland, held many warships in port, and the War Department was worried that if the bridge were to be blown up by the enemy, passage to and from the bay would be hopelessly blocked.
    II. Though many skeptics were opposed to the idea of building such an enormous bridge, the most vocal opposition came from a surprising source: the United States War Department.
    III. The War Department's concerns led to a showdown at San Francisco City Hall between Strauss and the Secretary of War, who demanded to know what would happen if a military enemy blew up the bridge.
    IV. In 1933, by submitting a construction cost estimate of $17 million, an engineer named Joseph Strauss won the contract to build the Golden Gate Bridge of San Francisco, which would then become one of the world's largest bridges.
    V. Strauss quickly ended the debate by explaining that the Golden Gate Bridge was to be a suspension bridge, whose roadway would hang in the air from cables strung between two huge towers, and would immediately sink into three hundred feet of water if it were destroyed.

    The BEST order is:
    A. II, III, I, IV, V   B. I, II, III, V, IV   C. IV, II, I, III, V   D. IV, I, III, V, II

    1.____

2. I. Plastic surgeons have already begun to use virtual reality to map out the complex nerve and tissue structures of a particular patient's face, in order to prepare for delicate surgery.
    II. A virtual reality program responds to these movements by adjusting the images that a person sees on a screen or through goggles, thereby creating an "interactive" world in which a person can see and touch three-dimensional graphic objects.
    III. No more than a computer program that is designed to build and display graphic images, the virtual reality program takes graphic programs a step further by sensing a person's head and body movements.
    IV. The computer technology known as virtual reality, now in its very first stages of development, is already revolutionizing some aspects of contemporary life.
    V. Virtual reality computers are also being used by the space program, most recently to simulate conditions for the astronauts who were launched on a repair mission to the Hubble telescope.

    2.____

The BEST order is:
A. IV, II, I, V, III   B. III, I, V, II, IV   C. IV, III, II, I, V   D. III, I, II, IV, V

3. I. Before you plant anything, the soil in your plant bed should be carefully raked level, a small section at a time, and any clods or rocks that can't be broken up should be removed.
   II. Your plant should be placed in a hole that will position it at the same level it was at the nursery, and a small indentation should be pressed into the soil around the plant in order to hold water near its roots.
   III. Before placing the plant in the soil, lightly separate any roots that may have been matted together in the container, cutting away any thick masses that can't be separated, so that the remaining roots will be able to grow outward.
   IV. After the bed is ready, remove your plant from its container by turning it upside down and tapping or pushing on the bottom —never remove it by pulling on the plant.
   V. When you bring home a small plant in an individual container from the nursery, there are several things to remember while preparing to plant it in your own garden.
   The BEST order is:
   A. V, IV, III, II, I   B. V, II, IV, III, II   C. I, IV, II, III, V   D. I, IV, V, II, III

4. I. The motte and its tower were usually built first, so that sentries could use it as a lookout to warn the castle workers of any danger that might approach the castle.
   II. Though the moat and palisade offered the bailey a good deal of protection, it was linked to the motte by a set of stairs that led to a retractable drawbridge at the motte's gate, to enable people to evacuate onto the motte in case of an attack.
   III. The motte of these early castles was a fortified hill, sometimes as high as one hundred feet, on which stood a palisade and tower.
   IV. The bailey was a clear, level spot below the motte, also enclosed by a palisade, which in turn was surrounded by a large trench or moat.
   V. The earliest castles built in Europe were not the magnificent stone giants that still tower over much of the European landscape, but simpler wooden constructions called motte-and-bailey castles.
   The BEST order is:
   A. V, III, I, IV, II   B. V, IV, I, II, III   C. I, IV, III, II, V   D. I, III, II, IV, V

5. I. If an infant is left alone or abandoned for a short while, its immediate response is to cry loudly, accompanying its screams with aggressive flailing of its legs and limbs.
   II. If a child has been abandoned for a longer period of time, it becomes completely still and quiet, as if realizing that now its only chance for survival is to shut its mouth and remain motionless.
   III. Along with their intense fear of the dark, the crying behavior of human infants offers insights into how prehistoric newborn children might have evolved instincts that would prevent them from becoming victims of predators.

IV. This behavior often surprises people who enter a hospital's maternity ward for the first time and encounter total silence from a roomful of infants.

V. This violent screaming response is quite different from an infant's cries of discomfort or hunger, and seems to serve as either the child's first line of defense against an unwanted intruder, or a desperate attempt to communicate its position to the mother.

The BEST order is:

A. III, II, IV, I, V   B. III, I, V, II, IV   C. I, V, IV, II, III   D. II, IV, I, V, III

6.
I. When two cats meet who are strangers, their first actions and gestures determine who the "dominant" cat will be, at least for the time being.

II. Unlike dogs, cats are typically a solitary animal species who avoid social interaction, but they do display specific social responses to each other upon meeting.

III. This is unlikely, however; before such a point of open hostility is reached, one of the cats will usually take the "submissive" position of crouching down while looking away from the other dat.

IV. If a cat desires dominance or sees the other cat as a threat to its territory, it will stare directly at the intruder with a lowered tail.

V. If the other cat responds with a similar gesture, or with the strong defensive posture of an arched back, laid-back ears and raised tail, a fight or chase is likely if neither cat gives in.

The BEST order is:

A. IV, II, I, V, III   B. I, II, IV, V, III   C. I, IV, V, III, II   D. II, I, IV, V, III

7.
I. A star or planet's gravitational force can best be explained in this way: anything passing through this "dent" in space will veer toward the star or planet as if it were rolling into a hole.

II. Objects that are massive or heavy, such as stars or planets, "sink" into this surface, creating a sort of dent or concavity in the surrounding space.

III. Black holes, the most massive objects known to exist in space, create dents so large and deep that the space surrounding them actually folds in on itself, preventing anything that falls in —even light —from ever escaping again.

IV. The sort of dent a star or planet makes depends on how massive it is; planets generally have weak gravitational pulls, but stars, which are larger and heavier, make a bigger "dent" that will attract more matter.

V. In outer space, the force of gravity works as if the surrounding space is a soft, flat surface.

The BEST order is:

A. III, V, II, I, IV   B. III, IV, I, V, II   C. V, II, I, IV, III   D. I, V, II, IV, III

8.
I. Eventually, the society of Kyoto gave the world one of its first and greatest novels when Japan's most promising writer, Lady Murasaki Shikibu, wrote her chronicle of Kyoto's society, *The Tale of Genji*, which preceded the first European novels by more than 500 years.

II. The society of Kyoto was dedicated to the pleasures of art; the courtiers experimented with new and colorful methods of sculpture, painting, writing, decorative gardening, and even making clothes.

III. Japanese culture began under the powerful authority of Chinese Buddhism, which influenced every aspect of Japanese life from religion to politics and art.
IV. This new, vibrant culture was so sophisticated that all the people in Kyoto's imperial court considered themselves poets, and the line between life and art hardly existed —lovers corresponded entirely through written verses, and even government officials communicated by writing poems to each other.
V. In the eighth century, when the emperor established the town of Kyoto as the capital of the Japanese empire, Japanese society began to develop its own distinctive style.

The BEST order is:
  A. V, II, IV, I, III   B. II, I, V, IV, III   C. V, III, IV, I, II   D. III, V, II, IV, I

9. I. Instead of wheels, the HSST uses two sets of magnets, one which sits on the track, and another that is carried by the train; these magnets generate an identical magnetic field which forces the two sets apart.
II. In the last few decades, railway travel has become less popular throughout the world, because it is much slower than travel by airplane, and not much less expensive.
III. The HSST's designers say that the train can take passengers from one town to another as quickly as a jet plane —while consuming less than half the energy.
IV. This repellent effect is strong enough to lift the entire train above the trackway, and the train, literally traveling on air, rockets along at speeds of up to 300 miles per hour.
V. The revolutionary technology of magnetic levitation, currently being tested by Japan's experimental HSST (High Speed Surface Transport), may yet bring passenger trains back from the dead.

The BEST order is:
  A. II, V, I, IV, III   B. II, I, IV, III, V   C. V, II, III, I, IV   D. V, I, III, IV, II

9.____

10. I. When European countries first began to colonize the African continent, their impression of the African people was of a vast group of loosely organized tribal societies, without any great centralized source of power or wealth.
II. The legend of Timbuktu persisted until the nineteenth century, when a French adventurer visited Timbuktu and found that raids by neighboring tribesmen had made the city a shadow of its former self.
III. In the fifteenth century, when the stories of travelers who had traveled Africa's Sudan region began circulating around Europe, this impression began to change.
IV. In 1470, an Italian merchant named Benedetto Dei traveled to Timbuktu and confirmed these rumors, describing a thriving metropolis where rich and poor people worshipped together in the city's many ornate mosques — there was even a university in Timbuktu, much like its European counterparts, where African scholars pursued their studies in the arts and sciences.

10.____

V. The travelers' legends told of an enormous city in the western Sudan, Timbuktu, where the streets were crowded with goods brought by faraway caravans, and where there was a stone palace as large as any in Europe.

The BEST order is:
A. III, V, I, IV, II B. I, II, IV, III, V C. I, III, V, IV, II D. II, I, III, IV, V

11.
I. Also, our reference points in sighting the moon make us believe that its size is changing; when the moon is rising through the trees, it seems huge, because our brains unconsciously compare the size of the moon with the size of the trees in the foreground.
II. To most people, the sky itself appears more distant at the horizon than directly overhead, and if the moon's size—which remains constant—is projected from the horizon, the apparent distance of the horizon makes the moon look bigger.
III. Up higher in the sky, the moon is set against tiny stars in the background, which will make the moon seem smaller.
IV. People often wonder why the moon becomes bigger when it approaches the horizon, but most scientists agree that this is a complicated optical illusion, produced by at least three factors.
V. The moon illusion may also be partially explained by a phenomenon that has nothing to do with errors in our perception—light that enters the earth's atmosphere is sometimes refracted, and so the atmosphere may act as a kind of magnifying glass for the moon's image.

The BEST order is:
A. IV, III, V, II, I B. IV, II, I, III, V C. V, II, I, III, IV D. II, I, III, IV, V

12.
I. When the Native Americans were introduced to the horses used by white explorers, they were amazed at their new alternative—here was an animal that was strong and swift, would patiently carry a person or other loads on its back, and they later discovered, was right at home on the plains.
II. Before the arrival of European explorers to North America, the natives of the American plains used large dogs to carry their travois-long lodgepoles loaded with clothing, gear, and food.
III. These horses, it is now known, were not really strangers to North America; the very first horses originated here, on this continent, tens of thousands of years ago, and migrated into Asia across the Bering Land Bridge, a strip of land that used to link our continent with the Eastern world.
IV. At first, the natives knew so little about horses that at least one tribe tried to feed their new animals pieces of dried meat and animal fat, and were surprised when the horses turned their heads away and began to eat the grass of the prairie.
V. The American horse eventually became extinct, but its Asian cousins were reintroduced to the New World when the European explorers brought them to live among the Native Americans.

The BEST order is:
A. II, I, IV, III, V B. II, IV, I, III, V C. I, II, IV, III, V D. I, III, V, II, IV

13. I. The dress worn by the dancer is believed to have been adorned in the past by shells which would strike each other as the dancer performed, creating a lovely sound.
    II. Today's jingle-dress is decorated with the tin lids of snuff cans, which are rolled into cones and sewn onto the dress,
    III. During the jingle-dress dance, the dancer must blend complicated footwork with a series of gentle hos that cause the cones to jingle in rhythm to a drumbeat.
    IV. When contemporary Native American tribes meet for a pow-wow, one of the most popular ceremonies to take place is the women's jingle-dress dance.
    V. Besides being more readily available than shells, the lids are thought by many dancers to create a softer, more subtle sound.
    The BEST order is:
    A. II, IV, V, I, III B. IV, II, I, III, V C. II, I, III, V, IV D. IV, I, II, V, III

14. I. If a homeowner lives where seasonal climates are extreme, deciduous shade trees—which will drop their leaves in the winter and allow sunlight to pass through the windows—should be planted near the southern exposure in order to keep the house cool during the summer.
    II. This trajectory is shorter and lower in the sky than at any other time of year during the winter, when a house most requires heating; the northern-facing parts of a house do not receive any direct sunlight at all.
    III. In designing an energy-efficient house, especially in colder climates, it is important to remember that most of the house's windows should face south.
    IV. Though the sun always rises in the east and sets in the west, the sun of the northern hemisphere is permanently situated in the southern portion of the sky.
    V. The explanation for why so many architects and builders want this "southern exposure" is related to the path of the sun in the sky.
    The BEST order is:
    A. III, I, V, IV, II B. III, V, IV, II, I C. I, III, IV, II, V D. I, II, V, IV, III

15. I. His journeying lasted twenty-four years and took him over an estimated 75,000 miles, a distance that would not be surpassed by anyone other than Magellan—who sailed around the world—for another six hundred years.
    II. Perhaps the most far-flung of these lesser-known travelers was Ibn Batuta, an African Moslem who left his birthplace of Tangier in the summer of 1325.
    III. Ibn Batuta traveled all over Africa and Asia, from Niger to Peking, and to the islands of Maldive and Indonesia.
    IV. However, a few explorers of the Eastern world logged enough miles and adventures to make Marco Polo's voyage look like an evening stroll.
    V. In America, the most well-known of the Old World's explorers are usually Europeans such as Marco Polo, the Italian who brought many elements of Chinese culture to the Western world.
    The BEST order is:
    A. V, IV, II, III, I B. V, IV, III, II, I C. III, II, I, IV, V D. II, III, I, IV, V

16.
    I. In the rainforests of South America, a rare species of frog practices a reproductive method that is entirely different from this standard process.
    II. She will eventually carry each of the tadpoles up into the canopy and drop each into its own little pool, where it will be easy to locate and safe from most predators.
    III. After fertilization, the female of the species, who lives almost entirely on the forest floor, lays between 2 and 16 eggs among the leaf litter at the base of a tree, and stands watch over these eggs until they hatch.
    IV. Most frogs are pond-dwellers who are able to deposit hundreds of eggs in the water and then leave them alone, knowing that enough eggs have been laid to insure the survival of some of their offspring.
    V. Once the tadpoles emerge, the female backs in among them, and a tadpole will wriggle onto her back to be carried high into the forest canopy, where the female will deposit it in a little pool of water cupped in the leaf of a plant.
    The BEST order is:
    A. I, IV, III, II, V   B. I, III, V, II, IV   C. IV, III, II, V, I   D. IV, I, III, V, II

17.
    I. Eratosthenes had heard from travelers that at exactly noon on June 21, in the ancient city of Aswan, Egypt, the sun cast no shadow in a well, which meant that the sun must be directly overhead.
    II. He knew the sun always cast a shadow in Alexandria, and so he figured that if he could measure the length of an Alexandria shadow at the time when there was no shadow in Aswan, he could calculate the angle of the sun, and therefore the circumference of the earth.
    III. The evidence for a round earth was not new in 1492; in fact, Eratosthenes, an Alexandrian geographer who lived nearly sixteen centuries before Columbus's voyage (275-195 B.C.), actually developed a method for calculating the circumference of the earth that is still in use today.
    IV. Eratosthenes's method was correct, but his result—28,700 miles—was about 15 percent too high, probably because of the inaccurate ancient methods of keeping time, and because Aswan was not due south of Alexandria, as Eratosthenes had believed.
    V. When Christopher Columbus sailed across the Atlantic Ocean for the first time in 1492, there were still some people in the world who ignored scientific evidence and believed that the earth was flat, rather than round.
    The BEST order is:
    A. I, II, V, III, IV   B. V, III, IV, I, II   C. V, III, I, II, IV   D. III, V, I, II, IV

18.
    I. The first name for the child is considered a trial naming, often impersonal and neutral, such as the Ngoni name *Chabwera*, meaning "it has arrived."
    II. This sort of name is not due to any parental indifference to the child, but is a kind of silent recognition of Africa's sometimes high infant death rate; most parents ease the pain of losing a child with the belief that it is not really a person until it has been given a final name.
    III. In many tribal African societies, families often give two different names to their children, at different periods in time.
    IV. After the trial naming period has subsided and it is clear that the child will survive, the parents choose a final name for the child, an act that symbolically completes the act of birth.

V. In fact, some African first-given names are explicitly uncomplimentary, translating as "I am dead" or "I am ugly," in order to avoid the jealousy of ancestral spirits who might wish to take a child that is especially healthy or attractive.

The BEST order is:

A. III, I, II, V, IV   B. III, IV, II, I, V   C. IV, III, I, II, V   D. IV, V, III, I, II

19. I. Though uncertain of the definite reasons for this behavior, scientists believe the birds digest the clay in order to counteract toxins contained in the seeds of certain fruits that are eaten by macaws.
    II. For example, all macaws flock to riverbanks at certain times of the year to eat the clay that is found in river mud.
    III. The macaws of South America are not only among the largest and most beautifully colored of the world's flying birds, but they are also one of the smartest.
    IV. It is believed that macaws are forced to resort to these toxic fruits during the dry season, when foods are more scarce.
    V. The macaw's intelligence has led to intense study by scientists, who have discovered some macaw behaviors that have not yet been explained.

    The BEST order is:

    A. III, IV, I, II, V   B. III, V, II, I, IV   C. V, II, I, IV, III   D. IV, I, II, III, V

20. I. Although Maggie Kuhn has since passed away, the Gray Panthers are still waging a campaign to reinstate the historical view of the elderly as people whose experience allows them to make their greatest contribution in their later years.
    II. In 1972, an elderly woman named Maggie Kuhn responded to this sort of treatment by forming a group called the Gray Panthers, an organization of both old and young adults with the common goal of creating change.
    III. This attitude is reflected strongly in the way elderly people are treated by our society; many are forced into early retirement, or are placed in rest homes in which they are isolated from their communities.
    IV. Unlike most other cultures around the world, Americans tend to look upon old age with a sense of dread and sadness.
    V. Kuhn believed that when the elderly are forced to withdraw into lives that lack purpose, society loses one of its greatest resources: people who have a lifetime of experience and wisdom to offer their communities.

    The BEST order is:

    A. IV, III, II, V, I   B. IV, II, I, III, V   C. II, IV, III, V, I   D. II, I, IV, III, V

21. I. The current theory among most anthropologists is that humans evolved from apes who lived in trees near the grasslands of Africa.
    II. Still, some anthropologists insist that such an invention was necessary for the survival of early humans, and point to the Kung Bushmen of central Africa as a society in which the sling is still used in this way.
    III. Two of these inventions—fire, and weapons such as spears and clubs—were obvious defenses against predators, and there is archaeological evidence to support the theory of their use.

IV. Once people had evolved enough to leave the safety of trees and walk upright, they needed the protection of several inventions in order to survive.
V. But another invention, a feather or fiber sling that allowed mothers to carry children while leaving their hands free to gather roots or berries, would certainly have decomposed and left behind no trace of itself.

The BEST order is:
A. I, II, III, V, IV   B. IV, I, II, III, V   C. I, IV, III, V, II   D. IV, III, V, II, I

22. I. The person holding the bird should keep it in hot water up to its neck, and the person cleaning should work a mild solution of dishwashing liquid into the bird's plumage, paying close attention to the head and neck.
II. When rinsing the bird, after all the oil has been removed, the running water should be directed against the lay of its feathers, until water begins to bead off the surface of the feathers—a sign that all the detergent has been rinsed out.
III. If you have rescued a sea bird from an oil spill and want to restore it to clean and normal living, you need a large sink, a constant supply of running hot water (a little over 100°F), and regular dishwashing liquid.
IV. This cleaning with detergent solution should be repeated as many times as it takes to remove all traces of oil from the bird's feathers, sometime over a period of several days.
V. But before you begin to clean the bird, you must find a partner because cleaning an oiled bird is a two-person job.

The BEST order is:
A. III, I, II, IV, V   B. III, V, I, IV, II   C. III, I, IV, V, II   D. III, IV, V, I, II

23. I. The most difficult time of year for the Tsaatang is the spring calving, when the reindeer leave their wintering ground and rush to their accustomed calving place, without stopping by night or by day.
II. Reindeer travel in herds, and though some animals are tamed by the Tsaatang for riding or milking, the herds are allowed to roam free.
III. This journey is hard for the Tsaatang, who carry all their possessions with them, but once it's over it proves worthwhile; the Tsaatang can immediately begin to gather milk from reindeer cows who have given birth.
IV. The Tsaatang, a small tribe who live in the far northwest corner of Mongolia, practice a lifestyle that is completely dependent on the reindeer, their main resource for food, clothing, and transport.
V. The people must follow their yearly migrations, living in portable shelters that resemble Native American tepees.

The BEST order is:
A. I, III, II, V, IV   B. I, IV, II, V, III   C. IV, I, III, V, II   D. IV II, V, I, III

24. I. The Romans later improved this system by installing these heated pipe networks throughout walls and ceilings, supplying heat to even the uppermost floors of a building—a system that, to this day, hasn't been much improved.
II. Air-conditioning, the method by which humans control indoor temperatures, was practiced much earlier than most people think.

III. The earliest heating devices other than open fires were used in 350 B.C. by the ancient Greeks, who directed air that had been heated by underground fires into baked clay pipes that ran under the floor.
IV. Ironically, the first successful cooling system, patented in England in 1831, used fire as its main energy source—fires were lit in the attic of a building, creating an updraft of air that drew cool air into the building through ducts that had underground openings near the river Thames.
V. Cooling buildings was more of a challenge, and wasn't attempted until 1500: a water-based system, designed by Leonardo da Vinci, does not appear to have been successful, since it was never used again.

The BEST order is:
A. III, V, IV, I, II   B. III, I, II, V, IV   C. II, III, I, V, IV   D. IV, II, III, I, V

25. I. Cold, dry air from Canada passes over the Rocky Mountains and sweeps down onto the plains, where it collides with warm, moist air from the waters of the Gulf of Mexico, and when the two air masses meet, the resulting disturbance sometimes forms a violent funnel cloud that strikes the earth and destroys virtually everything in its path.
II. Hurricanes, storms which are generally not this violent and last much longer, are usually given names by meteorologists, but this tradition cannot be applied to tornados, which have a life span measured in minutes and disappear in the same way as they are born—unnamed.
III. A tornado funnel forms rotating columns of air whose speed reaches three hundred miles an hour—a speed that can only be estimated, because no wind-measuring devices in the direct path of a storm have ever survived.
IV. The natural phenomena known as tornados occur primarily over the Midwestern grasslands of the United States.
V. It is here, meteorologists tell us, that conditions for the formation of tornados are sometimes perfect during the spring months.

The BEST order is:
A. II IV, V, I, III   B. II, III, I, V, IV   C. IV, V, I, III, II   D. IV, III, I, V, II

KEY (CORRECT ANSWERS)

1.	C		11.	B
2.	C		12.	A
3.	B		13.	D
4.	A		14.	B
5.	B		15.	A
6.	D		16.	D
7.	C		17.	C
8.	D		18.	A
9.	A		19.	B
10.	C		20.	A

21. C
22. B
23. D
24. C
25. C

EXAMINATION SECTION
TEST 1

DIRECTIONS: The sentences listed below are part of a meaningful paragraph, but they are not given in their proper order. You are to decide what would be the BEST order to put sentences to form a well-organized paragraph. Each sentence has a place in the paragraph; there are no extra sentences. *PRINT THE LETTER OF THE CORRECT ANSWER IN THE SPACE AT THE RIGHT.*

Questions 1-3.

DIRECTIONS: Questions 1 through 3 are to be answered on the basis of the following passage.

Almost half of the increase in Chicago came from five neighborhoods, including West Garfield Park. He was 12 years old and had just been recruited into a gang by his older brothers and cousin. A decade later, he sits in Cook County jail, held without bail and awaiting trial on three cases, including felony drug charges and possession of a weapon. Violence in Chicago erupted last year, with the city recording 771 murders—a 58% jump from 2015. They point to a $95 million police-training center in West Garfield Park, public-transit improvements on Chicago's south side and efforts to get major corporations such as Whole Foods and Wal-Mart to invest. Chicago city officials say that they are making strategic investments in ailing neighborhoods. Amarley Coggins remembers the first time he dealt heroin, discreetly approaching a car coming off an interstate highway and into West Garfield park, the neighborhood where he grew up on Chicago's west side.

1. When organized correctly, the first sentence of the paragraph begins with 1.____
   A. "Amarley Coggins remembers..."   B. "He was 12 years old..."
   C. "They point to a..."   D. "Violence in Chicago..."

2. After correctly organizing the paragraph, the author wishes to replace a word 2.____
   in the last sentence with its synonym *enterprises*. Which word does the author wish to replace?
   A. murders   B. neighborhoods
   C. corporations   D. improvements

3. If put together correctly, the second to last sentence would end with the words 3.____
   A. "...Chicago's west side."   B. "...in ailing neighborhoods."
   C. "...older brother and cousins."   D. "...and Wal-Mart to invest."

Questions 4-6.

DIRECTIONS: Questions 4 through 6 are to be answered on the basis of the following passage.

Critics argue that driverless vehicles pose too many risks, including cyberattacks, computer malfunctions, relying on algorithms to make ethical decisions, and fewer transportation jobs. Driverless vehicles, also called autonomous vehicles and self-driving vehicles, are vehicles that can operate without human intervention. And algorithms make decisions based on data obtained from sensors and connectivity. Driverless vehicles rely primarily on three technologies: sensors, connectivity, and algorithms. Sensors observe multiple directions simultaneously. Connectivity accesses information on traffic, weather, road hazards, and navigation. Supporters argue that driverless vehicles have many benefits, including fewer traffic accidents and fatalities, more efficient traffic flows, greater mobility for those who cannot drive, and less pollution. Once the realm of science fiction, driverless vehicles could revolutionize automotive travel over the next few decades.

4. When all of the sentences are organized in correct order, the first sentence starts with
   A. "Connectivity accesses information..."
   B. "Critics argue that..."
   C. "Once the realm of..."
   D. "Driverless vehicles, also called..."

4.____

5. If the above paragraph appeared in correct order, which of the following transition words would be MOST appropriate in the beginning of the sentence that starts "Critics argue that..."
   A. Additionally
   B. To begin,
   C. In conclusion,
   D. Conversely,

5.____

6. When the paragraph is properly arranged, it ends with the words
   A. "...over the next few decades."
   B. "...fewer transportation jobs."
   C. "...and less pollution."
   D. "...without human intervention"

6.____

Questions 7-10.

DIRECTIONS: Questions 7 through 10 are to be answered on the basis of the following passage.

This method had some success, but also carried fatal risks. Various people across Europe independently developed vaccination as an alternative during the later years of the eighteenth century, but Edward Jenner (1749-1823) popularized the practice. Vaccination has been called a miracle of modern medicine, but it has a long and controversial history stretching back to the ancient world. In 1803 the Royal Jennerian Institute was founded in England, and vaccination programs initially drew enormous public support. In 429 BCE in Greece, the historian Thucydides (c.460-c.395 BCE) noted that survivors of smallpox did not become reinfected in subsequent epidemics. Variolation as a means of preventing severe smallpox infection became an accepted practice in China in the tenth century CE, and its popularity spread across Asia,

Europe, and to the Americas by the seventeenth century. Variolation required either inhalation of smallpox dust, or putting scabs or parts of the smallpox pustules under the skin. Widespread inoculation against smallpox was purported to have been part of Ayurvedic tradition as far back as at least 1000 BCE, when Indian doctors traveled to households before the rainy season each year.

7. When arranged properly, what does "This method" refer to in the sentence that begins "This method had some success..."? 7.____
   A. Vaccination   B. Inoculation
   C. Variolation   D. Hybridization

8. When organized correctly, the paragraph's third sentence should begin 8.____
   A. "In 429 BCE in Greece..."   B. "Variolation required..."
   C. "In 1803 the..."   D. "Vaccination has been called..."

9. If put in the correct order, this paragraph should end with the words 9.____
   A. "...under the skin."   B. "...to the ancient world."
   C. "...enormous public support." D. "...by the seventeenth century."

10. In the second sentence, the author is thinking about using the word immunization instead of which of its synonyms? 10.____
    A. Variolation   B. Vaccination   C. Inhalation   D. Inoculation

Questions 11-13.

DIRECTIONS: Questions 11 through 13 are to be answered on the basis of the following passage.

Summers are hot—often north of 100 degrees—and because it lies at the far end of a San Diego Gas & Electric transmission line, the town has suffered frequent power outages. Another way is that microgrids can ease the entry of intermittent renewable energy sources, like wind and solar, into the modern grid. Utilities are also interested in microgrids because of the money they can save by deferring the need to build new transmission lines. "If you're on the very end of a utility line, everything that happens, happens 10 times worse for you," says Mike Gravely, team leader for energy systems integration at the California Energy Commission. The town has a lot of senior citizens, who can be frail in the heat. Borrego Springs, California, is a quaint town of about 3,400 people set against the Anza-Borrego Desert about 90 miles east of San Diego. High winds, lightning strikes, forest fires and flash floods can bust up that line and kill the electricity. But today, Borrego Springs has a failsafe against power outages: a microgrid. Resiliency is one of the main reasons the market in microgrids is booming, with installed capacity in the United States projected to be more than double between 2017 and 2022, according to a new report on microgrids from GTM Research. "Without air conditioning," says Linda Haddock, head of the local Chamber of Commerce, "people will die."

11. When the sentences above are organized correctly, the paragraph should start with the sentence that begins 11.____
    A. "Borrego Springs, California..."   B. "But today, Borrego Springs..."
    C. "Summers are hot..."   D. "Utilities are also interested..."

12. If the author wanted to split this paragraph into two smaller paragraphs, the first sentence of the second paragraph would start with the words
    A. "High winds, lightning strikes, forest fires…"
    B. "But today, Borrego Springs…"
    C. "Resiliency is one of the main…"
    D. "If you're on the very end…"

13. Assuming the paragraph were organized correctly, the second to last sentence would end
    A. "…to build new transmission lines."
    B. "…be frail in the heat."
    C. "…into the modern grid."
    D. "…east of San Diego."

Questions 14-17.

DIRECTIONS: Questions 14 through 17 are to be answered on the basis of the following passage.

Exhaustive search is not typically a successful approach to problem solving because most interesting problems have search spaces that are simply too large to be dealt with in this manner, even by the fastest computers. Thus, in order to ignore a portion of a search space, some guiding knowledge or insight must exist so that the solution will not be overlooked. This partial understanding is reflected in the fact that a rigid algorithmic solution—a routine and predetermined number of computational steps—cannot be applied. A large part of the intelligence of chess players resides in the heuristics they employ. When search is used to explore the entire solution space, it is said to be exhaustive. Chess is a classic example where humans routinely employ sophisticated heuristics in a search space. Therefore, if one hopes to find a solution (or a reasonably good approximation of a solution) to such a problem, one must selectively explore the problem's search space. Rather, the concept of search is used to solve such problems. Heuristics is a major area of AI that concerns itself with how to limit effectively the exploration of a search space. Many problems that humans are confronted with are not fully understood. The difficulty here is that if part of the search space is not explored, one runs the risk that the solution one seeks will be missed. A chess player will typically search through a small number of possible moves before selecting a move to play. Not every possible move and countermove sequence is explored. Only reasonable sequences are examined.

14. When correctly organized, the paragraph above should begin with the words
    A. "Many problems that…"
    B. "Therefore, if one hopes to…"
    C. "Only reasonable sequences are…"
    D. "The difficulty here is…"

15. If the paragraph was organized correctly, the fourth sentence would begin with the words
    A. "Chess is a classic…"
    B. "Heuristics is a major…"
    C. "Exhaustive search is not…"
    D. "The difficulty here is…"

16. If the author wished to separate this paragraph into two equally sized paragraphs, the sentence that begins the second paragraph would END with the words
    A. "...heuristics they employ."
    B. "...in a search space."
    C. "...are not fully employed."
    D. "...will be missed."

17. When organized correctly, the paragraph would end with the words
    A. "...the heuristics they employ."
    B. "...will not be overlooked."
    C. "...said to be exhaustive."
    D. "...are not fully understood."

Questions 18-21.

DIRECTIONS: Questions 18 through 21 are to be answered on the basis of the following passage.

Asian-Americans soon found themselves the targets of ridicule and attacks. Prior to the bombing he had tried to enlist in the military but was turned down due to poor health. His case, Korematsu v. The United States, is still considered a blemish on the record of the Supreme Court and has received heightened scrutiny given the indefinite confinement of many prisoners after the terrorist attacks on September 11, 2001. On February 19, 1942, President Franklin D. Roosevelt issued Executive Order 9066, which granted the leaders of the armed forces permission to create Military Areas and authorizing the removal of any and all persons from those areas. Fred Korematsu was a 22-year-old welder when the Japanese bombed Pearl Harbor on December 7, 1941. A Nisei—which means an American citizen born to Japanese parents—he was one of four brothers and grew up working in his parents' plant nursery in Oakland, California. This statement effectively pronounced Japanese-Americans on the West Coast as traitors because even though Executive Order 9066 allowed the military to remove any person from designated areas, only those of Japanese descent were ordered to leave. Before Pearl Harbor, he was employed by a defense contractor in California. At the time of the attack, he was having a picnic with his Italian-American girlfriend. Asian-American Fred Korematsu (1919-2005) is most remembered for challenging the legality of Japanese internment during World War II. It was for this simple reason that he eventually became known as a civil rights leader. American reaction to an attack on United States' soil was both swift and harsh. Awarded the Presidential Medal of Honor, he is considered a leader of the civil rights movement in the United States. Roosevelt justified these actions in the opening paragraph of the order by declaring, "the successful prosecution of the war requires every possible protection against espionage, and against sabotage to national-defense material, national-defenses premises and national-defense utilities." Years later he told the San Francisco Chronicle, "I was just living my life, and that's what I wanted to do."

18. When put together correctly, the above paragraph would begin with the words
    A. "It was for this simple reason..."
    B. "A Nisei—which means..."
    C. "Awarded the Presidential Medal of Honor..."
    D. "Asian-American Fred Korematsu..."

19. If the author wished to separate this piece into two separate paragraphs, the sentence that would be the BEST way to start the second paragraph would begin with the words
    A. "Awarded the Presidential Medal of Honor..."
    B. "Fred Korematsu was a..."
    C. "Roosevelt justified these actions..."
    D. "Before Pearl Harbor, he was..."

19._____

20. In the sentence that begins "A Nisei—which means...", who does "he" refer to in the paragraph?
    A. Roosevelt
    B. A sibling of Korematsu
    C. Fred Korematsu
    D. Japanese-Americans on the West Coast

20._____

21. If organized correctly, the fourth sentence should begin with the words
    A. "At the time of the attack..."
    B. "His case, Korematsu v. The United States..."
    C. "Fred Korematsu was a..."
    D. "This statement effectively pronounced..."

21._____

22. When put together correctly, the last sentence of the paragraph should end with the words
    A. "...that's what I wanted to do."   B. "...were ordered to leave."
    C. "...during World War II."   D. "...was both swift and harsh."

22._____

Questions 23-25.

DIRECTIONS: Questions 23 through 25 are to be answered on the basis of the following passage.

Over the past two decades, her personal finances have been eroded by illness, divorce, the cost of raising two children, the housing bust, and the economic downturn. "There are more people attending college, more people taking out loans, and more people taking out a higher dollar amount of loans," says Matthew Ward, associate director of media relations at the New York Fed. Anderson, who is 57, told her complicated story at a recent Senate Aging Committee hearing (she's previously appeared on the CBS Evening News). Some 3 percent of U.S. households that are headed by a senior citizen now hold federal student debt, mostly debt they took on to finance their own educations, according to a new report from the Government Accountability Office (GAO), an independent agency. She hasn't been able to afford payments on her loans for nearly eight years. Rosemary Anderson has a master's degree, a good job at the University of California (Santa Cruz), and student loans that she could be paying off until she's 81. Student debt has risen across every age group over the past decade, according to a Federal Reserve Bank of New York analysis of credit report data... "As the baby boomers continue to move into retirement, the number of older Americans with defaulted loans will only continue to increase," the report warned. She first enrolled in college in her thirties.

23. When organized correctly, the first sentence should begin with the words
    A. "She first enrolled…" B. "Anderson, who is 57…"
    C. "Some 3 percent of…" D. "Rosemary Anderson has…"

24. If the author wished to split the paragraph into two paragraphs (not necessarily equal in length), the first sentence of the second paragraph would begin with the words
    A. "Some 3 percent of…" B. "There are more people…"
    C. "Over the past two decades…" D. "She first enrolled…"

25. When put in the correct order, the second to last sentence should end with the words
    A. "…an independent agency." B. "…of credit report data."
    C. "…at the New York Fed." D. "…in her thirties."

KEY (CORRECT ANSWERS)

1. A   11. A
2. C   12. B
3. B   13. C
4. D   14. A
5. D   15. C

6. B   16. D
7. C   17. A
8. A   18. D
9. C   19. B
10. D 20. C

21. C
22. B
23. D
24. A
25. B

TEST 2

DIRECTIONS: The sentences listed below are part of a meaningful paragraph, but they are not given in their proper order. You are to decide what would be the BEST order to put sentences to form a well-organized paragraph. Each sentence has a place in the paragraph; there are no extra sentences. *PRINT THE LETTER OF THE CORRECT ANSWER IN THE SPACE AT THE RIGHT.*

Questions 1-3.

DIRECTIONS: Questions 1 through 3 are to be answered on the basis of the following passage.

According to the World Health Organization (WHO), exposure to ambient (outdoor) air pollution causes 3 million premature deaths around the world each year, largely due to heart and lung diseases. Air pollution also contributes to such environmental threats as smog, acid rain, depletion of the ozone layer, and global climate change. The U.S. Environmental Protection Agency (EPA) sets National Ambient Air Quality Standards (NAAQS) for those four pollutants as well as carbon monoxide (CO) and lead. The EPA also regulates 187 toxic air pollutants, such as asbestos, benzene, dioxin, and mercury. Finally, the EPA places limits on emissions of greenhouse gases like carbon dioxide (CO_2) and methane, which contribute to global climate change. The WHO has established Air Quality Guidelines (ACGs) to identify safe levels of exposure to the emission of four harmful air pollutants worldwide: particulate matter (PM), ozone (O_3), nitrogen dioxide (NO_2), and sulfur dioxide (SO_2). Since EPA criteria define the allowable concentrations of these six substances in ambient air throughout the United States, they are known as criteria air pollutants. Air pollution refers to the release into the air of chemicals and other substances, known as pollutants, that are potentially harmful to human health and the environment.

1. When organized correctly, the first sentence of this paragraph should begin   1.____
   A. "Air pollution refers…"
   B. "The EPA also regulates..,"
   C. "The WHO has established…"
   D. "According to the…"

2. When put in the correct order, the fourth sentence should end with the words   2.____
   A. "…to global climate change."
   B. "…as criteria air pollutants."
   C. "…nitrogen dioxide (NO_2), and sulfur dioxide (SO_2)."
   D. "…health and the environment."

3. If put in the most logical order, the paragraph would end with the words   3.____
   A. "…as criteria air pollutants."
   B. "…to global climate change."
   C. "…benzene, dioxin, and mercury."
   D. "…human health and the environment."

Questions 4-6.

DIRECTIONS: Questions 4 through 6 are to be answered on the basis of the following passage.

Although gentrification has been associated with some positive impacts, such as urban revitalization and lower crime rates, critics charge that it marginalizes racial and ethnic minorities and destroys the character of urban neighborhoods. British sociologist Ruth Glass is credited with coining the term "gentrification" in her 1964 book *London: Aspects of Change*, which described the transformation that occurred when members of the gentry (an elite or privileged social class) took over working-class districts of London. Gentrification is a type of neighborhood change, a broader term that encompasses various physical, demographic, social, and economic processes that affect distinct residential areas. The arrival of wealthier people leads to new economic development and an increase in property values and rent, which often makes housing unaffordable for longtime residents. Gentrification is a transformation process that typically occurs in urban neighborhoods when higher-income people move in and displace lower-income existing residents.

4. When organized in the correct order, the first sentence of the paragraph should begin with the words
    A. "Gentrification is a type of…"
    B. "British sociologist Ruth…"
    C. "The arrival of…"
    D. "Gentrification is a transformation…"

4.____

5. If put together in the correct order, the second to last sentence in the paragraph would end with the words
    A. "…lower-income existing residents."
    B. "…that affect distinct residential areas."
    C. "…character of urban neighborhoods."
    D. "…working-class districts of London."

5.____

6. If the author wished to change the beginning of the final sentence to "in the end." to better signal the finish of the paragraph, which of the following words would the phrase appear in front of?
    A. British
    B. Gentrification
    C. Although
    D. The

6.____

Questions 7-11.

DIRECTIONS: Questions 7 through 11 are to be answered on the basis of the following passage.

The primary signs of ADHD include a persistent pattern of inattention or hyperactivity lasting in duration for six months or longer with an onset before 12 years of age. Children with ADHD often experience peer rejection, neglect, or teasing and family interactions may contain high levels of discord and negative interactions (APA, 2013). Two primary types of the disorder include inattentive and hyperactive/impulsive, with a combined type when both inattention and hyperactivity occur together. Inattentive ADHD is evidenced by executive functioning deficits such as being off task, lacking sustained focus, and being disorganized. Hyperactive ADHD is evidenced by excessive talkativeness and fidgeting, with an inability to control impulses that may result in harm. Attention Deficit Hyperactivity Disorder (ADHD) is a commonly diagnosed childhood behavioral disorder affecting millions of children in the U.S. every year (National Institute of Mental Health [NIMH], 2012), with prevalence rates between 5% and 11% of the population. Other research has examined singular traits such as executive function deficits in the school setting, task performance in the school setting (Berk, 1986), driving and awareness of time. However, researching academic aspects of the school experience does not provide a comprehensive understanding of the systemic effects of ADHD in the school environment. Historically, much research on ADHD has focused on the academic impact of behavioral symptoms such as reading and mathematics. These behaviors are inappropriate for the child's age level and symptoms typically interfere with functioning in multiple environments.

7. If the author put the paragraph into a logical order, the first sentence would begin with the words
   A. "Inattentive ADHD is..."
   B. "Historically, much research..."
   C. "These behaviors are..."
   D. "Attention Deficit Hyperactivity Disorder..."

7.____

8. When put in the correct order, what does the author mean by "These behaviors" in the sentence that begins "These behaviors are..."?
   A. Inattention or hyperactivity   B. Reading and Mathematics
   C. Peer rejection   D. Sustained focus

8.____

9. If the author wished to split this paragraph into two paragraphs (not necessarily equal parts), the first sentence of the second paragraph would BEGIN with the words
   A. "Historically, much research..."
   B. "Other research has examined..."
   C. "Two primary types of..."
   D. "Inattentive ADHD is evidenced..."

9.____

10. When put in the correct order, the third sentence in the paragraph would END with the words
    A. "...an onset before 12 years of age."
    B. "...5% and 11% of the population."
    C. "...such as reading and mathematics."
    D. "...in multiple environments."

10.____

11. If the above paragraph was organized correctly, its ending words of the last sentence would be
    A. "...sustained focus, and being disorganized."
    B. "...an onset before 12 years of age."
    C. "...in the school environment."
    D. "...inattention and hyperactivity occur together."

11.____

Questions 12-15.

DIRECTIONS: Questions 12 through 15 are to be answered on the basis of the following passage.

Health care fraud imposes huge costs on society. In prosecutions of fraud, the DOJ employs the resources of its own criminal and civil divisions, as well as those of the U.S. Attorneys' Offices, HHS, and the FBI. The FBI estimates that health care fraud accounts for at least three and possibly up to ten percent of total health care expenditures, or somewhere between $82 billion and $272 billion each year. Providers are also careful to screen hires for excluded persons or entities lest they be subject to civil monetary penalties. Several government agencies are involved in fighting health care fraud. Individual states assist the HHS Office of the Inspector General ("OIG") and Centers for Medicare & Medicaid Services ("CMS") to initiate and pursue investigations of Medicare and Medicaid fraud. In addition, the OIG uses its permissive exclusion authority to exclude individuals and entities convicted of health care related crimes from federally funded health care services in order to induce providers to help track fraud through a voluntary disclosure program. $30 to $98 billion dollars of that (approximately 36%) is fraud against the public health programs Medicare and Medicaid. The Department of Justice ("DOJ") and the Department of Health and Human Services ("HHS") enforce federal health care fraud law and regulations.

12. When put together in a logical order, the second sentence of the paragraph would end with the words
   A. "...in fighting health care fraud."
   B. "...$272 billion each year."
   C. "...voluntary disclosure program."
   D. "...to civil monetary penalties."

13. In order to organize the paragraph correctly, the sentence that begins "In addition, the OIG..." should FOLLOW the sentence that begins with the words
   A. "$30 to $98 billion dollars of that..."
   B. "Health care fraud..."
   C. "Individual states assist..."
   D. "In prosecutions of fraud..."

14. The author wishes to split the paragraph into a smaller introductory paragraph followed by a slightly longer body paragraph. Which of the following sentences would be BEST to start the second paragraph?
   A. "$30 to $98 billion dollars of that (approximately 36%) is fraud against the public health care programs Medicare and Medicaid."
   B. "Several government agencies are involved in fighting health care fraud."
   C. "In prosecutions of fraud, the DOJ employs the resources of its own criminal and civil divisions, as well as those of the U.S. Attorneys' Offices, HHS, and the FBI."
   D. "Health care fraud imposes huge costs on society."

15. If put together correctly, the paragraph should end with the words 15.____
    A. "...Attorneys' Offices, HHS, and the FBI."
    B. "...huge costs on society."
    C. "...fighting health care fraud."
    D. "...of Medicare and Medicaid fraud."

Questions 16-19.

DIRECTIONS: Questions 16 through 19 are to be answered on the basis of the following passage.

President Abraham Lincoln advocated for granting amnesty to former Confederates to heal the country after the devastating war. Adams and his fellow Federalist Party members in Congress used the law to jail more than a dozen of his political rivals. In 1977, President Jimmy Carter lifted the restrictions on draft dodgers, granting them unconditional amnesty. The issue of amnesty again arose shortly after the U.S. Civil War (1861-1865). Some U.S. government officials, including Vice President Andrew Johnson, advocating placing severe punishments on the military and civilian leaders of the secessionist Confederate States of America. A century later, the controversial nature of the Vietnam War (1964-1975), combined with the compulsory draft for military service, compelled many young men of eligible age to violate the law to avoid the draft. When Thomas Jefferson, Adams' Vice President and opponent of the Alien and Sedition Acts, won the 1800 presidential election, he declared amnesty for those found to have violated the law. Other young men who were drafted deserted the army and refused to serve. In May 1865, when serving as president following Lincoln's assassination, Johnson issued the Proclamation of Amnesty and Reconstruction, which granted the rights of voting and holding office to most former Confederates. In 1974, President Gerald Ford granted amnesty to deserters and "draft dodgers" on the condition that they swear allegiance to the United States and engage in two years of community service. In 1798, President John Adams signed the Alien and Sedition Acts, a set of four laws that restricted criticism of the federal government.

16. When put in the correct order, the paragraph would begin with the following words. 16.____
    A. "Some U.S. government..."   B. "In May 1865, when..."
    C. "A century later, the..."   D. "In 1798, President..."

17. If put in logical order, what sentence number would the sentence that begins 17.____
    "President Abraham Lincoln..." be?
    A. One   B. Six   C. Five   D. Two

18. The author wants to split this paragraph into three separate paragraphs. The 18.____
    THIRD paragraph should begin with the words
    A. "The issue of amnesty again..."   B. "In 1798, President..."
    C. "In 1977, President Jimmy..."   D. "A century later, the..."

19. When organized in sequential order, the last sentence of the paragraph 19.____
    would end with the words
    A. "...of his political rivals."   B. "...after the devastating war."
    C. "...them unconditional amnesty."   D. "...of the federal government."

6 (#2)

Questions 20-22.

DIRECTIONS: Questions 20 through 22 are to be answered on the basis of the following passage.

Throughout history, militias have played an important role in national defense against foreign invaders or oppressors. In the original American colonies, state militias served to keep order and played an important role in the fight for independence from the British during the American Revolutionary War. Since that time, state-level militias have continued to exist in the United States alongside a national standing army, providing additional reserve defense and emergency assistance when needed. Some countries still rely almost entirely on public militias for civil defense. In Switzerland, for example, all able-bodied males must serve as part of the Swiss military or civilian service for several months starting when they turn 20 years old and remain reserve militia for years after. Similarly, in Israel, all non-Arab citizens over the age of 18 are required to serve in the Israel Defense Forces for at least two years; Israel is unique in that it requires military service from female citizens as well as males.

20. When put into the correct order, the paragraph should begin with the words 20.____
    A. "Throughout history, militias..."   B. "Similarly, in Israel..."
    C. "Some countries still rely..."   D. "Since that time, state-level..."

21. The fifth sentence of the paragraph should end with the words 21.____
    A. "...against foreign invaders or oppressors."
    B. "...militias for civil defense."
    C. "...reserve militia for years after."
    D. "...citizens as well as males."

22. The last sentence of the paragraph should end with the words 22.____
    A. "...militias for civil defense."
    B. "...citizens as well as males."
    C. "...against foreign invaders or oppressors."
    D. "...during the American Revolutionary War."

Questions 23-25.

DIRECTIONS: Questions 23 through 25 are to be answered on the basis of the following passage.

Medicines such as herbal and homeopathic remedies differ radically from those typically prescribed by mainstream physicians. These practices derive from different cultural traditions and scientific premises. As of 2012, the Memorial Sloan-Kettering Cancer Center offered hypnosis and tai chi, which is an ancient Chinese exercise, to help eases the pains associated with conventional cancer treatments. Some medical professionals staunchly dismiss a number of alternative techniques and theories as quackery. The concept of alternative medicine encompasses an extremely wide range of therapeutic modalities, from acupuncture to yoga. As of 2012, nearly 40 percent of Americans use some alternative medicines or therapies, according to the National Institutes of Health's National Center for Complementary and Alternative Medicine. Alternative approaches to health, fitness, disease prevention, and treatment are sometimes referred to as holistic health care or natural medicine. These names suggest some of the philosophical foundations shared by traditions such as homeopathy, naturopathy, traditional Chinese medicine and herbal medicine. A University of Pennsylvania study in 2010 found that more than 70 percent of U.S. cancer centers offered information on complementary therapies. Increasingly, health care providers are encouraging patients to combine alternative and conventional (or allopathic) treatments, a practice known as complementary or integrative medicine. In the contemporary United States, the phrase alternative medicine has come to mean virtually any healing or wellness practice not based within the conventional system of medical doctors, nurses, and hospitals. Some of these alternative treatments include acupuncture to alleviate pain and nausea and yoga to help reduce stress and manage pain. Yet taken as a whole, the alternative sector of the health field is enormously popular and rapidly growing. The Health Services Research Journal reported in 2011 that three out of four U.S. health care workers used complementary or alternative medicine practices themselves. Other studies have shown that more medical professionals are recommending that cancer patients seek alternative treatments to deal with the side effects of conventional treatments, such as chemotherapy, radiation, and surgery.

23. When put in the correct order, the first sentence should begin with the words   23.____
    A. "A University of Pennsylvania study…"
    B. "Other studies have shown that…"
    C. "Increasingly, health care providers…"
    D. "In the contemporary United States…"

24. If the author were to split the paragraph into two separate ones, the first   24.____
    sentence of the second paragraph should begin with the words
    A. "Alternative approaches to health…"
    B. "The concept of alternative medicine…"
    C. "As of 2012, nearly 40%..."
    D. "These names suggest some…"

25. When put into the correct logical sequence, the paragraph should end with   25.____
    the words
    A. "…Complementary and Alternative Medicine."
    B. "…system of medical doctors, nurses, and hospitals."
    C. "…associated with conventional cancer treatments."
    D. "…health care or natural medicine."

KEY (CORRECT ANSWERS)

1.	A	11.	C
2.	C	12.	B
3.	B	13.	C
4.	D	14.	B
5.	B	15.	A
6.	C	16.	D
7.	D	17.	B
8.	A	18.	D
9.	A	19.	C
10.	D	20.	A

21. C
22. B
23. D
24. A
25. C

PHILOSOPHY, PRINCIPLES, PRACTICES, AND TECHNICS
OF
SUPERVISION, ADMINISTRATION, MANAGEMENT, AND ORGANIZATION

TABLE OF CONTENTS

	Page
MEANING OF SUPERVISION	1
THE OLD AND THE NEW SUPERVISION	1
THE EIGHT (8) BASIC PRINCIPLES OF THE NEW SUPERVISION	1
I. Principle of Responsibility	1
II. Principle of Authority	2
III. Principle of Self-Growth	2
IV. Principle of Individual Worth	2
V. Principle of Creative Leadership	2
VI. Principle of Success and Failure	2
VII. Principle of Science	3
VIII. Principle of Cooperation	3
WHAT IS ADMINISTRATION?	3
I. Practices Commonly Classed as "Supervisory"	3
II. Practices Commonly Classed as "Administrative"	3
III. Practices Commonly Classed as Both "Supervisory" and "Administrative"	4
RESPONSIBILITIES OF THE SUPERVISOR	4
COMPETENCIES OF THE SUPERVISOR	4
THE PROFESSIONAL SUPERVISOR-EMPLOYEE RELATIONSHIP	4
MINI-TEXT IN SUPERVISION, ADMINISTRATION, MANAGEMENT, AND ORGANIZATION	5
I. Brief Highlights	5
A. Levels of Management	6
B. What the Supervisor Must Learn	6
C. A Definition of Supervision	6
D. Elements of the Team Concept	6
E. Principles of Organization	6
F. The Four Important Parts of Every Job	7
G. Principles of Delegation	7
H. Principles of Effective Communications	7
I. Principles of Work Improvement	7
J. Areas of Job Improvement	7
K. Seven Key Points in Making Improvements	8

	L.	Corrective Techniques for Job Improvement	8
	M.	A Planning Checklist	8
	N.	Five Characteristics of Good Directions	9
	O.	Types of Directions	9
	P.	Controls	9
	Q.	Orienting the New Employee	9
	R.	Checklist for Orienting New Employees	9
	S.	Principles of Learning	10
	T.	Causes of Poor Performance	10
	U.	Four Major Steps in On-the-Job Instructions	10
	V.	Employees Want Five Things	10
	W.	Some Don'ts in Regard to Praise	11
	X.	How to Gain Your Workers' Confidence	11
	Y.	Sources of Employee Problems	11
	Z.	The Supervisor's Key to Discipline	11
	AA.	Five Important Processes of Management	12
	BB.	When the Supervisor Fails to Plan	12
	CC.	Fourteen General Principles of Management	12
	DD.	Change	12
II.	Brief Topical Summaries		13
	A.	Who/What is the Supervisor?	13
	B.	The Sociology of Work	13
	C.	Principles and Practices of Supervision	14
	D.	Dynamic Leadership	14
	E.	Processes for Solving Problems	15
	F.	Training for Results	15
	G.	Health, Safety, and Accident Prevention	16
	H.	Equal Employment Opportunity	16
	I.	Improving Communications	16
	J.	Self-Development	17
	K.	Teaching and Training	17
		1. The Teaching Process	17
		a. Preparation	17
		b. Presentation	18
		c. Summary	18
		d. Application	18
		e. Evaluation	18
		2. Teaching Methods	18
		a. Lecture	18
		b. Discussion	18
		c. Demonstration	19
		d. Performance	19
		e. Which Method to Use	19

PHILOSOPHY, PRINCIPLES, PRACTICES, AND TECHNICS
OF
SUPERVISION, ADMINISTRATION, MANAGEMENT, AND ORGANIZATION

MEANING OF SUPERVISION

The extension of the democratic philosophy has been accompanied by an extension in the scope of supervision. Modern leaders and supervisors no longer think of supervision in the narrow sense of being confined chiefly to visiting employees, supplying materials, or rating the staff. They regard supervision as being intimately related to all the concerned agencies of society, they speak of the supervisor's function in terms of "growth," rather than the "improvement" of employees.

This modern concept of supervision may be defined as follows: Supervision is leadership and the development of leadership within groups which are cooperatively engaged in inspection, research, training, guidance, and evaluation.

THE OLD AND THE NEW SUPERVISION

TRADITIONAL
1. Inspection
2. Focused on the employee
3. Visitation
4. Random and haphazard
5. Imposed and authoritarian
6. One person usually

MODERN
1. Study and analysis
2. Focused on aims, materials, methods, supervisors, employees, environment
3. Demonstrations, intervisitation, workshops, directed reading, bulletins, etc.
4. Definitely organized and planned (scientific)
5. Cooperative and democratic
6. Many persons involved (creative)

THE EIGHT (8) BASIC PRINCIPLES OF THE NEW SUPERVISION

I. Principle of Responsibility
   Authority to act and responsibility for acting must be joined.
   A. If you give responsibility, give authority.
   B. Define employee duties clearly.
   C. Protect employees from criticism by others.
   D. Recognize the rights as well as obligations of employees.
   E. Achieve the aims of a democratic society insofar as it is possible within the area of your work.
   F. Establish a situation favorable to training and learning.
   G. Accept ultimate responsibility for everything done in your section, unit, office, division, department.
   H. Good administration and good supervision are inseparable.

II. Principle of Authority
The success of the supervisor is measured by the extent to which the power of authority is not used.
   A. Exercise simplicity and informality in supervision
   B. Use the simplest machinery of supervision
   C. If it is good for the organization as a whole, it is probably justified.
   D. Seldom be arbitrary or authoritative.
   E. Do not base your work on the power of position or of personality.
   F. Permit and encourage the free expression of opinions.

III. Principle of Self-Growth
The success of the supervisor is measured by the extent to which, and the speed with which, he is no longer needed.
   A. Base criticism on principles, not on specifics.
   B. Point out higher activities to employees.
   C. Train for self-thinking by employees to meet new situations.
   D. Stimulate initiative, self-reliance, and individual responsibility
   E. Concentrate on stimulating the growth of employees rather than on removing defects.

IV. Principle of Individual Worth
Respect for the individual is a paramount consideration in supervision.
   A. Be human and sympathetic in dealing with employees.
   B. Don't nag about things to be done.
   C. Recognize the individual differences among employees and seek opportunities to permit best expression of each personality.

V. Principle of Creative Leadership
The best supervision is that which is not apparent to the employee.
   A. Stimulate, don't drive employees to creative action.
   B. Emphasize doing good things.
   C. Encourage employees to do what they do best.
   D. Do not be too greatly concerned with details of subject or method.
   E. Do not be concerned exclusively with immediate problems and activities.
   F. Reveal higher activities and make them both desired and maximally possible.
   G. Determine procedures in the light of each situation but see that these are derived from a sound basic philosophy.
   H. Aid, inspire, and lead so as to liberate the creative spirit latent in all good employees.

VI. Principle of Success and Failure
There are no unsuccessful employees, only unsuccessful supervisors who have failed to give proper leadership.
   A. Adapt suggestions to the capacities, attitudes, and prejudices of employees.
   B. Be gradual, be progressive, be persistent.
   C. Help the employee find the general principle; have the employee apply his own problem to the general principle.
   D. Give adequate appreciation for good work and honest effort.
   E. Anticipate employee difficulties and help to prevent them.
   F. Encourage employees to do the desirable things they will do anyway.
   G. Judge your supervision by the results it secures.

VII. Principle of Science
Successful supervision is scientific, objective, and experimental. It is based on facts, not on prejudices.
- A. Be cumulative in results.
- B. Never divorce your suggestions from the goals of training.
- C. Don't be impatient of results.
- D. Keep all matters on a professional, not a personal, level.
- E. Do not be concerned exclusively with immediate problems and activities.
- F. Use objective means of determining achievement and rating where possible.

VIII. Principle of Cooperation
Supervision is a cooperative enterprise between supervisor and employee.
- A. Begin with conditions as they are.
- B. Ask opinions of all involved when formulating policies.
- C. Organization is as good as its weakest link.
- D. Let employees help to determine policies and department programs.
- E. Be approachable and accessible—physically and mentally.
- F. Develop pleasant social relationships.

WHAT IS ADMINISTRATION

Administration is concerned with providing the environment, the material facilities, and the operational procedures that will promote the maximum growth and development of supervisors and employees. (Organization is an aspect and a concomitant of administration.)

There is no sharp line of demarcation between supervision and administration; these functions are intimately interrelated and, often, overlapping. They are complementary activities.

I. Practices Commonly Classed as "Supervisory"
- A. Conducting employees' conferences
- B. Visiting sections, units, offices, divisions, departments
- C. Arranging for demonstrations
- D. Examining plans
- E. Suggesting professional reading
- F. Interpreting bulletins
- G. Recommending in-service training courses
- H. Encouraging experimentation
- I. Appraising employee morale
- J. Providing for intervisitation

II. Practices Commonly Classified as "Administrative"
- A. Management of the office
- B. Arrangement of schedules for extra duties
- C. Assignment of rooms or areas
- D. Distribution of supplies
- E. Keeping records and reports
- F. Care of audio-visual materials
- G. Keeping inventory records
- H. Checking record cards and books

I. Programming special activities
J. Checking on the attendance and punctuality of employees

III. Practices Commonly Classified as Both "Supervisory" and "Administrative"
   A. Program construction
   B. Testing or evaluating outcomes
   C. Personnel accounting
   D. Ordering instructional materials

RESPONSIBILITIES OF THE SUPERVISOR

A person employed in a supervisory capacity must constantly be able to improve his own efficiency and ability. He represent the employer to the employees and only continuous self-examination can make him a capable supervisor.

Leadership and training are the supervisor's responsibility. An efficient working unit is one in which the employees work with the supervisor. It is his job to bring out the best in his employees. He must always be relaxed, courteous, and calm in his association with his employees. Their feelings are important, and a harsh attitude does not develop the most efficient employees.

COMPETENCES OF THE SUPERVISOR

I. Complete knowledge of the duties and responsibilities of his position.
II. To be able to organize a job, plan ahead, and carry through.
III. To have self-confidence and initiative.
IV. To be able to handle the unexpected situation and make quick decisions.
V. To be able to properly train subordinates in the positions they are best suited for.
VI. To be able to keep good human relations among his subordinates.
VII. To be able to keep good human relations between his subordinates and himself and to earn their respect and trust.

THE PROFESSIONAL SUPERVISOR-EMPLOYEE RELATIONSHIP

There are two kinds of efficiency: one kind is only apparent and is produced in organizations through the exercise of mere discipline; this is but a simulation of the second, or true, efficiency which springs from spontaneous cooperation. If you are a manager, no matter how great or small your responsibility, it is your job, in the final analysis, to create and develop this involuntary cooperation among the people whom you supervise. For, no matter how powerful a combination of money, machines, and materials a company may have, this is a dead and sterile thing without a team of willing, thinking, and articulate people to guide it.

The following 21 points are presented as indicative of the exemplary basic relationship that should exist between supervisor and employee:

1. Each person wants to be liked and respected by his fellow employee and wants to be treated with consideration and respect by his superior.
2. The most competent employee will make an error. However, in a unit where good relations exist between the supervisor and his employees, tenseness and fear do not exist. Thus, errors are not hidden or covered up, and the efficiency of a unit is not impaired.

3. Subordinates resent rules, regulations, or orders that are unreasonable or unexplained.
4. Subordinates are quick to resent unfairness, harshness, injustices, and favoritism.
5. An employee will accept responsibility if he knows that he will be complimented for a job well done, and not too harshly chastised for failure; that his supervisor will check the cause of the failure, and, if it was the supervisor's fault, he will assume the blame therefore. If it was the employee's fault, his supervisor will explain the correct method or means of handling the responsibility.
6. An employee wants to receive credit for a suggestion he has made, that is used. If a suggestion cannot be used, the employee is entitled to an explanation. The supervisor should not say "no" and close the subject.
7. Fear and worry slow up a worker's ability. Poor working environment can impair his physical and mental health. A good supervisor avoids forceful methods, threats, and arguments to get a job done.
8. A forceful supervisor is able to train his employees individually and as a team, and is able to motivate them in the proper channels.
9. A mature supervisor is able to properly evaluate his subordinates and to keep them happy and satisfied.
10. A sensitive supervisor will never patronize his subordinates.
11. A worthy supervisor will respect his employees' confidences.
12. Definite and clear-cut responsibilities should be assigned to each executive.
13. Responsibility should always be coupled with corresponding authority.
14. No change should be made in the scope or responsibilities of a position without a definite understanding to that effect on the part of all persons concerned.
15. No executive or employee, occupying a single position in the organization, should be subject to definite orders from more than one source.
16. Orders should never be given to subordinates over the head of a responsible executive. Rather than do this, the officer in question should be supplanted.
17. Criticisms of subordinates should, whoever possible, be made privately, and in no case should a subordinate be criticized in the presence of executives or employees of equal or lower rank.
18. No dispute or difference between executives or employees as to authority or responsibilities should be considered too trivial for prompt and careful adjudication.
19. Promotions, wage changes, and disciplinary action should always be approved by the executive immediately superior to the one directly responsible.
20. No executive or employee should ever be required, or expected, to be at the same time an assistant to, and critic of, another.
21. Any executive whose work is subject to regular inspection should, wherever practicable, be given the assistance and facilities necessary to enable him to maintain an independent check of the quality of his work.

MINI-TEXT IN SUPERVISION, ADMINISTRATION, MANAGEMENT, AND ORGANIZATION

I. Brief Highlights

   Listed concisely and sequentially are major headings and important data in the field for quick recall and review.

A. Levels of Management
   Any organization of some size has several levels of management. In terms of a ladder, the levels are:

   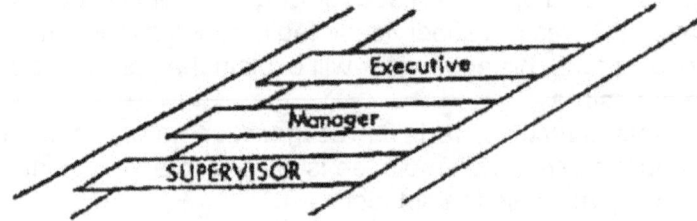

   The first level is very important because it is the beginning point of management leadership.

B. What the Supervisor Must Learn
   A supervisor must learn to:
   1. Deal with people and their differences
   2. Get the job done through people
   3. Recognize the problems when they exist
   4. Overcome obstacles to good performance
   5. Evaluate the performance of people
   6. Check his own performance in terms of accomplishment

C. A Definition of Supervisor
   The term supervisor means any individual having authority, in the interests of the employer, to hire, transfer, suspend, lay-off, recall, promote, discharge, assign, reward, or discipline other employees or responsibility to direct them, or to adjust their grievances, or effectively to recommend such action, if, in connection with the foregoing, exercise of such authority is not of a merely routine or clerical nature but requires the use of independent judgment.

D. Elements of the Team Concept
   What is involved in teamwork? The component parts are:
   1. Members
   2. A leader
   3. Goals
   4. Plans
   5. Cooperation
   6. Spirit

E. Principles of Organization
   1. A team member must know what his job is.
   2. Be sure that the nature and scope of a job are understood.
   3. Authority and responsibility should be carefully spelled out.
   4. A supervisor should be permitted to make the maximum number of decisions affecting his employees.
   5. Employees should report to only one supervisor.
   6. A supervisor should direct only as many employees as he can handle effectively.
   7. An organization plan should be flexible.

8. Inspection and performance of work should be separate.
9. Organizational problems should receive immediate attention.
10. Assign work in line with ability and experience.

F. The Four Important Parts of Every Job
1. Inherent in every job is the *accountability* for results.
2. A second set of factors in every job is *responsibilities*.
3. Along with duties and responsibilities one must have the *authority* to act within certain limits without obtaining permission to proceed.
4. No job exists in a vacuum. The supervisor is surrounded by key *relationships*.

G. Principles of Delegation
Where work is delegated for the first time, the supervisor should think in terms of these questions:
1. Who is best qualified to do this?
2. Can an employee improve his abilities by doing this?
3. How long should an employee spend on this?
4. Are there any special problems for which he will need guidance?
5. How broad a delegation can I make?

H. Principles of Effective Communications
1. Determine the media.
2. To whom directed?
3. Identification and source authority.
4. Is communication understood?

I. Principles of Work Improvement
1. Most people usually do only the work which is assigned to them.
2. Workers are likely to fit assigned work into the time available to perform it.
3. A good workload usually stimulates output.
4. People usually do their best work when they know that results will be reviewed or inspected.
5. Employees usually feel that someone else is responsible for conditions of work, workplace layout, job methods, type of tools/equipment, and other such factors.
6. Employees are usually defensive about their job security.
7. Employees have natural resistance to change.
8. Employees can support or destroy a supervisor.
9. A supervisor usually earns the respect of his people through his personal example of diligence and efficiency.

J. Areas of Job Improvement
The areas of job improvement are quite numerous, but the most common ones which a supervisor can identify and utilize are:
1. Departmental layout
2. Flow of work
3. Workplace layout
4. Utilization of manpower
5. Work methods
6. Materials handling

　　　　7.　Utilization
　　　　8.　Motion economy

　K.　Seven Key Points in Making Improvements
　　　　1.　Select the job to be improved
　　　　2.　Study how it is being done now
　　　　3.　Question the present method
　　　　4.　Determine actions to be taken
　　　　5.　Chart proposed method
　　　　6.　Get approval and apply
　　　　7.　Solicit worker participation

　l.　Corrective Techniques of Job Improvement
　　　Specific Problems
　　　　1.　Size of workload
　　　　2.　Inability to meet schedules
　　　　3.　Strain and fatigue
　　　　4.　Improper use of men and skills
　　　　5.　Waste, poor quality, unsafe conditions
　　　　6.　Bottleneck conditions that hinder output
　　　　7.　Poor utilization of equipment and machine
　　　　8.　Efficiency and productivity of labor

　　　General Improvement
　　　　1.　Departmental layout
　　　　2.　Flow of work
　　　　3.　Work plan layout
　　　　4.　Utilization of manpower
　　　　5.　Work methods
　　　　6.　Materials handling
　　　　7.　Utilization of equipment
　　　　8.　Motion economy

　　　Corrective Techniques
　　　　1.　Study with scale model
　　　　2.　Flow chart study
　　　　3.　Motion analysis
　　　　4.　Comparison of units produced to standard allowance
　　　　5.　Methods analysis
　　　　6.　Flow chart and equipment study
　　　　7.　Down time vs. running time
　　　　8.　Motion analysis

　M.　A Planning Checklist
　　　　1.　Objectives
　　　　2.　Controls
　　　　3.　Delegations
　　　　4.　Communications
　　　　5.	Resources
　　　　6.	Manpower

7. Equipment
8. Supplies and materials
9. Utilization of time
10. Safety
11. Money
12. Work
13. Timing of improvements

N. Five Characteristics of Good Directions
In order to get results, directions must be:
1. Possible of accomplishment
2. Agreeable with worker interests
3. Related to mission
4. Planned and complete
5. Unmistakably clear

O. Types of Directions
1. Demands or direct orders
2. Requests
3. Suggestion or implication
4. volunteering

P. Controls
A typical listing of the overall areas in which the supervisor should establish controls might be:
1. Manpower
2. Materials
3. Quality of work
4. Quantity of work
5. Time
6. Space
7. Money
8. Methods

Q. Orienting the New Employee
1. Prepare for him
2. Welcome the new employee
3. Orientation for the job
4. Follow-up

R. Checklist for Orienting New Employees

		Yes	No
1.	Do you appreciate the feelings of new employees when they first report for work?	___	___
2.	Are you aware of the fact that the new employee must make a big adjustment to his job?	___	___
3.	Have you given him good reasons for liking the job and the organization?	___	___
4.	Have you prepared for his first day on the job?	___	___
5.	Did you welcome him cordially and make him feel needed?	___	___

	Yes	No

6. Did you establish rapport with him so that he feels free to talk and discuss matters with you? ___ ___
7. Did you explain his job to him and his relationship to you? ___ ___
8. Does he know that his work will be evaluated periodically on a basis that is fair and objective? ___ ___
9. Did you introduce him to his fellow workers in such a way that they are likely to accept him? ___ ___
10. Does he know what employee benefits he will receive? ___ ___
11. Does he understand the importance of being on the job and what to do if he must leave his duty station? ___ ___
12. Has he been impressed with the importance of accident prevention and safe practice? ___ ___
13. Does he generally know his way around the department? ___ ___
14. Is he under the guidance of a sponsor who will teach the right way of doing things? ___ ___
15. Do you plan to follow-up so that he will continue to adjust successfully to his job? ___ ___

S. Principles of Learning
   1. Motivation
   2. Demonstration or explanation
   3. Practice

T. Causes of Poor Performance
   1. Improper training for job
   2. Wrong tools
   3. Inadequate directions
   4. Lack of supervisory follow-up
   5. Poor communications
   6. Lack of standards of performance
   7. Wrong work habits
   8. Low morale
   9. Other

U. Four Major Steps in On-The-Job Instruction
   1. Prepare the worker
   2. Present the operation
   3. Tryout performance
   4. Follow-up

V. Employees Want Five Things
   1. Security
   2. Opportunity
   3. Recognition
   4. Inclusion
   5. Expression

W. Some Don'ts in Regard to Praise
1. Don't praise a person for something he hasn't done.
2. Don't praise a person unless you can be sincere.
3. Don't be sparing in praise just because your superior withholds it from you.
4. Don't let too much time elapse between good performance and recognition of it

X. How to Gain Your Workers' Confidence
Methods of developing confidence include such things as:
1. Knowing the interests, habits, hobbies of employees
2. Admitting your own inadequacies
3. Sharing and telling of confidence in others
4. Supporting people when they are in trouble
5. Delegating matters that can be well handled
6. Being frank and straightforward about problems and working conditions
7. Encouraging others to bring their problems to you
8. Taking action on problems which impede worker progress

Y. Sources of Employee Problems
On-the-job causes might be such things as:
1. A feeling that favoritism is exercised in assignments
2. Assignment of overtime
3. An undue amount of supervision
4. Changing methods or systems
5. Stealing of ideas or trade secrets
6. Lack of interest in job
7. Threat of reduction in force
8. Ignorance or lack of communications
9. Poor equipment
10. Lack of knowing how supervisor feels toward employee
11. Shift assignments

Off-the-job problems might have to do with:
1. Health
2. Finances
3. Housing
4. Family

Z. The Supervisor's Key to Discipline
There are several key points about discipline which the supervisor should keep in mind:
1. Job discipline is one of the disciplines of life and is directed by the supervisor.
2. It is more important to correct an employee fault than to fix blame for it.
3. Employee performance is affected by problems both on the job and off.
4. Sudden or abrupt changes in behavior can be indications of important employee problems.
5. Problems should be dealt with as soon as possible after they are identified.
6. The attitude of the supervisor may have more to do with solving problems than the techniques of problem solving.
7. Correction of employee behavior should be resorted to only after the supervisor is sure that training or counseling will not be helpful.

8. Be sure to document your disciplinary actions.
9. Make sure that you are disciplining on the basis of facts rather than personal feelings.
10. Take each disciplinary step in order, being careful not to make snap judgments, or decisions based on impatience.

AA. Five Important Processes of Management
1. Planning
2. Organizing
3. Scheduling
4. Controlling
5. Motivating

BB. When the Supervisor Fails to Plan
1. Supervisor creates impression of not knowing his job
2. May lead to excessive overtime
3. Job runs itself—supervisor lacks control
4. Deadlines and appointments missed
5. Parts of the work go undone
6. Work interrupted by emergencies
7. Sets a bad example
8. Uneven workload creates peaks and valleys
9. Too much time on minor details at expense of more important tasks

CC. Fourteen General Principles of Management
1. Division of work
2. Authority and responsibility
3. Discipline
4. Unity of command
5. Unity of direction
6. Subordination of individual interest to general interest
7. Remuneration of personnel
8. Centralization
9. Scalar chain
10. Order
11. Equity
12. Stability of tenure of personnel
13. Initiative
14. Esprit de corps

DD. Change

Bringing about change is perhaps attempted more often, and yet less well understood, than anything else the supervisor does. How do people generally react to change? (People tend to resist change that is imposed upon them by other individuals or circumstances.

Change is characteristic of every situation. It is a part of every real endeavor where the efforts of people are concerned.

1. Why do people resist change?
   People may resist change because of:
   a. Fear of the unknown
   b. Implied criticism
   c. Unpleasant experiences in the past
   d. Fear of loss of status
   e. Threat to the ego
   f. Fear of loss of economic stability

2. How can we best overcome the resistance to change?
   In initiating change, take these steps:
   a. Get ready to sell
   b. Identify sources of help
   c. Anticipate objections
   d. Sell benefits
   e. Listen in depth
   f. Follow up

II. Brief Topical Summaries

   A. Who/What is the Supervisor?
      1. The supervisor is often called the "highest level employee and the lowest level manager."
      2. A supervisor is a member of both management and the work group. He acts as a bridge between the two.
      3. Most problems in supervision are in the area of human relations, or people problems.
      4. Employees expect: Respect, opportunity to learn and to advance, and a sense of belonging, and so forth.
      5. Supervisors are responsible for directing people and organizing work. Planning is of paramount importance.
      6. A position description is a set of duties and responsibilities inherent to a given position.
      7. It is important to keep the position description up-to-date and to provide each employee with his own copy.

   B. The Sociology of Work
      1. People are alike in many ways; however, each individual is unique.
      2. The supervisor is challenged in getting to know employee differences. Acquiring skills in evaluating individuals is an asset.
      3. Maintaining meaningful working relationships in the organization is of great importance.
      4. The supervisor has an obligation to help individuals to develop to their fullest potential.
      5. Job rotation on a planned basis helps to build versatility and to maintain interest and enthusiasm in work groups.
      6. Cross training (job rotation) provides backup skills.

7. The supervisor can help reduce tension by maintaining a sense of humor, providing guidance to employees, and by making reasonable and timely decisions. Employees respond favorably to working under reasonably predictable circumstances.
8. Change is characteristic of all managerial behavior. The supervisor must adjust to changes in procedures, new methods, technological changes, and to a number of new and sometimes challenging situations.
9. To overcome the natural tendency for people to resist change, the supervisor should become more skillful in initiating change.

C. Principles and Practices of Supervision
1. Employees should be required to answer to only one superior.
2. A supervisor can effectively direct only a limited number of employees, depending upon the complexity, variety, and proximity of the jobs involved.
3. The organizational chart presents the organization in graphic form. It reflects lines of authority and responsibility as well as interrelationships of units within the organization.
4. Distribution of work can be improved through an analysis using the "Work Distribution Chart."
5. The "Work Distribution Chart" reflects the division of work within a unit in understandable form.
6. When related tasks are given to an employee, he has a better chance of increasing his skills through training.
7. The individual who is given the responsibility for tasks must also be given the appropriate authority to insure adequate results.
8. The supervisor should delegate repetitive, routine work. Preparation of recurring reports, maintaining leave and attendance records are some examples.
9. Good discipline is essential to good task performance. Discipline is reflected in the actions of employees on the job in the absence of supervision.
10. Disciplinary action may have to be taken when the positive aspects of discipline have failed. Reprimand, warning, and suspension are examples of disciplinary action.
11. If a situation calls for a reprimand, be sure it is deserved and remember it is to be done in private.

D. Dynamic Leadership
1. A style is a personal method or manner of exerting influence.
2. Authoritarian leaders often see themselves as the source of power and authority.
3. The democratic leader often perceives the group as the source of authority and power.
4. Supervisors tend to do better when using the pattern of leadership that is most natural for them.
5. Social scientists suggest that the effective supervisor use the leadership style that best fits the problem or circumstances involved.
6. All four styles—telling, selling, consulting, joining—have their place. Using one does not preclude using the other at another time.

7. The theory X point of view assumes that the average person dislikes work, will avoid it whenever possible, and must be coerced to achieve organizational objectives.
8. The theory Y point of view assumes that the average person considers work to be a natural as play, and, when the individual is committed, he requires little supervision or direction to accomplish desired objectives.
9. The leader's basic assumptions concerning human behavior and human nature affect his actions, decisions, and other managerial practices.
10. Dissatisfaction among employees is often present, but difficult to isolate. The supervisor should seek to weaken dissatisfaction by keeping promises, being sincere and considerate, keeping employees informed, and so forth.
11. Constructive suggestions should be encouraged during the natural progress of the work.

E. Processes for Solving Problems
1. People find their daily tasks more meaningful and satisfying when they can improve them.
2. The causes of problems, or the key factors, are often hidden in the background. Ability to solve problems often involves the ability to isolate them from their backgrounds. There is some substance to the cliché that some persons "can't see the forest for the trees."
3. New procedures are often developed from old ones. Problems should be broken down into manageable parts. New ideas can be adapted from old one.
4. People think differently in problem-solving situations. Using a logical, patterned approach is often useful. One approach found to be useful includes these steps:
    a. Define the problem
    b. Establish objectives
    c. Get the facts
    d. Weigh and decide
    e. Take action
    f. Evaluate action

F. Training for Results
1. Participants respond best when they feel training is important to them.
2. The supervisor has responsibility for the training and development of those who report to him.
3. When training is delegated to others, great care must be exercised to insure the trainer has knowledge, aptitude, and interest for his work as a trainer.
4. Training (learning) of some type goes on continually. The most successful supervisor makes certain the learning contributes in a productive manner to operational goals.
5. New employees are particularly susceptible to training. Older employees facing new job situations require specific training, as well as having need for development and growth opportunities.
6. Training needs require continuous monitoring.
7. The training officer of an agency is a professional with a responsibility to assist supervisors in solving training problems.

8. Many of the self-development steps important to the supervisor's own growth are equally important to the development of peers and subordinates. Knowledge of these is important when the supervisor consults with others on development and growth opportunities.

G. Health, Safety, and Accident Prevention
1. Management-minded supervisors take appropriate measures to assist employees in maintaining health and in assuring safe practices in the work environment.
2. Effective safety training and practices help to avoid injury and accidents.
3. Safety should be a management goal. All infractions of safety which are observed should be corrected without exception.
4. Employees' safety attitude, training and instruction, provision of safe tools and equipment, supervision, and leadership are considered highly important factors which contribute to safety and which can be influenced directly by supervisors.
5. When accidents do occur, they should be investigated promptly for very important reasons, including the fact that information which is gained can be used to prevent accidents in the future.

H. Equal Employment Opportunity
1. The supervisor should endeavor to treat all employees fairly, without regard to religion, race, sex, or national origin.
2. Groups tend to reflect the attitude of the leader. Prejudice can be detected even in very subtle form. Supervisors must strive to create a feeling of mutual respect and confidence in every employee.
3. Complete utilization of all human resources is a national goal. Equitable consideration should be accorded women in the work force, minority-group members, the physically and mentally handicapped, and the older employee. The important question is: "Who can do the job?"
4. Training opportunities, recognition for performance, overtime assignments, promotional opportunities, and all other personnel actions are to be handled on an equitable basis.

I. Improving Communications
1. Communications is achieving understanding between the sender and the receiver of a message. It also means sharing information—the creation of understanding.
2. Communication is basic to all human activity. Words are means of conveying meanings; however, real meanings are in people.
3. There are very practical differences in the effectiveness of one-way, impersonal, and two-way communications. Words spoken face-to-face are better understood. Telephone conversations are effective, but lack the rapport of person-to-person exchanges. The whole person communicates.
4. Cooperation and communication in an organization go hand in hand. When there is a mutual respect between people, spelling out rules and procedures for communicating is unnecessary.
5. There are several barriers to effective communications. These include failure to listen with respect and understanding, lack of skill in feedback, and misinterpreting the meanings of words used by the speaker. It is also common

practice to listen to what we want to hear, and tune out things we do not want to hear.
6. Communication is management's chief problem. The supervisor should accept the challenge to communicate more effectively and to improve interagency and intra-agency communications.
7. The supervisor may often plan for and conduct meetings. The planning phase is critical and may determine the success or the failure of a meeting.
8. Speaking before groups usually requires extra effort. Stage fright may never disappear completely, but it can be controlled.

J. Self-Development
1. Every employee is responsible for his own self-development.
2. Toastmaster and toastmistress clubs offer opportunities to improve skills in oral communications.
3. Planning for one's own self-development is of vital importance. Supervisors know their own strengths and limitations better than anyone else.
4. Many opportunities are open to aid the supervisor in his developmental efforts, including job assignments; training opportunities, both governmental and non-governmental—to include universities and professional conferences and seminars.
5. Programmed instruction offers a means of studying at one's own rate.
6. Where difficulties may arise from a supervisor's being away from his work for training, he may participate in televised home study or correspondence courses to meet his self-development needs.

K. Teaching and Training
1. The Teaching Process
Teaching is encouraging and guiding the learning activities of students toward established goals. In most cases this process consists of five steps: preparation, presentation, summarization, evaluation, and application.

   a. Preparation
   Preparation is two-fold in nature; that of the supervisor and the employee. Preparation by the supervisor is absolutely essential to success. He must know what, when, where, how, and whom he will teach. Some of the factors that should be considered are:
   1) The objectives
   2) The materials needed
   3) The methods to be used
   4) Employee participation
   5) Employee interest
   6) Training aids
   7) Evaluation
   8) Summarization

   Employee preparation consists in preparing the employee to receive the material. Probably the most important single factor in the preparation of the employee is arousing and maintaining his interest. He must know the objectives of the training, why he is there, how the material can be used, and its importance to him.

b. Presentation
In presentation, have a carefully designed plan and follow it. The plan should be accurate and complete, yet flexible enough to meet situations as they arise. The method of presentation will be determined by the particular situation and objectives.

c. Summary
A summary should be made at the end of every training unit and program. In addition, there may be internal summaries depending on the nature of the material being taught. The important thing is that the trainee must always be able to understand how each part of the new material relates to the whole.

d. Application
The supervisor must arrange work so the employee will be given a chance to apply new knowledge or skills while the material is still clear in his mind and interest is high. The trainee does not really know whether he has learned the material until he has been given a chance to apply it. If the material is not applied, it loses most of its value.

e. Evaluation
The purpose of all training is to promote learning. To determine whether the training has been a success or failure, the supervisor must evaluate this learning.
In the broadest sense, evaluation includes all the devices, methods, skills, and techniques used by the supervisor to keep himself and the employees informed as to their progress toward the objectives they are pursuing. The extent to which the employee has mastered the knowledge, skills, and abilities, or changed his attitudes, as determined by the program objectives, is the extent to which instruction has succeeded or failed.
Evaluation should not be confined to the end of the lesson, day, or program but should be used continuously. We shall note later the way this relates to the rest of the teaching process.

2. Teaching Methods
A teaching method is a pattern of identifiable student and instructor activity used in presenting training material.
All supervisors are faced with the problem of deciding which method should be used at a given time.

a. Lecture
The lecture is direct oral presentation of material by the supervisor. The present trend is to place less emphasis on the trainer's activity and more on that of the trainee.

b. Discussion
Teaching by discussion or conference involves using questions and other techniques to arouse interest and focus attention upon certain areas, and by doing so creating a learning situation. This can be one of the most

valuable methods because it gives the employees an opportunity to express their ideas and pool their knowledge.

    c. Demonstration
The demonstration is used to teach how something works or how to do something. It can be used to show a principle or what the results of a series of actions will be. A well-staged demonstration is particularly effective because it shows proper methods of performance in a realistic manner.

    d. Performance
Performance is one of the most fundamental of all learning techniques or teaching methods. The trainee may be able to tell how a specific operation should be performed but he cannot be sure he knows how to perform the operation until he has done so.
As with all methods, there are certain advantages and disadvantages to each method.

    e. Which Method to Use
Moreover, there are other methods and techniques of teaching. It is difficult to use any method without other methods entering into it. In any learning situation, a combination of methods is usually more effective than any one method alone.

Finally, evaluation must be integrated into the other aspects of the teaching-learning process.

It must be used in the motivation of the trainees; it must be used to assist in developing understanding during the training; and it must be related to employee application of the results of training.

This is distinctly the role of the supervisor.

AN HISTORIC LOOK AT REAL PROPERTY TAX ASSESSMENTS IN NEW YORK

CONTENTS

	Page
How the Property Tax Bill is Determined	1
Total Tax Levies	2
Assessed Value	2
Equalization Rates	3
Property Appraisal	3
Equalizing to Full Value	4
Importance of Accurate Equalization Rates	6
Property Subject to Tax	6
Full Value Assessment	7
Computer-Assisted Assessments	9
Assessors	10
Taxpayer Complaint and Appeal Provisions	11
Some Implications for Assessing Units	12
County and State Services for Local Assessors	13
County Services	13
State Services	14
The Gap Between Law and Practice	14
Conclusion	15

AN HISTORIC LOOK AT
REAL PROPERTY TAX ASSESSMENTS IN NEW YORK

The property tax bill—its amount and the fairness with which it is shared—has been a public issue for apparently as long as we have had such a tax. Its history in New York goes back to early colonial times.

A combination of events in the late 70s has pushed the issue forward again as an important public question that is likely to be debated for at least the next few years. Among the events are recent New York court decisions that appear to require a major overhaul of property assessment practices and may substantially alter the distribution of property taxes among taxpayers.

The real property tax remains the most important and continuing source of revenues raised by local governments. It has come to be exceeded in New York by the totals of state and federal aid received by these local governments. Federal and state taxes, which do not include the property tax, have become several times larger than local collections. The property tax thus plays a much less important part in the total tax picture—federal, state, and local—than it did earlier in the century. Real property tax collections in New York State have long been rising, however, and still exceed those of either the state personal income tax or state and local sales taxes.[1]

A thorough study of why property taxes have increased is beyond the scope of this discussion, but a few reasons may be mentioned. Local governmental expenditures have expanded even more than revenues from these taxes. Wages, salaries, and fringe benefits of employees, and the prices of materials and supplies have increased. Payments to aid the needy and sick have moved up as the cost of living and of medical care have risen. The introduction of new functions and the expansion of existing ones in response to public demand have added to local tax requirements. These changes have taken place against an economic background of growing incomes for most individuals and families and of rising market values for most real estate.

As property taxes have increased and property values have risen, issues relating to assessment or valuation of property for tax purposes have become more acute. Assessment changes tend to lag behind changes in the market. All properties or types of property have not shared in rising market values to the same degree. As a result, assessed values, which probably never have reflected real values accurately in most communities, have become more and more remotely related to current conditions. Even if properties once were assessed with reasonable equity in relation to one another, a long lag in adjusting assessments to changing values usually produces substantial inequities among property taxpayers.

HOW THE PROPERTY TAX BILL IS DETERMINED

Three factors influence the amount of property taxes that a property owner pays. They are:
1. The total amount of taxes levied by local authorities.
2. The assessed value placed on the property as compared with all other taxable properties in a town (or other assessing district).
3. The equalization rates fixed by the state and the county.

---

[1] For 1975, revenues from the property tax were $6.7 billion; from income tax, $5.4 billion; and from sales tax, $3.5 billion. In 2017 they were, respectively: $2.4 billion; $51.5 billion; and from sales tax plus excise and user taxes, $15.7 billion.

Total Tax Levies

Three "layers" of local government cover New York State and are supported in part by the property tax. In addition, other local governments may be supported, depending upon where the property is located.

The state outside of New York City is divided into 57 counties. Each county is divided into towns, or towns and cities. The state is also divided into school districts. Property is therefore located in (1) a county, (2) a town or city, and (3) a school district.

One or more incorporated villages may be in a town. Special taxing or improvement districts also are laid out in many towns for fire protection, water supply, street lighting, and the like. Property in villages or districts helps to support the services provided.

Generally, property taxes are included in budgets that the local governments prepare. The amount of tax is usually determined by the difference between estimated expenditures for the coming year and estimated receipts from sources other than the property tax.

Passing judgment upon budgets and levying property taxes usually are the responsibility of local governing bodies, with the important qualification that they must abide by the requirements of state laws and the State Constitution. The more important governing bodies in rural areas are the town board, the county board (variously named county legislature board of supervisors, or board of representatives), the school board and annual school district meeting, and the village board of trustees.

These governing bodies, not the assessors, determine the total amount of property taxes needed.

Assessed Value

The work of the assessors is essentially concerned with dividing among individual property owners the total amounts of taxes that are levied by other authorities. The assessors do this by placing a value upon each property in their assessing district (in rural areas, principally the town).

Let us use a greatly simplified example. Suppose a town needs $300 of property taxes to help meet expenses for the coming year. There are three properties in the town. The assessor has assessed or valued each one at $10,000. The total assessed value is then $30,000. The rate required to yield the $300 is $10 per $1,000 of assessed value or 10 mills per dollar ($300 divided by $30,000). A $10 per $1,000 tax rate on property assessed at $10,000 yields $100. The $300 tax levy for town purposes is divided equally among the three properties because each is assessed at the same figure.

If one property were assessed at $15,000, another at $5,000, and the third at $10,000 the total assessed value would be the same, and so would the tax rate, but the taxes payable on the first property would be $150; on the second, $50; and on the third, $100. The taxes have been divided differently by changing the relationship between the assessed value on two properties as compared with the total assessed value.

We may, therefore, conclude that once the total amount of the town tax levy is determined the share of the tax that is payable on a piece of property depends on the assessed value placed on that property compared with the total valuation in the town.

Note that the tax payable does not depend on the assessed value of the property alone, but also upon the total valuation in the town. The assessed value on a piece of property may be changed without changing the amount of tax if the total assessed value in the town is changed to the same degree. To illustrate, let us return to the example above where the three properties in a town are assessed at $10,000 each. Suppose the assessor doubles the $10,000 assessment on one of the properties and changes the assessment on the others so that the total assessed valuation in the town is also doubled. The total value is then $60,000. The tax rate required to yield $300 is then cut in half to $5 per $1,000 of assessed value ($300 divided by $60,000). A $5 tax rate on the new assessment of $20,000 yields the same tax as before, or $100.

Often this important fact is not understood. The assessor of a town may attempt to raise the general level of assessments in order to bring them more nearly into line with realistic levels of value. Protests often follow, partly because of the apparently widespread belief that raising the assessed value on a property necessarily involves increased taxes.

Increased taxes on a property result only if the total levy is increased or if the assessed value of the property is aided by a greater percentage than the total valuation. Assume that the assessed values of $10,000 each for the three properties in the example are changed to $30,000, $20,000, and $10,000. The total assessed value has been doubled, from $30,000 to $60,000. The tax rate needed to raise $300 has been halved from $10 to $5 per $1,000 of assessed value. The original tax of $100 payable on each property has been changed to $150 for the first, $100 for the second, and $50 for the third. Taxes against the first property have increased because its assessed value was tripled while the total was doubled. Taxes payable on the second property remain unchanged because its assessed value was increased at the same rate as the total assessed value. Taxes due on the third property are reduced because its assessed value was not changed while the total assessed value for the town was doubled.

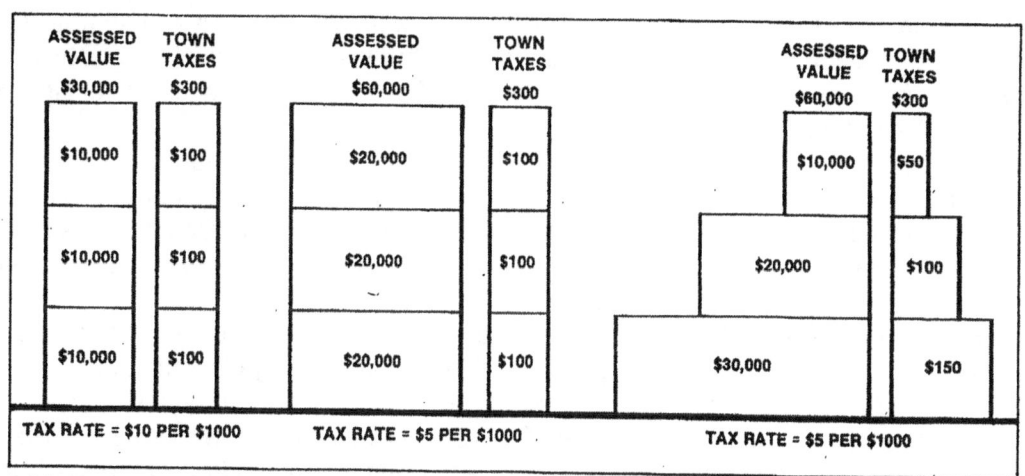

Relative assessments determine the share of the total property tax bill each individual pays.
The assessor's work essentially is to divide tax levies among taxpayers. Increased assessments do not necessarily mean increased taxes.

Equalization Rates

The Real Property Tax Law of New York (Section 306) requires that property be assessed at its full value. A common concept of full value in court decisions is the price at which a property would change hands under ordinary circumstances between a buyer who is willing but not compelled to buy and a seller who is willing but not compelled to sell. Full value thus is market value. Such a definition of full value cannot apply in all cases such as those involving highly specialized industrial properties which do not ordinarily change hands in the market. It is, however, applicable for more common types of property for which there is a market.

Property Appraisal. Placing a value on a property ultimately involves a subjective judgment by the appraiser. Well-established procedures are available, however, to make this decision as objective as possible. The three generally accepted methods of appraisal include not only the market approach, but also the income approach, but also the income approach and the cost approach.[2]

In the market approach, value is estimated by comparing the property with similar properties that have been sold recently (known by appraisers as "comparable sales"). The market approach approximates a value based on the amount a willing buyer would pay and a willing seller would take, neither being under undue pressure ("arm's-length sale"). Adjustments must be made for important differences between the property being appraised and the "comparable sales." This approach is useful and generally accurate when the market is active enough to make meaningful comparisons, and properties are fairly similar in nature, such as single family residences. A major limitation is the availability of comparable sales.

The income approach estimates values by treating the income earned or rental value of a property as a return on its capital value. Several methods are used to estimate property values through income capitalization. The reliability of this approach depends on the accuracy of income and rent as an indication of value and the extent to which the capitalization process actually exists in the market place. The value of a dairy farm, for example, may be estimated partly by the number of cows it will carry, and the income thereby yielded.

The third method of appraisal is the cost approach. The value of land must be estimated separately, using either the market or income approach. The replacement cost for new structures is estimated and then depreciated for loss in value over time. The depreciated value of buildings and structures is then added to the value of the land to provide an estimate for the parcel. The cost approach has many serious limitations, but is often used when adequate sales and income data are unavailable, such as for a section of a railroad, a power line facility, or a steel rolling mill of a complex corporation.

In actual practice, a careful appraiser or assessor may use a combination of these three approaches when the information is available. Where the real estate market is active and considerable construction is occurring, assessors may check their judgments on market value of a property against what they know about current construction costs, and may also estimate on the basis of potential rental or income value.

Equalizing to Full Value. Notwithstanding the Real Property Tax Law, most properties are assessed at less than full value in the great majority of assessing jurisdictions in New York. Further, wide variation exists in the average level or percentage of full value at which assessors in different districts assess property. To correct for these variations, the law provides that adjustments shall be made in specified situations where equitable allocation of the tax burden is affected. The adjustments are made by means of an equalization rate. The rate is simply a percentage figure that is expected to represent the average percentage of full value at which the assessor in an assessing district, such as a town, values properties.

The same law (Section 202 and Article 12) requires that the State Board of Equalization and Assessment establish sate equalization rates for each county, town, city, and village. To establish these rates, the Board regularly conducts market-value surveys on a sample of properties in each district and obtains information concerning valid, "arm's-length" sales of real estate.

The apportionment or allocation of taxes for county purposes among the towns and cities of a county is one situation where equalization rates are important. Town and city assessors assess property for county as well as town and city tax purposes. Typically, substantial differences exist among these local governments in a county in the average percentage of full value at which properties are assessed. To apportion taxes for county purposes among towns

---

[2] Hollis A. Swett, "Real Estate Value and the Property Tax, Some Basic Concepts," paper presented at the Association of Towns Annual Meeting, New York, New York, February 1976.

and cities in proportion to total assessed values in each town and city would be manifestly unfair. Equalization rates, therefore, are used to make adjustment.

Let us illustrate by a greatly simplified example. Suppose a county needs $900 of property taxes to help meet expenses for the coming, year. There are only two towns (and no cities) in the county, each with its own assessor. In Town A there are only three properties, each assessed at its full value of $30,000, $20,000, and $10,000. Total assessed value in Town A is, therefore, $60,000. The equalization rate, or average percentage of full value, at which properties are assessed is, therefore, the same as assessed value, $60,000.

In Town B, there are also three properties, each identical in full value to those in Town A. The assessor, however, has assessed each one at $10,000, making a total assessed value of $30,000, or one-half the total in Town A. The equalization rate for Town B should, therefore, be 50 percent. The $30,000 divided by 50 percent yields a full value of $60,000.

Let us further suppose that the tax levy of $900 for county purposes were to be apportioned between the two towns in proportion to their assessed values of $60,000 and $30,000. Taxpayers in Town A would bear two-thirds of the levy, or $600, since assessed value in Town A is two-thirds of the county total of $90,000. Taxpayers in Town B would bear one-third of the levy, or $300. Taxpayers in Town A would be paying double the amount of county tax compared with those in Town B although the full value of taxable property is identical in the two towns. The assessor for Town A, in conscientiously appraising each property at full value, would have penalized the taxpayers of the town. In Town B, the assessor has not only assessed all but one property at less than full value, but has failed to assess the three properties at a reasonably uniform percentage of their full value.

The law, therefore, provides for equalizing or adjusting assessed values of towns and cities in allocating county taxes. The equalization rate is the major factor in this adjustment. Essentially, taxes for county purposes are apportioned in proportion to full value of taxable property in each town or city.

To return to the example above, the assessed value of $60,000 in Town A divided by the equalization rate of 100 percent yields a full value of $60,000. The $30,000 assessed value in Town B divided by the 50 percent equalization rate yields a full value of $60,000. If the $900 of county taxes are apportioned in proportion to full value, the taxpayers of each town bear one-half the levy, or $450. Each town shares equally in the levy because the total full valuation in each town is the same.

The equalization rates correct for differences in average levels of assessment between the two towns. Note, however, that they do not correct for inequitable assessments on individual properties within a town. In Town B, for example, the three properties are assessed at $10,000 each although their value is $30,000, $20,000, and $10,000, respectively. Each property owner would have to pay one-third of the $450 county tax apportioned to the town although the full value of the first property is three times that of the third. In Town A, on the other hand, the three properties identical in value to those in Town B, have been assessed at full value, totaling $60,000. The tax rate of $7.50 per $1,000 required to raise $450 for county purposes in Town A would result in taxes of $225 against the $30,000 property, $150 against the $20,000 property, and #$75 against the $10,000 property. The assessor of Town B can correct inequitable assessments among individual properties in that town. An equalization rate cannot do this.

The assessor of Town B could correct the inequities by raising all assessments to full value as in Town A, by assessing each property at the current equalization rate level of 50 percent of full value, or by assessing each property at some other uniform percentage of full value. Instead of assessing the three properties at $10,000 each, the assessor could value the $30,000 property at $15,000, the $20,000 property at $10,000, and the $10,000 property at $5,000. Total assessed value would remain at $30,000, the equalization rate at 50 percent, and full value at $60,000. A tax rate of $15 per $1,000 assessed value would then be required to raise $450 of county taxes. Then, as in Town A, there would be taxes of $225 against the $30,000 property (assessed at $15,000), $150 against the $20,000 property (assessed at $10,000), and $75 against the $10,000 property (assessed at $5,000).

Importance of Accurate Equalization Rates. Although equalization rates do not correct for inequitable assessments on individual properties within a town, they can, as illustrated, effectively adjust for variations among towns (and cities) in average levels of value at which properties are assessed. They can do this to the degree that they are accurate.

Grossly inaccurate rates may be worse than none at all. For example, if the equalization rates in the illustration above were fixed at 100 percent for both Towns A and B, assessed value would be the same as full value in each town, and Town A would be penalized for its full value assessments. In effect, there would be no equalization rates or equalization of the tax levy for county purposes. If the equalization rates of both towns were fixed at 50 percent, the effect would be the same. If the rate for Town A were made lower than for Town B, Town A would be better off if the process were abolished. In any of these cases, Town A's assessor would have strong incentive to cut assessments on properties, and both towns could embark upon competitive undervaluation with chaotic results.

Two kinds of authorities are required to establish equalization rates annually: the state and the county. The state fixes rates for towns, cities, and villages. The county governing board, or a county equalization commission in a few counties, fixes rates for each town and city in that county. Appeal procedures are provided by state law for local jurisdictions that believe the state or county rates are unfair.

The county rates are used in apportioning taxes for county purposes among the towns and cities in the county. A county may adopt the state rates, and many do.

The state rates serve a variety of purposes. One of them, for example, is in distributing certain forms of state aid, especially state aid to school districts. A major part of state aid for education is distributed according to formulas that include as one factor the full valuation of taxable property in a school district. Full valuation is obtained by dividing assessed valuation by the state equalization rate, as in the illustrations above. School districts with a low full value of taxable property per pupil generally receive more state aid per pupil than their opposites.

The belief sometimes gains currency that raising the levels of assessed values in a community will curtail state aid for schools. As the examples above illustrate, this is not true so long as the state equalization rates reflect levels of assessment with reasonable accuracy, and the state uses the rates to calculate state aid.

In the present system of property taxation in New York, reasonably accurate equalization rates are essential for equitable allocation of property taxes and state aid, and for other purposes. They also help to assure those assessors who conscientiously try to readjust assessed values of properties in their communities that their efforts will not be penalized through apportionment of taxes and state aid.

PROPERTY SUBJECT TO TAX

Only real estate or real property (as defined in the Real Property Tax Law) is subject to the property tax in New York State, contrary to practice in many other states where all or part of personal property is also supposed to be included. All real property in the state is taxable unless exempt by law or other provision.

Exemptions, however, are substantial. In some assessing jurisdictions, they comprise the lion's share of all real estate. The more the exemptions, of course, the less the taxable property that remains to bear tax levies.

Exempt property includes not only that of governments (federal, state, and local) with certain exceptions, but also a variety of kinds of real estate held by various kinds of private organizations and individuals for various purposes. For example, property of churches, colleges, hospitals and charitable organizations used exclusively for nonprofit purposes is exempt. Certain railroad real property is entitled to partial exemption, as are certain agricultural and forest lands and business investments in real estate improvement. Property of war veterans and certain near relatives is entitled to exemption of up to $5,000, if purchased wi6th funds obtained from pensions and other sources provided by the federal or New York governments. Persons over 65 years old with limited incomes may be eligible for partial exemption of their homes. These examples are by no means comprehensive.

Generally, the kinds of exemptions have been growing in scope and complexity over a long period. The intended effect of state (and local) legislation of exemptions is, of course, to aid worthy causes, organizations, or individuals. A side effect is gradual erosion of the tax base as the list of exempt properties lengthens.

FULL VALUE ASSESSMENT

In no New York assessing jurisdiction—town, city, village or county—are all properties assessed precisely at full value. In very few does even the average level of assessment approximate 100 percent of full value.

These deficiencies in the statutory standard of perfection have a variety of causes. One is that property appraisal is not a precise science. Another is the lag between changing real estate values and the capacity of the governmental assessment machinery to keep up with them. Still another over the sweep of the long history of the state has been the absence of substantial support among local and state officials and other citizens for assessments uniformly approximating full value, except for occasional upsurges of revivalistic fervor in some localities, and even more rarely in the state capitol.

The Governor's Advisory Panel of Consultants reported in 1976 on an analysis of a sample of residential properties drawn from the 1973 state equalization survey.[3] The average ratio of assessment to sales was calculated, and then the average deviation of the assessment-to-sales ratio of each property from the sample average was determined (the coefficient of variation). In only 68 of 991 towns and cities in the state (excluding New York City) was the average deviation within 20 percent of the average assessment-sales ratio for that municipality. The average deviation was over 60 percent in 91 cities and towns. Said the panel, "[In] all but a handful of assessing units in New York State, assessments of residential property are scattered with appalling randomness over a wide range of deviation from the simple mean."[4] This comment was inspired, not simply by the failure to assess residences at full value, but by the failure to assess with reasonable consistency at any ratio of full value.

The panel chose to study residences probably partly because there are many more of them than other kinds of property and they are easier to appraise with some consistency. Other information shows wide variation in assessment of other properties and in average assessments of different classes of property.

As for overall average levels of assessment within assessing units, the state equalization rates for assessment rolls completed in 1975, the latest available year, are revealing. In only 60 of the 991 towns and cities were the rates within 10 percent of the full value standard (100

---

[3] Governor Hugh L. Carey, Educational Finance and the New York State Real Property Tax—*The Inescapable Relationship*, May 1976, Education Study Unit, N.Y. State Division of the Budget, State Capitol, Albany, New York 12224, 32 pp.
[4] Ibid., p. 7.

percent).⁵ The rates themselves reflect market values at the January 1, 1973 price level, indicating that the State Board of Equalization and Assessment, like the local assessing units, has problems keeping up with changing real estate values.

The extreme range in equalization rates among towns and cities was from 1.16 percent in the town of Highland, Sullivan County to 136.36 percent in the Town of Manlius, Onondaga County. Within some counties the range was similarly very great. Within Ulster County, for example, the rates were 131.86 and 3.55 percent, respectively, in the Towns of Denning and Hardenburgh. In Westchester County, the Town of Cortlandt had a rate of 17.18 percent, and North Salem, 105.94 percent. In New York City, which is a single assessing district, the range among its five counties was from 36.57 percent in Richmond to 70.29 percent in New York.

Equalization rates were below 30 percent in 616 of the 991 towns and cities, and below 50 percent in 778. They exceeded 100 percent in 43 municipalities. In recent years, the rates have tended rapidly downward as the rise in real estate prices has accelerated faster than the great majority of assessors have reappraised their assessment rolls. One indication of the trend is that the State Board of Equalization and Assessment decided to add two decimals to the equalization rates beginning with 1974 assessment rolls; some are so low (for instance, the Town of Highland cited above) that a change of one whole percentage point would raise full value by a very large proportion.

In this situation of "appalling randomness" of assessment of individual properties, and declining equalization rates in a rising real estate market, the New York Court of Appeals, the highest state court, decided that the New York Real Property Tax Law requires assessment at full (market) value. On June 5, 1975, the court ordered that the Town of Islip in Suffolk County assess all real property within the Town at full value by December 31, 1976 (a deadline that was later delayed).⁶ Although the "Hellerstein" decision was directed only to the Town of Islip, it binds the lower courts to uphold a similar challenge in any other assessing district. As of April 1977, at least 36 "Hellerstein-type" actions had been filed in courts throughout the state, and more undoubtedly will follow.

One of the taxpayer suits was against the Nassau County Board of Assessors, which a lower state court ordered in May 1977 to complete new assessment rolls at full value by May 1, 1980. The chairman of the board was quoted as saying, "Our present rolls date back to 1938...Since then the value of residential property has climbed sharply while commercial property has not risen as much."⁷ The 1975 equalization rate for the county was 17.12 percent.

These developments are stimulating widespread interest in bringing assessments to full value and maintaining them from year to year at that changing level. These are difficult goals not attained statewide over the nearly 200 years that the state law has required assessment at full value or its equivalent. They had not been attained in other states with comparable assessment standards although the high courts of several states have rendered similar decisions—among them New Jersey, 1975; Connecticut, 1957; and Massachusetts, 1961.

The potential benefits of full value assessments are substantial. First, taxes on similar properties in the same tax districts would be equalized. (The same result would of course follow from consistent assessment at some fraction of full value.) Second, taxpayers are more likely to have some knowledge of the accuracy of their properties' assessed values in comparison to their market values, as opposed to some (often unknown) average fractional assessment in the district. Finally, taxpayers are more likely to challenge an excessive assessment if it exceeds their estimate of true value; a fractional assessment at far less than full value is less likely to

---

⁵ N.Y. State Board of Equalization and Assessment, *State Equalization Rates for 1975 Assessment Rolls for Cities, Towns and Villages*, October 1976, 23 pp.
⁶ Pauline Hellerstein v. The Assessor of the Town of Islip.
⁷ *New York Times*, May 24, 1977.

create taxpayer concern, even if it is excessive in relation to assessments of comparable properties.

Full value assessment (or for that matter, consistent assessment at a percentage of full value) would inevitably cause a shift of taxes among individual properties and among different classes of property. This is an inevitable outcome of equalizing assessments of properties having equal full or market value. The studies done for the governor's panel (cited above) by the State Board of Equalization and Assessment and the Education Unit of the State Division of the Budget indicate that the shifts in taxes within the residential property class from one property to another would total far more than the shift from other property classes to the residential category.[8] Among classes, however, estimated statewide totals indicate a probable net tax shift to residential, vacant land, and farm property classes from the commercial, apartment, industrial, and utility classes.

It is hazardous to generalize from these statewide totals to a specific local situation because there is so much variation among assessing units. For example, these analyses indicate that, on the average over the state, commercial properties are over-assessed compared with residential and farm properties, but in a specific town this average relationship may not hold and the reverse situation can even be true. The average relationship is still less likely to prevail in comparing individual properties in a town, because the variation in ratios of assessment to full value within a property class such as residences is extreme in many towns and cities.

Once a number of revaluation programs have been completed in many assessing units, it will be possible to determine whether particular classes of taxpayers are unduly burdened. If such a burden results, some sort of relief could be granted by the State Legislature. Among many alternatives is legislating that certain types of property be assessed at a specified percentage of full value. If fractional assessment is authorized, however, it will still be necessary to determine the full values upon which the fractions can be based in a consistent manner. Other alternatives, such as partial exemption of single family residences, are also likely to require determining full values as a yardstick for exemptions.

COMPUTER-ASSISTED ASSESSMENTS

In trying to make assessment rolls conform more nearly to the statutory standard of full value or some uniform percentage of full value in a thorough-going, professional and equitable way, the assessors have commonly reappraised or revalued all properties. Alternatively, local governments have contracted with appraisal firms to do the work with the resulting values subject to acceptance by their assessors. Counties have often contracted for revaluation for their constituent towns and cities in anticipation of greater countywide uniformity in assessment.

A major limitation of this procedure has been the difficulty of keeping the information and values up-to-date once they have been compiled. Massive amounts of data must be accumulated and analyzed on a continuing basis. This is usually much beyond the capacity of the assessing office with the resources commonly available. Revaluations have quickly become outdated because of rapidly changing real estate values and changes in existing properties, such as new construction, demolition, or other destruction of property.

Attempts to apply computer technology in recent years to these mass appraisal procedures offer promise of making it possible for the first time to keep assessment roll listings and valuations reasonably current. Computers may well make it practical for assessing districts to implement the Hellerstein decision by revaluing properties and keeping abreast of changing market values thereafter.

---

[8] Governor Hugh L. Carey, op. cit., p. 17.

The New York State Board of Equalization and Assessment over the past few years has been developing what it terms the Real Property Information System, which includes computer assistance for property valuation. The system has been implemented by assessors of several local governments beginning with the Town of Ramapo (Rockland County). It provides assessors with the means of processing and updating market value information for all properties on assessment rolls.

Basically, the computer-assisted assessment procedure involves tabulating and recording all recent property sales in a jurisdiction. When a single-family residence is subjected to value estimating, this process is carried out:

1. The computer selects the five properties from the sales file that most closely resemble the one being appraised.
2. The computer calculates a predicted value for the subject residence. These calculations are based on the procedures customarily used by appraisers in judging value.
3. Once the computer estimates are generated, each one is reviewed by a professional appraisal at the property. If errors are found, appropriate information is fed back into the computer.

Computer-assisted assessments are most accurate for single-family residences, primarily because accurate comparable sales data for them are more readily available than for other kinds of property. Approximately 70 percent of the properties in the State (not including New York City) are in the residential class.[9] More than half the remainder, or almost a fifth of the total, is in the "vacant lands" class. The next most numerous properties are in the "commercial" and "farm" classes.

There are nearly 1,000 town, city, and county assessing districts in the state with approximately 3.5 million parcels outside New York City to be assessed. At best, full-scale implementation of computerized assessments will be a lengthy process. Current budgetary and staff restrictions, and attrition of the State Board of Equalization and Assessment's experienced professional personnel, will make it even more protracted. Historically, the state and the public have shown only desultory interest in matching assessment performance with statutory standards and these cutbacks are consistent with that record.[10]

ASSESSORS

Assessing units in New York include almost all towns and cities, some villages, two counties, and the state itself. The State Board of Equalization and Assessment is responsible for assessing some properties, principally special franchises and railroad property in connection with fixing ceilings for partial exemptions. Special franchise property is generally property of public utilities located in public lands, for example, a power or telephone line in a highway right of way.

Two counties—Nassau and Tompkins—are assessing units.[11] Elsewhere in the state, the 918 towns and 59 cities are assessing units; and their assessment rolls are used for town and city, special district, county and school taxation. The village board of trustees can also elect to

---

[9] Governor Hugh L. Carey, op. cit., p. 23.
[10] See Postscript at end of this bulletin. Recent legislation may speed implementation of computer-assisted assessments.
[11] In Nassau, the two cities (Glen Cove and Long Beach) and the 65 villages may assess for city and village tax purposes, respectively.

have town assessments used for village taxation, rather than to have separate village assessments.

The "Assessment Improvement Law" of 1970, how officially Article 15-A of the Real Property Tax Law, made substantial changes in the assessment organization affecting local assessors, except in the villages and New York City.

One such change required the appointment of one assessor in each district meeting minimum qualification standards who was to undergo training determined by the State Board of Equalization and Assessment. This assessor is appointed by the local legislative body (or chief executive in some cases) for a six-year term, unless the position has an indefinite term in the competitive civil service. The appointee may be removed, but only for just cause. Exceptions to this appointive single assessor requirement were made for Nassau County and cities of 100,000 or more population (New York, Buffalo, Rochester, Yonkers, Syracuse, Albany). Another important exception is that over half the towns and a few smaller cities opted before the prescribed deadline in 1971 to retain their traditional practice of electing a single assessor, or, as in most towns, a three-person board (two elected at each biennial town election, one for a two-year and the other for a four-year term). The only qualification the law requires of a candidate for election as an assessor has been that he or she be a voter of the town. Municipalities that exercised the option of electing their assessors, nevertheless, must conform with the assessor training and other requirements of the Assessment Improvement Law. These municipalities may also opt to shift to appointing a single assessor, and some have since 1971. It should be said that a number of cities and towns had appointed professional assessors and assessment staffs long before this law was passed.

A second change required by Article 15-A for cities and towns is appointment of a board of assessment review composed of persons who are not assessors and a majority of whom are not officers or employees of the local government. The board hears taxpayer complaints on grievance day. Prior to the new law, the assessors of most local governments sat as a board of review. The intent of the change was to meet criticism of long standing that the assessors sat as judges of their own work, to hear and make decisions on taxpayer appeals from their own work.

The governing body of the local government must appoint from three to five review board members who have knowledge of property values in the locality. Membership could include, for example, individuals engaged in banking, insurance, real estate, professional appraising and similar occupations, and persons formerly assessors. Appointments are for five-year staggered terms.

TAXPAYER COMPLAINT AND APPEAL PROVISIONS

Assessors in each town and city not governed by special provisions are expected to assess all real property within their jurisdiction (except special franchises) according to its condition and ownership as of May 1.[12] The law requires completion of the tentative assessment roll on or before June 1. A copy must be left with the assessor or the town clerk for public inspection, and notices must be posted in the town and published in a newspaper. At least ten days before grievance day, the assessor must mail notices to those on whose property assessments have been increased.

---

[12] There are differences from the dates named in this section for the special "tax act" counties of Erie, Monroe, Nassau, Suffolk, and Westchester. Tompkins is such a county also, but the dates do not differ except for the city of Ithaca. For most villages, the date of taxable status is January 1; for tentative completion of the village assessment roll, February 1; and for village grievance day, the 3rd Tuesday in February.

Grievance day is held on the third Tuesday in June at the time and place specified in the public notices. Complaining taxpayers may file a statement under oath indicating why the assessment of their property is incorrect. The board of assessment review receives and hears complaints on grievance day, and may adjust up or down the assessments under question. The assessor must attend (in other words, sit with) the tentative assessment roll on at least three days of the public inspection period prior to grievance day. He or she must also attend the review board hearings, and has the right to respond to any complaint. Informal complaints may of course be made to assessors the year-round.

On or before August 1, the assessor completes the assessment roll. The assessor then must file a certified copy of the roll with the town or city clerk where it is open for public inspection. Notices to this effect must be published in a local newspaper, and, in towns, posted at the town clerk's office. The original roll is delivered to the clerk of the county legislative body, and town, special district, and county taxes are entered on it usually late in the fall. It is delivered to the tax collector with a warrant for collection, usually by the first of the year. The taxes must also be entered on the copy of the roll that remains in the town clerk's office as a public record.

If a complaining taxpayer fails to obtain the relief desired at the grievance day proceedings, he or she may carry an appeal to the courts. In presenting the case to a court, the taxpayer must establish the full market value of his or her property and the average level of assessment in the assessing unit. Court appeals, historically an expensive and time-consuming process used by few taxpayers, have been substantially simplified in the last several years by amendments to the law, and more recently by important court decisions. In *Ed Guth Realty v. Gingold*, a case from the City of Syracuse, the Court of Appeals ruled in 1974 that the state equalization rate can be used as the most significant evidence toward satisfying the burden of proof of the average level of assessment in the assessing unit. Shortly thereafter, the ruling was regarded as applicable in another local government in the case of *860 Executive Towers Inc. v. The Board of Assessors of the County of Nassau*. The court (Appellate Division) further concluded that, although the methods used by the State Board of Equalization and Assessment can be improved, they cannot be challenged in a proceeding to review an assessment.[13]

The taxpayer thus has to show in court only that the level of assessment on his or her property is higher than the average level of assessment indicated by the state equalization rate.[14] A customarily long and costly process for the taxpayer of appraising a sample of comparable properties in the jurisdiction is thereby apparently eliminated.

As a result of these decisions, it is said that thousands of similar cases are pending throughout the state.

SOME IMPLICATIONS FOR ASSESSING UNITS

The court decisions in the Guth and Hellerstein cases have helped to open a Pandora's box for assessors, the courts, local governments, state legislative and executive agencies, and perhaps many taxpayers.

Any taxpayer willing to go to the trouble and expense may ask a court to require a revaluation of the assessment rolls at full value in his or her town or city, relying on the Hellerstein case. Any taxpayers who feel that their properties are assessed at a substantially higher ratio than the equalization rate for their towns or cities, may apply to a court for a reduction in assessment, relying on the Guth case rulings.

---

[13] Association of Towns of the State of New York, *Assessors Topics*, October 1976, Albany, New York.
[14] The 1977 State Legislature amended the Real Property Tax Law to qualify in an uncertain way the impact of the Guth decision. See Postscript for further discussion of this change.

An assessing unit can, as many have, anticipate the prospect of a revaluation at full value, and prepare for it. Computer-assisted assessment is one possible line of action already discussed. In practical terms, however, this alternative is probably contingent upon the availability of competent and persistent state support. The prospects for it on the massive scale needed to work with large numbers of local governments and parcels of property are not encouraging in this period of retrenchment. However, one favorable development is 1977 legislation that provides state aid for part of the cost of local revaluation.

The assessing unit, because of the Guth case and for other reasons, also can examine carefully the data used by the State Board of Equalization and Assessment in fixing the equalization rate for that unit. When a Guth-type case arises, it is too late to question the rate in court. The state sampling, appraisals, and other steps and information in the rate-fixing process, can be challenged with solid evidence when found questionable, but this should be done as early in the procedure as possible, and at least by the time the State Board sends notice of the tentative equalization rate.

It is to the advantage of the state as well as local governments and taxpayers that its equalization rates be as accurate as practicable. To improve accuracy, local assessors and governments have customarily been encouraged to contribute information. Among other ways of eliciting information, the State Board has sought through field staff to check its sampling with local officials. The Board has also freely supplied local officials with the data behind its equalization rate, and has acted upon information supplied by them when it is pertinent, substantial, and objective.

In the current period of curtailment and retrenchment, the open relations between state and local governments desired for more accurate equalization rates are in jeopardy. From the local viewpoint, the State Board has reduced local contacts, supplied data less promptly and freely, and given notice of tentative equalization rates so late that studied response is impractical. Efforts toward improving equity in assessment, according to its statutory definition, can be crippled in such a situation. Equalization rates also can gradually deteriorate—as they in fact did earlier in the history of the state[15]—and the state becomes quite remote to a city or town assessor.

COUNTY AND STATE SERVICES FOR LOCAL ASSESSORS

Another major provision of the Assessment Improvement Law of 1970 is that counties and the State Board of Equalization and Assessment provide various forms of technical and professional aid to local assessing units.[16]

County Services. Each county except the two (Nassau and Tompkins) now acting as assessing units has been required to establish a real property tax service agency, and to appoint a director for a six-year term to head it. The law has required the director to meet minimum qualifications set by the State Board, and complete the training courses it prescribes, as with town and city assessors. Appraisers employed by the county agency must meet the same conditions.

In general, the purpose of the agency is to assist towns and cities with assessments and assessing work, and to do work for the county that has been associated with assessing and taxing real property. It must prepare tax maps, keep them up-to-date and provide copies to city,

---

[15] For example, grossly inaccurate rates led to creating in 1949 the present State Board of Equalization and Assessment.
[16] Real Property Tax Law, Article 15-A.

town, and village assessors and others. The initial maps must be completed and State Board approved applied for by October 1, 1979.

At the request of the chief executive or assessor of cities and towns in the county, the agency was to be ready by October 1, 1976, to perform advisory appraisals of "moderately complex properties" requiring engineering skills, or economic analyses of "substantial complexity." The State Board determines the specific types of property included in this provision. It must also review agency appraisals if the town or city assessor thinks them inaccurate or unreasonable and applies for review. The appraisals are not binding upon city or town assessors but must be considered by them.

The county agency must also advise assessors concerning assessment rolls, property record cards, appraisal cards, and other records. It must provide appraisal cards in the form prescribed by the State Board and cooperate in training programs of the Board. It must also provide useful information to the county authorities for fixing town and city equalization rates for county tax purposes, and perform other duties.

State Services. An important responsibility of the State Board not already described is that it was to be prepared by October 1, 1976, to do advisory appraisals of (1) privately owned forest lands in excess of 500 acres, (2) "highly complex properties" requiring highly specialized engineering skills or highly complex economic analyses, and (3) taxable public utility property. These appraisals must be done, as in the case of the county, at the request of the local government's chief executive or assessor.

THE GAP BETWEEN LAW AND PRACTICE

The gap between the legal requirement of full value assessment and local performance is great, and so is the gap between what the state is supposed to do and actually does.

With respect to local deficiencies, many factors contribute to the "appalling randomness" of assessment described by the Governor's Panel. Among them is the deviation of local practice from the idea embodied in the Assessment Improvement Law of 1970 that assessing personnel should be appointed by local governing boards rather than elected, that these individuals should have at least a minimum of prior professional training or experienced or both, and that they should have some assurance of at least a minimum job tenure consistent with conscientious work performance. Approximately half the towns and a few cities apparently continue to elect assessors and each biennial local election results in high turnover, with sometimes cavalier voter disregard for consistent and persistent assessment. Building expertise in functions such as computer-assisted assessments in a locality under these circumstances is probably impossible.

Local boards of assessment review ideally have a quasi-judicial role of correcting injustice, when they hear formal complaints, by referring to the Guth case and related high court decisions and laws. Some local boards can make a shambles of uniform assessment by granting practically any request for reduced valuation. Others can tolerate poor assessment by refusing relief, however, judicially justified it may be.

With respect to counties, considerable variation exists in their capacity to complete and maintain tax maps, perform advisory appraisals, and assist town and city assessing units in other ways prescribed by the Assessment Improvement Law of 1970.

The gap between State Board performance and the requirements of the Real Property Tax Law is substantial. The Board is not providing systematic training for local assessing and appraisal personnel. It has postponed advisory appraisals beyond the legal deadline of October 1, 1976. It lacks the capacity to lend technical assistance and support for widespread local implementation of computer-assisted assessments and other aspects of its Real Property

Information System. It is making more difficult local opportunity for close scrutiny of equalization rates.

Curtailment and retrenchment of State Board activities is inconsistent with the expansion of state responsibilities required by law and recent major judicial decisions. Such reduction is at least partly the result of the more general and severe fiscal pressures upon the state.

The state and local situations do not, and should not, encourage taxpayer belief in early achievement of statewide equity of property assessment according to the statutory definition of equity. It is possible, however, to improve local performance within the present framework in those localities where the will exists and resources are committed to achieve improvement.

CONCLUSION

Inequities in assessing properties are common in New York except in those communities taking vigorous steps to bring assessed value into line with current real estate market values. Reducing inequities by a thorough revaluation or reassessment does not necessarily result in increased taxes for individuals. It will result in a larger share of taxes for those whose properties have been under-assessed compared with their neighbors. A smaller share will be borne by property owners over-assessed theretofore compared with their neighbors.

GLOSSARY OF REAL ESTATE TERMS

CONTENTS

	Page
Abstract of Title................Appraisal by Summation	1
Appurtenance.......................Cancellation Clause	2
Caveat Emptor..................................Conveyance	3
County Clerk's Certificate.... Documentary Evidence	4
Duress......................................Exclusive Agency	5
Exclusive Right to Sell.......................Ground Rent	6
Habendum Clause................................ Landlord	7
Lease.................................…...Mortgagee	8
Mortgagor...Party Wall	9
Percentage Lease....................................Release	10
Release Clause....................Subordination Clause	11
Subscribing Witness..............................Valuation	12
Vendee's Lien…. ....Zoning Ordinance	13

GLOSSARY OF REAL ESTATE TERMS

A

Abstract of Title—A summary of all of the recorded instruments and proceedings which affect the title to property, arranged in chronological order.

Accretion—The addition to land through processes of nature, as by streams or wind.

Accrued Interest—Accrue: to grow; to be added to. Accrued interest is interest that has been earned but not due and payable.

Acknowledgment—A formal declaration before a duly authorized officer by a person who has executed an instrument that such execution is the person's act and deed.

Acquisition—An act or process by which a person procures property.

Acre—A measure of land equaling 160 square rods or 4,840 square yards or 43,560 feet.

Adjacent—Lying near to but not necessarily in actual contact with.

Adjoining—Contiguous; attaching, in actual contact with.

Administrator—A person appointed by court to administer the estate of a deceased person who left no will; i.e., who died intestate.

Ad Valorem—According to valuation.

Adverse Possession—A means of acquiring title where an occupant has been in actual, open, notorious, exclusive, and continuous occupancy of property under a claim of right for the required statutory period.

Affidavit—A statement or declaration reduced to writing, and sworn to or affirmed before some officer who is authorized to administer an oath or affirmation.

Affirm—To confirm, to ratify, to verify.

Agency—That relationship between principal and agent which arises out of a contract either expressed or implied, written or oral, wherein an agent is employed by a person to do certain acts on the person's behalf in dealing with a third party.

Agent—One who undertakes to transact some business or to manage some affair for another by authority of the latter.

Agreement of Sale—A written agreement between seller and purchaser in which the purchaser agrees to buy certain real estate and the seller agrees to sell upon terms and conditions set forth therein.

Alienation—A transferring of property to another; the transfer of property and possession of lands, or other things, from one person to another

Amortization—A gradual paying off of a debt by periodical installments.

Apportionments—Adjustment of the income, expenses or carrying charges of real estate usually computed to the date of closing of title so that the seller pays all expenses to that date. The buyer assumes all expenses commencing the date the deed is conveyed to the buyer.

Appraisal—An estimate of a property's valuation by an appraiser who is usually presumed to be expert in this work.

Appraisal by Capitalization—An estimate of value by capitalization of productivity and income.

Appraisal by Comparison—Comparability with the sale prices of other similar properties.

Appraisal by Summation—Adding together all parts of a property separately appraised to form a whole: e.g., value of the land considered as vacant added to the cost of reproduction of the building, less depreciation.

Appurtenance—Something which is outside the property itself but belongs to the land and adds to its greater enjoyment such as a right of way or a barn or a dwelling.

Assessed Valuation—A valuation placed upon property by a public officer or a board, as a basis for taxation.

Assessment—A charge against real estate made by a unit of government to cover a proportionate cost of an improvement such as a street or sewer.

Assessor—An official who has the responsibility of determining assessed values.

Assignee—The person to whom an agreement or contract is assigned.

Assignment—The method or manner by which a right, a specialty, or contract is transferred from one person to another.

Assignor—A party who assigns or transfers an agreement or contract to another.

Assumption of Mortgage—The taking of title to property by a grantee, wherein the grantee assumes liability for payment of an existing note or bond secured by a mortgage against a property and becomes personally liable for the payment of such mortgage debt.

Attest—To witness to; to witness by observation and signature.

Avulsion—The removal of land from one owner to another, when a stream suddenly changes its channel.

B

Beneficiary—The person who receives or is to receive the benefits resulting from certain acts.

Bequeath—To give or hand down by will; to leave by will.

Bequest—That which is given by the terms of a will.

Bill of Sale—A written instrument given to pass title of personal property from vendor to vendee.

Binder—An agreement to cover the down payment for the purchase of real estate as evidence of good faith on the part of the purchaser.

Blanket Mortgage—A single mortgage which covers more than one piece of real estate.

Bona Fide—In good faith, without fraud.

Bond—The evidence of a personal debt which is secured by a mortgage or other lien on real estate.

Building Codes—Regulations established by local governments stating fully the structural requirements for building.

Building Line—A line fixed at a certain distance from the front and/or sides of a lot, beyond which no building can project.

Building Loan Agreement—An agreement whereby the lender advances money to an owner with provisional payments at certain stages of construction.

C

Cancellation Clause—A provision in a lease which confers upon one or more or all of the parties to the lease the right to terminate the party's or parties' obligations thereunder upon the occurrence of the condition or contingency set forth in the said clause.

Caveat Emptor—Let the buyer beware. The buyer must examine the goods or property and buy at the buyer's own risk.

Cease and Desist Order—An order executed by the Secretary of State directing broker recipients to cease and desist from all solicitation of homeowners whose names and addresses appear on the list(s) forwarded with such order. The order acknowledges petition filings by homeowners listed evidencing their premises are not for sale, thereby revoking the implied invitation to solicit. The issuance of a Cease and Desist Order does not prevent an owner from selling or listing his premises for sale. It prohibits soliciting by licensees served with such order and subjects violators to penalties of suspension or revocation of their licenses as provided in section 441-c of the Real Property Law.

Cease and Desist Petition—A statement filed by a homeowner showing address of premises owned which notifies the Department of State that such premises are not for sale and does not wish to be solicited. In so doing, petitioner revokes the implied invitation to be solicited, by any means with respect thereto, by licensed real estate brokers and salespersons.

Certiorari—A proceeding to review in a competent court the action of an inferior tribunal board or officer exercising judicial functions.

Chain of Title—A history of conveyances and encumbrances affecting a title from the time the original patent was granted, or as far back as records are available.

Chattel—Personal property, such as household goods or fixtures.

Chattel Mortgage—A mortgage on personal property.

Client—The one by whom a broker is employed and by whom the broker will be compensated on completion of the purpose of the agency.

Closing Date—The date upon which the buyer takes over the property; usually between 30 and 60 days after the signing of the contract. Cloud on the Title An outstanding claim or encumbrance which, if valid, would affect or impair the owner's title.

Collateral—Additional security pledged for the payment of an obligation.

Color of Title—That which appears to be good title, but which is not title in fact.

Commission—A sum due a real estate broker for services in that capacity.

Commitment—A pledge or a promise or affirmation agreement.

Condemnation—Taking private property for public use, with fair compensation to the owner; exercising the right of eminent domain.

Conditional Sales Contract—A contract for the sale of property stating that delivery is to be made to the buyer, title to remain vested in the seller until the conditions of the contract have been fulfilled.

Consideration—Anything of value given to induce entering into a contract; it may be money, personal services, or even love and affection.

Constructive Notice—Information or knowledge of a fact imputed by law to a person because the person could have discovered the fact by proper diligence and inquiry; (public records).

Contract—An agreement between competent parties to do or not to do certain things for a legal consideration, whereby each party acquires a right to what the other possesses.

Conversion—Change from one character or use to another.

Conveyance—The transfer of the title of land from one to another. The means or medium by which title of real estate is transferred.

County Clerk's Certificate—When an acknowledgment is taken by an officer not authorized in the state or county where the document is to be recorded, the instrument which must be attached to the acknowledgment is called a county clerk's certificate. It is given by the clerk of the county where the officer obtained his/her authority and certifies to the officer's signature and powers.

Covenants—Agreements written into deeds and other instruments promising performance or nonperformance of certain acts, or stipulating certain uses or nonuse's of the property.

D

Damages—The indemnity recoverable by a person who has sustained an injury, either to his/her person, property or relative rights, through the act or default of another.

Decedent—One who is dead.

Decree Order issued by one in authority; an edict or law; a judicial decision.

Dedication—A grant and appropriation of land by its owner for some public use, accepted for such use, by an authorized public official on behalf of the public.

Deed—An instrument in writing duly executed and delivered, that conveys title to real property.

Deed Restriction—An imposed restriction in a deed for the purpose of limiting the use of the land such as: A restriction against the sale of liquor thereon. A restriction As to the size, type, value or placement of improvements that may be erected thereon.

Default—Failure to fulfill a duty or promise, or to discharge an obligation; omission or failure to perform any acts.

Defendant—The party sued or called to answer in any suit, civil or criminal, at law or in equity.

Deficiency Judgment—A judgment given when the security for a loan does not entirely satisfy the debt upon its default.

Delivery—The transfer of the possession of a thing from one person to another.

Demising Clause—A clause found in a lease whereby the landlord (lessor) leases and the tenant (lessee) takes the property.

Depreciation—Loss of value in real property brought about by age, physical deterioration, or functional or economic obsolescence.

Descent—When an owner of real estate dies intestate, the owner's property descends, by operation of law, to the owner's distributees.

Devise—A gift of real estate by will or last testament.

Devisee—One who receives a bequest of real estate made by will.

Devisor—One who bequeaths real estate by will.

Directional Growth—The location or direction toward which the residential sections of a city are destined or determined to grow.

Dispossess Proceedings—Summary process by a landlord to oust a tenant and regain possession of the premises for nonpayment of rent or other breach of conditions of the lease or occupancy.

Distributee—Person receiving or entitled to receive land as representative of the former owner.

Documentary Evidence—Evidence in the form of written or printed papers.

Duress—Unlawful constraint exercised upon a person whereby the person is forced to do some act against his will.

Earnest Money—Down payment made by a purchaser of real estate as evidence of good faith.

Easement—A right that may be exercised by the public or individuals on, over or through the lands of others.

Ejectment—A form of action to regain possession of real property, with damages for the unlawful retention; used when there is no relationship of landlord and tenant.

Eminent Domain—A right of the government to acquire property for necessary public use by condemnation; the owner must be fairly compensated.

Encroachment—A building, part of a building, or obstruction which intrudes upon or invades a highway or sidewalk or trespasses upon the property of another.

Encumbrance—Any right to or interest in land that diminishes its value. (Also Incumbrance)

Endorsement—An act of signing one's name on the back of a check or note, with or without further qualifications.

Equity—The interest or value which the owner has in real estate over and above the liens against it.

Equity of Redemption—A right of the owner to reclaim property before it is sold through foreclosure proceedings, by the payment of the debt, interest and costs.

Erosion—The wearing away of land through processes of nature, as by streams and winds.

Escheat—The reversion to the state of property in event the owner thereof dies, without leaving a will and has no distributees to whom the property may pass by lawful descent.

Escrow—A written agreement between two or more parties providing that certain instruments or property be placed with a third party to be delivered to a designated person upon the fulfillment or performance of some act or condition.

Estate—The degree, quantity, nature and extent of interest which a person has in real property.

Estate for Life—An estate or interest held during the terms of some certain person's life.

Estate in Reversion—The residue of an estate left for the grantor, to commence in possession after the termination of some particular estate granted by the grantor.

Estate at Will—The occupation of lands and tenements by a tenant for an indefinite period, terminable by one or both parties at will.

Estoppel Certificate—An instrument executed by the mortgagor setting forth the present status and the balance due on the mortgage as of the date of the execution of the certificate. A legal proceeding by a lessor landlord to recover possession of real property.

Eviction, Actual—Where one is, either by force or by process of law, actually put out of possession.

Eviction, Constructive—Any disturbance of the tenant's possessions by the landlord whereby the premises are rendered unfit or unsuitable for the purpose for which they were leased.

Eviction, Partial—Where the possessor of the premises is deprived of a portion thereof.

Exclusive Agency—An agreement of employment of a broker to the exclusion of all other brokers; if sale is made by any other broker during term of employment, broker holding exclusive agency is entitled to commissions in addition to the commissions payable to the broker who effected the transaction.

Exclusive Right to Sell—An agreement of employment by a broker under which the exclusive right to sell for a specified period is granted to the broker; if a sale during the term of the agreement is made by the owner or by any other broker, the broker holding such exclusive right to sell is nevertheless entitled to compensation.

Executor—A male person or a corporate entity or any other type of organization named or designated in a will to carry out its provisions as to the disposition of the estate of a deceased person.

Executrix—A woman appointed to perform the duties similar to those of an executor.

Extension Agreement—An agreement which extends the life of the mortgage to a later date.

F

Fee; Fee Simple; Fee Absolute—Absolute ownership of real property; a person has this type of estate where the person is entitled to the entire property with unconditional power of disposition during the person's life and descending to the person's distributees and legal representatives upon the person's death intestate.

Fiduciary—A person who on behalf of or for the benefit of another transacts business or handles money on property not the person's own; such relationship implies great confidence and trust.

Fixtures—Personal property so attached to the land or improvements as to become part of the real property.

Foreclosure—A procedure whereby property pledged as security for a debt is sold to pay the debt in the event of default in payments or terms.

Forfeiture—Loss of money or anything of value, by way of penalty due to failure to perform.

Freehold—An interest in real estate, not less than an estate for life. (Use of this term discontinued Sept. 1, 1967.)

Front Foot—A standard measurement, one foot wide, of the width of land, applied at the frontage on its street line. Each front foot extends the depth of the lot.

G

Grace Period—Additional time allowed to perform an act or make a payment before a default occurs.

Graduated Leases—A lease which provides for a graduated change at stated intervals in the amount of the rent to be paid; used largely in long term leases.

Grant—A technical term used in deeds of conveyance of lands to indicate a transfer. Grantee The party to whom the title to real property is conveyed.

Grantor—The person who conveys real estate by deed; the seller.

Gross Income—Total income from property before any expenses are deducted.

Gross Lease—A lease of property whereby the lessor is to meet all property charges regularly incurred through ownership.

Ground Rent—Earnings of improved property credited to earning of the ground itself after allowance made for earnings of improvements.

H

Habendum Clause—The "To Have and To Hold" clause which defines or limits the quantity of the estate granted in the premises of the deed.

Hereditaments—The largest classification of property; including lands, tenements and incorporeal property, such as rights of way.

Holdover Tenant—A tenant who remains in possession of leased property after the expiration of the lease term.

Hypothecate—To give a thing as security without the necessity of giving up possession of it.

I

In Rem—A proceeding against the realty directly; as distinguished from a proceeding against a person. (Used in taking land for nonpayment of taxes, etc.)

Incompetent—A person who is unable to manage his/her own affairs by reason of insanity, inbecility or feeble-mindedness.

Incumbrance—Any right to or interest in land that diminishes its value. (Also Encumbrance)

Injunction—A writ or order issued under the seal of a court to restrain one or more parties to a suit or proceeding from doing an act which is deemed to be inequitable or unjust in regard to the rights of some other party or parties in the suit or proceeding.

Installments—Parts of the same debt, payable at successive periods as agreed; payments made to reduce a mortgage.

Instrument—A written legal document; created to effect the rights of the parties. Interest

Rate—The percentage of a sum of money charged for its use.

Intestate—A person who dies having made no will, or leaves one which is defective in form, in which case the person's estate descends to the person's distributees.

Involuntary Lien—A lien imposed against property without consent of the owner, i.e., taxes, special assessments.

Irrevocable—Incapable of being recalled or revoked; unchangeable; unalterable.

J

Jeopardy—Peril, danger.

Joint Tenancy—Ownership of realty by two or more persons, each of whom has an undivided interest with the "right of survivorship."

Judgment—Decree of a court declaring that one individual is indebted to another, and fixing the amount of such indebtedness.

Junior Mortgage—A mortgage second in lien to a previous mortgage.

L

Laches—Delay or negligence in asserting one's legal rights.

Land, Tenements and Hereditaments—A phrase used in the early English Law, to express all sorts of property of the immovable class.

Landlord—One who rents property to another.

Lease—A contract whereby, for a consideration, usually termed rent, one who is entitled to the possession of real property transfers such rights to another for life, for a term of years, or at will. Leasehold The interest or estate which a lessee of real estate has therein by virtue of the lessee's lease.

Lessee—A person to whom property is rented under a lease.

Lessor—One who rents property to another under a lease.

Lien—A legal right or claim upon a specific property which attaches to the property until a debt is satisfied.

Lien (Mechanic's)—A notice filed with the County Clerk stating that payment has not been made for an improvement to real property. Life Estate The conveyance of title to property for the duration of the life of the grantee.

Life Tenant—The holder of a life estate.

Lis Pendens—A legal document, filed in the office of the county clerk giving notice that an action or proceeding is pending in the courts affecting the title to the property.

Listing—An employment contract between principal and agent, authorizing the agent to perform services for the principal involving the latter's property.

Litigation—The act of carrying on a lawsuit.

M

Mandatory—Requiring strict conformity or obedience.

Market Value—The highest price which a buyer, willing but not compelled to buy, would pay, and the lowest a seller, willing but not compelled to sell, would accept.

Marketable Title—A title which a court of equity considers to be so free from defect that it will enforce its acceptance by a purchaser.

Mechanic's Lien—A lien given by law upon a building or other improvement upon land, and upon the land itself, to secure the price of labor done upon, and materials furnished for, the improvement.

Meeting of the Minds—Whenever all parties to a contract agree to the exact terms thereof.

Metes and Bounds—A term used in describing the boundary lines of land, setting forth all the boundary lines together with their terminal points and angles.

Minor—A person under an age specified by law; under 18 years of age.

Monument—A fixed object and point established by surveyors to establish land locations.

Moratorium—An emergency act by a legislative body to suspend the legal enforcement of contractual obligations.

Mortgage—An instrument in writing, duly executed and delivered, that creates a lien upon real estate as security for the payment of a specified debt, which is usually in the form of a bond.

Mortgage Commitment—A formal indication, by a lending institution that it will grant a mortgage loan on property, in a certain specified amount and on certain specified terms. Mortgage Reduction Certificate An instrument executed by the mortgagee, setting forth the present status and the balance due on the mortgage as of the date of the execution of the instrument.

Mortgagee—The party who lends money and takes a mortgage to secure the payment thereof.

Mortgagor—A person who borrows money and gives a mortgage on the person's property as security for the payment of the debt.

Multiple Listing—An arrangement among Real Estate Board of Exchange Members, whereby each broker presents the broker's listings to the attention of the other members so that if a sale results, the commission is divided between the broker bringing the listing and the broker making the sale.

N

Net Listing—A price below which an owner will not sell the property, and at which price a broker will not receive a commission; the broker receives the excess over and above the net listing as the broker's commission.

Notary Public—A public officer who is authorized to take acknowledgments to certain classes of documents, such as deeds, contracts, mortgages, and before whom affidavits may be sworn.

O

Obligee—The person in whose favor an obligation is entered into.

Obligor—The person who binds himself/herself to another; one who has engaged to perform some obligation; one who makes a bond.

Obsolescence—Loss in value due to reduced desirability and usefulness of a structure because its design and construction become obsolete; loss because of becoming old-fashioned, and not in keeping with modern means, with consequent loss of income.

Open End Mortgage—A mortgage under which the mortgagor may secure additional funds from the mortgagee, usually up to but not exceeding the original amount of the existing amortizing mortgage.

Open Listing—A listing given to any number of brokers without liability to compensate any except the one who first secures a buyer ready, willing and able to meet the terms of the listing, or secures the acceptance by the seller of a satisfactory offer; the sale of the property automatically terminates the listing.

Open Mortgage—A mortgage that has matured or is overdue and, therefore, is "open" to foreclosure at any time.

Option—A right given for a consideration to purchase or lease a property upon specified terms within a specified time; if the right is not exercised the option holder is not subject to liability for damages; if exercised, the grantor of option must perform.

P

Partition—The division which is made of real property between those who own it in undivided shares.

Party Wall—A party wall is a wall built along the line separating two properties, partly on each, which wall either owner, the owner's heirs and assigns has the right to use; such right constituting an easement over so much of the adjoining owner's land as is covered by the wall.

Percentage Lease—A lease of property in which the rental is based upon the percentage of the volume of sales made upon the leased premises, usually provides for minimum rental.

Personal Property—Any property which is not real property.

Plat Book—A public record containing maps of land showing the division of such land into streets, blocks and lots and indicating the measurements of the individual parcels.

Plottage—Increment in unity value of a plot of land created by assembling smaller ownerships into one ownership.

Police Power—The right of any political body to enact laws and enforce them, for the order, safety, health, morals and general welfare of the public.

Power of Attorney—A written instrument duly signed and executed by an owner of property, which authorizes an agent to act on behalf of the owner to the extent indicated in the instrument.

Premises—Lands and tenements; an estate; the subject matter of a conveyance.

Prepayment Clause—A clause in a mortgage which gives a mortgagor the privilege of paying the mortgage indebtedness before it becomes due.

Principal—The employer of an agent or broker; the broker's or agent's client.

Probate—To establish the will of a deceased person.

Purchase Money Mortgage—A mortgage given by a grantee in part payment of the purchase price of real estate.

Q

Quiet Enjoyment—The right of an owner or a person legally in possession to the use of property without interference of possession.

Quiet Title Suit—A suit in court to remove a defect, cloud or suspicion regarding legal rights of an owner to a certain parcel of real property.

Quitclaim Deed—A deed which conveys simply the grantor's rights or interest in real estate, without any agreement or covenant as to the nature or extent of that interest, or any other covenants; usually used to remove a cloud from the title.

R

Real Estate Board—An organization whose members consist primarily of real estate brokers and salespersons.

Real Property—Land, and generally whatever is erected upon or affixed thereto.

Realtor—A coined word which may only be used by an active member of a local real estate board, affiliated with the National Association of Real Estate Boards.

Recording—The act of writing or entering in a book of public record instruments affecting the title to real property.

Redemption—The right of a mortgagor to redeem the property by paying a debt after the expiration date and before sale at foreclosure; the right of an owner to reclaim the owner's property after the sale for taxes.

Release—The act or writing by which some claim or interest is surrendered to another.

Release Clause—A clause found in a blanket mortgage which gives the owner of the property the privilege of paying off a portion of the mortgage indebtedness, and thus freeing a portion of the property from the mortgage.

Rem—(See In Rem)

Remainder—An estate which takes effect after the termination of a prior estate such as a life estate.

Remainderman—The person who is to receive the property after the death of a life tenant.

Rent—The compensation paid for the use of real estate.

Reproduction Cost—Normal cost of exact duplication of a property as of a certain date.

Restriction—A limitation placed upon the use of property contained in the deed or other written instrument in the chain of title. Reversionary Interest The interest which a person has in lands or other property upon the termination of the preceding estate.

Revocation—An act of recalling a power of authority conferred, as the revocation of a power of attorney, a license, an agency, etc.

Right of Survivorship—Right of the surviving joint owner to succeed to the interests of the deceased joint owner, distinguishing feature of a joint tenancy or tenancy by the entirety.

Right of Way—The right to pass over another's land more or less frequently according to the nature of the easement.

Riparian Owner—One who owns land bounding upon a river or watercourse.

Riparian Rights—The right of a landowner to water on, under or adjacent to his land.

S

Sales Contract—A contract by which the buyer and seller agree to terms of sale.

Satisfaction Piece—An instrument for recording and acknowledging payment of an indebtedness secured by a mortgage.

Seizin—The possession of land by one who claims to own at least an estate for life therein.

Set Back—The distance from the curb or other established line, within which no buildings may be erected.

Severalty—The ownership of real property by an individual, as an individual.

Special Assessment—An assessment made against a property to pay for a public improvement by which the assessed property is supposed to be especially benefited.

Specific Performance—A remedy in a court of equity compelling a defendant to carry out the terms of an agreement or contract.

Statute—A law established by an act of the Legislature.

Statute of Frauds—State law which provides that certain contracts must be in writing in order to be enforceable at law.

Stipulations—The terms within a written contract.

Straight Line Depreciation—A definite sum set aside annually from income to pay costs of replacing improvements, without reference to the interest it earns.

Subdivision—A tract of land divided into lots or plots suitable for home building purposes.

Subletting—A leasing by a tenant to another, who holds under the tenant.

Subordination Clause—A clause which permits the placing of a mortgage at a later date which takes priority over an existing mortgage.

Subscribing Witness—One who writes his/her name as witness to the execution of an instrument.

Surety—One who guarantees the performance of another; guarantor.

Surrender—The cancellation of a lease by mutual consent of the lessor and the lessee.

Surrogate's Court (Probate Court)—A court having jurisdiction over the proof of wills, the settling of estates and of citations.

Survey—The process by which a parcel of land is measured and its area ascertained; also the blueprint showing the measurements, boundaries and area.

T

Tax Sale—Sale of property after a period of nonpayment of taxes.

Tenancy in Common—An ownership of realty by two or more persons, each of whom has an undivided interest, without the "right of survivorship."

Tenancy by the Entirety—An estate which exists only between husband and wife with equal right of possession and enjoyment during their joint lives and with the "right of survivorship."

Tenancy at Will—A license to use or occupy lands and tenements at the will of the owner.

Tenant—One who is given possession of real estate for a fixed period or at will.

Tenant at Sufferance—One who comes into possession of lands by lawful title and keeps it afterwards without any title at all.

Testate—Where a person dies leaving a valid will.

Title—Evidence that owner of land is in lawful possession thereof; evidence of ownership.

Title Insurance—A policy of insurance which indemnifies the holder for any loss sustained by reason of defects in the title.

Title Search—An examination of the public records to determine the ownership and encumbrances affecting real property.

Torrens Title—System of title records provided by state law: it is a system for the registration of land titles whereby the state of the title, showing ownership and encumbrances, can be readily ascertained from an inspection of the "register of titles" without the necessity of a search of the public records.

Tort—A wrongful act, wrong, injury; violation of a legal right.

Transfer Tax—A tax charged under certain conditions on the property belonging to an estate.

U

Unearned Increment—An increase in value of real estate due to no effort on the part of the owner; often due to increase in population.

Urban Property—City property; closely settled property.

Usury—On a loan, claiming a rate of interest greater than that permitted by law.

V

Valid—Having force, or binding force; legally sufficient and authorized by law.

Valuation—Estimated worth or price. The act of valuing by appraisal.

Vendee's Lien—A lien against property under contract of sale to secure deposit paid by a purchaser.

Verification—Sworn statements before a duly qualified officer to the correctness of the contents of an instrument.

Violations—Act, deed or conditions contrary to law or permissible use of real property.

Void—To have no force or effect; that which is unenforceable.

Voidable—That which is capable of being adjudged void, but is not void unless action is taken to make it so.

W

Waiver—The renunciation, abandonment or surrender of some claim, right or privilege.

Warranty Deed—A conveyance of land in which the grantor warrants the title to the grantee.

Will—The disposition of one's property to take effect after death.

Without Recourse—Words used in endorsing a note or bill to denote that the future holder is not to look to the endorser in case of nonpayment.

Z

Zone—An area set off by the proper authorities for specific use; subject to certain restrictions or restraints.

Zoning Ordinance—Act of city or county or other authorities specifying type and use to which property may be put in specific areas.

www.ingramcontent.com/pod-product-compliance
Lightning Source LLC
Chambersburg PA
CBHW081806300426
44116CB00014B/2259